THE
WRAPAROUND
GUIDE

How to Gather Student Voice,

Build Community Partnerships,

and Cultivate Hope

LEIGH COLBURN & LINDA BEGGS

Solution Tree | Press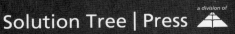

555 North Morton Street
Bloomington, IN 47404
800.733.6786 (toll free) / 812.336.7700
FAX: 812.336.7790

email: info@SolutionTree.com
SolutionTree.com

Visit **go.SolutionTree.com/leadership** to download the free reproducibles in this book.

Printed in the United States of America

Library of Congress Cataloging-in-Publication Data

Names: Colburn, Leigh, author. | Beggs, Linda, author.
Title: The wraparound guide : how to gather student voice, build community
   partnerships, and cultivate hope / Leigh Colburn, Linda Beggs.
Description: Bloomington, IN : Solution Tree Press, [2020] | Includes
   bibliographical references and index.
Identifiers: LCCN 2020020355 (print) | LCCN 2020020356 (ebook) | ISBN
   9781951075071 (paperback) | ISBN 9781951075088 (ebook)
Subjects: LCSH: Student assistance programs--United States. | School
   children--Services for. | School improvement programs--United States. |
   Community and school--United States.
Classification: LCC LB3430.5 .C65 2020 (print) | LCC LB3430.5 (ebook) |
   DDC 371.7--dc23
LC record available at https://lccn.loc.gov/2020020355
LC ebook record available at https://lccn.loc.gov/2020020356

Solution Tree
Jeffrey C. Jones, CEO
Edmund M. Ackerman, President

Solution Tree Press
President and Publisher: Douglas M. Rife
Associate Publisher: Sarah Payne-Mills
Art Director: Rian Anderson
Managing Production Editor: Kendra Slayton
Senior Production Editor: Todd Brakke
Content Development Specialist: Amy Rubenstein
Copy Editor: Jessi Finn
Proofreader: Elisabeth Abrams
Text and Cover Designer: Laura Cox
Editorial Assistants: Sarah Ludwig and Elijah Oates

DEDICATION

Education is an ornament in prosperity and a refuge in adversity.

—Aristotle

This book is dedicated to the thousands of children and teens who were willing to share their circumstance and their voice and who informed our efforts in launching wraparound services in their schools:

Felicia, R'moni, Mirakal, CJ, Moises, Enjolie, Storey, Parentheses, Tavarious, Grant, Tavio, Molly, Blessing, Ariana, John, Iman, Chloe, Max, Will, Stefan, Emma, Juanita, Delon, Jermel, Maureen, Nikki, Leo, Grace, Fatima, Henley, Kendall, Journie, Brittany, TJ, Shelbea, Isaiah, Amber, Sasha, Adrian, Abigail, Elizabeth, Caleb, Raven, Shamar, Daneasha, Andre, Donte, Amaree, Amy, Danielle, Julio, Raphael, Kahlie, Jessica, Jaydon, Emir, Steve, Ami, Dina, Chandler, Naomi, Nasir, Edgar, Erick, Yazleik, Johan, Mariah, Jose, Bikrom, Rueben, Grant, Dahnya, Abraham, Cristofer, Fozia, Tianna, Chase, Haley, Josh, Elijah, Joshua, Jaylen, Jared, Jason, Legion, Sam, Madison, Amie, Destiny, Kassie, Jazzmyn, Kolby, Hannah, Bernardo, Nick, Dana, Ellie, Emmie, J.B., Alex, Emmanuel, Alec, DonNeshia, Aniyah, Yanathe, Waldemar, Dakota, Blake, Dylan, Steven, Tana, Malik, Shaniya, Kayvon, Keke, Sarah, Elisha, Maya, Andrea, Whitney, Damon, Connor, Cristian, Unique, Ethan, China, Brian, Andrea, Alexus, Laysha, Caleb, Shelby, Jocelyn, Joe, Skye, Amia, Devan, Jeffrey, Avian, Porscha, Matt, Monica, Katie, Bailey, Wilson, Amelyah, Claire, Jackson, Emily, Abraham, Destiny, Colton, Evelin, Lisandra, Tyler, Kellie, Alejandro, Edgar, Halle, Ismael, Leslie, Esmerelda, Jerome, Alma, Sandra, Kassie, Chanarith, and more.

You are our inspiration.

ACKNOWLEDGMENTS

So many people have been a part of the journey to make this book a reality. We've found inspiration in the countless students who opened up their hearts and minds to share their stories and the courageous leaders willing to embrace innovation.

The first seeds of wraparound germinated in our minds after reading the work of Bob Barr and Emily Gibson. In their seminal book *Building a Culture of Hope* (Barr & Gibson, 2013), they laid out a vision where schools can help students develop resilience through a sense of optimism, self-worth, belonging, and purpose. They have since added self-regulation in their sequel *Building the Resilient School* (Barr & Gibson, 2020). What began as professional respect has blossomed into warm friendships. We are grateful they have accepted us into their sphere of hope, and we are appreciative of the advice and encouragement they gave us throughout the process of writing this book.

A special thanks belongs to the Marietta City Schools 2015 Board of Education, Emily Lembeck, Dayton Hibbs, and the community partners who helped start what is now the Marietta Student Life Center. Through their collective efforts, our students and their families had access to the wealth of assets in our town. The work in Marietta gave us a firsthand glimpse at what can happen in a teen's life when he or she connects with consistent, caring, and engaged adults willing to open doors for his or her future. Especially, we would like to express our appreciation to the 2015–2017 staff of the Graduate Marietta Student Success Center: Gaspar, Granville, Sheila, Marge, Joyce, Brenda, Matt, Terrance, Nicole, Jasmine, Jessica, Melanie, Chris, Tom, Grachelle, Sissy, Eunice, Barry, Richard, Stacy, Lester, Valarie, Kristin, Milena, Adrienne, and Maureen.

We've also been blessed by the stalwart support of Stephanie Johnson at the Georgia Department of Education. As a turnaround principal, she showed unflinching commitment to removing barriers her students face. Now, in her role as deputy superintendent for school improvement, she brings her unique brand of energy, smarts, and courage to the task of making equity a reality. Georgia is fortunate to have her!

The leaders from Gainesville City School System (GCSS) deserve their own note of recognition as well. They opened their wraparound center (The Hub) in January 2020. Sarah Bell began championing the concept of wraparound support before we met her in the summer of 2017. She paved the way by connecting us with superintendent Jeremy Williams and his cabinet, who embraced the idea with unwavering support. Gainesville High School principal Jamie Green has proven himself to be a passionate student advocate who is never too busy to listen. Finally, a huge thank-you to Tonya Sanders, director of The Hub, who has taken wraparound to the next level and created a space for Gainesville students to find their place in the world. They have assembled a dream team, and we are grateful to have been by their side through their journey.

Our graphic designer, Samantha Beggs, does a great job of translating our *very rough* sketches into crisp graphics. She is part mind reader, part magician, and 100 percent artist. Her ability to turn our half-baked ideas into fully formed cohesive images continually amazes us. We couldn't do our work without her.

Many thanks to the wraparound directors and their school districts who help keep us inspired and motivated, especially to Rona, Igola, Derrick, Rachel, Natalie, Dianne, Tonya, and Kay. Thank you for working with compassion and passion on behalf of your kids. Your work matters!

Many colleagues and fellow thought leaders have been valuable sounding boards and sources of encouragement: Mark Wilson, Carla Foley, Daniel Marshall, Chad Flatt, Ron Brookins, Joe and Dardi Hendershott, Jill Sims, Allyson Morgan, Allison McMahon, Beverly McAfee, Donna Ryan, Alisa Leckie, Taylor Norman, Jason Byars, Connie Ryals, Ashley Collier, Rachel Spates, Stanley Leone, Sharon Kherat, Dexter "The Godfather" Mills, John Floresta, Sheila Colquitt, Marie Sherbondy, Jason Meade, Debbie Woolard, and many others. Thank you for sharing your ideas and listening to ours.

Two people were especially helpful when writing about funding: Brian Campbell from Columbia County School System and Margaux Brown from Augusta University. Their knowledge and expertise were invaluable.

A special thank-you goes to Dan Rea, retired from Georgia Southern University and as the director of the National Youth-At-Risk Conference. We connected to him through his excellent scholarship on creating a framework for equity, the 5HHF, which is a must-read for anyone interested in wraparound. Thank you for working with us and supporting our vision for wraparound services. We think the tools we have developed together will continue to be of service to schools wanting to create a culture that supports the development of the whole child.

As first-time authors, we could not have found ourselves in better hands than with our Solution Tree team. We are indebted to the incomparable Douglas Rife for seeing the promise in this hopeful work and taking a risk on two new authors. Throughout this process, he's provided his steady counsel and encouragement—as well as delightful conversations ranging from cemeteries to presidential histories to dance contests! Quite a gentleman. Thanks also to Amy Rubenstein, who guided us through the first draft. Her eye for detail and lightning turnaround were invaluable in hitting some tight deadlines. The art and marketing departments, headed by Rian Anderson and Kelly Rockhill, respectively, also deserve a special thanks for getting us ready to publish. Special thanks to Todd Brakke, our eagle-eyed and patient editor who refined our writing and made the final text so much better.

A special thanks to our family, who gave us lots of leeway while we labored in "the cave" for weeks at a time. Fortunately for us, our cave was actually the beach, thanks to Rosemary Beggs arranging space for us at St. Simons Island for our writing retreats. Our husbands,

Doug and Phillip, spent many a week patiently "batching" and picking up more than their fair share of dog care. Leigh's sons John and Phillip, plus John's wife April, along with Linda's daughters Georgia and Samantha, were a continual source of encouragement.

Finally, none of this would be possible without the thousands of students who have willingly given us their time to share their thoughts, experiences, hopes, challenges, and dreams. You are the reason for everything we do.

—Leigh Colburn & Linda Beggs

Solution Tree Press would like to thank the following reviewers:

Louis Angelo
Principal
Upper St. Clair High School
Upper St. Clair, Pennsylvania

Margaux H. Brown
Assistant Professor of Counselor Education
Augusta University
Augusta, Georgia

Brian Campbell
Director of Title I and School Improvement
Columbia County Schools
Evans, Georgia

Sheila Colquitt
Wraparound Specialist
First District RESA
Brooklet, Georgia

John Floresta
Chief Strategy and Accountability Officer
Cobb County School District
Marietta, Georgia

Laura Hesson
School Board Member
Washington County School District
Saint George, Utah

Karla Jacobs
Commissioner
Georgia Commission on Women
Marietta, Georgia

Brandon Johnson
Principal
Lake Ridge High School
Mansfield, Texas

Stephanie Johnson
Deputy Superintendent of School Improvement
Georgia Department of Education
Atlanta, Georgia

Benjamin Kitslaar
Principal
West Side Elementary School
Elkhorn, Wisconsin

Robert Mackey
Superintendent
Unadilla Valley Central School District
New Berlin, New York

Daniel Marshall
School Counselor
Gilmer High School
Ellijay, Georgia

Clay McDonald
Assistant Principal
Yukon High School
Yukon, Oklahoma

Laura Mooiman
International Consultant
Mooiman Consulting
The Hague, Netherlands

Michelle Poppen
Assistant Principal
Maricopa High School
Maricopa, Arizona

Connie Ryals
Wraparound Specialist
Central Savannah River Area Regional
Educational Service Agency
Dearing, Georgia

Karen Smits
Retired Administrator
Marietta City Schools
Marietta, Georgia

Visit **go.SolutionTree.com/leadership** to
download the free reproducibles in this book.

TABLE OF CONTENTS

Reproducibles are in italics.

ABOUT THE AUTHORS

 **Leigh Colburn** is a career educator, community leader, and educational consultant. She began her career in elementary school—teaching in all K–5 grades before moving into elementary administration and becoming a principal. Leigh transitioned to high school administration and proudly served as the principal of Marietta High School for ten years until founding the *Graduate Marietta Student Success Center* on July 1, 2015. As director of this center, she established dynamic partnerships with the Marietta Board of Education, city council, public safety departments, and community agencies and organizations to improve the quality of life for Marietta's students. Under her leadership, the *Graduate Marietta Student Success Center* was named the 2016 Charter System Innovator of the Year for the state of Georgia.

Leigh founded the Centergy Project to bring her expertise to districts wishing to promote equity by offering wraparound service opportunities for their students and families. Her experience in both elementary and high school positions her to guide school leaders to take a whole child approach to addressing the needs of their students. Leigh is also a popular speaker at events such as the National Youth-At-Risk Conference, the National Elementary and Secondary Education Act (ESEA) Conference, and regional educational conferences.

Leigh earned degrees from Kennesaw State University, the University of Mississippi, and the University of Alabama. Leigh and her husband, Doug, have raised two sons. Her oldest, John, is a pastor in Birmingham, Alabama, and her youngest, Phillip, is a public safety officer while also serving proudly as a member of the United States Army Reserve. Leigh spends her free time enjoying outdoor activities from her northern Georgia mountain home.

 **Linda Beggs** is a cofounder of the Centergy Project, a Georgia-based education consultancy working with school districts wanting to offer embedded wraparound services. She brings over thirty years of consulting experience focused on organizational development with expertise in culture, change, and team effectiveness. Working with corporate, government, education, and nonprofit organizations has prepared Linda to engage schools to create the high-trust culture essential to implementing wraparound resource centers.

Linda has certifications in the Myers-Briggs Type Indicator and the EQ-i. She traveled nationwide for over ten years while working as a consultant with Franklin Covey and Pritchett & Associates, holding a variety of certifications in their content areas, such as *The Speed of Trust*, *The 7 Habits of Highly Effective People*, and *Business as Unusual*.

Linda is active in her community, having served on various boards and committees, including Marietta's College & Career Academy Steering Committee, Mentoring for Leadership, and liveSAFE Women of Achievement. She is a graduate and past chair of Leadership Cobb.

Linda is a proud graduate of the University of Georgia's Terry College of Business. She and her husband, Phillip, live in Marietta, Georgia. They have two daughters, Georgia, who works in home improvement, and Samantha, who is studying graphic design. They also have a spoiled whippet. In her free time, she enjoys spending time in the garden and studying with the Anne Hudgins Shakespeare Class.

To book Leigh Colburn or Linda Beggs for professional development, contact pd@SolutionTree.com.

FOREWORD

By Robert D. Barr

Hang on to your chair. You are about to be introduced to an idea that might just rock your world. And while the idea is cloaked in the seemingly genteel title of *The Wraparound Guide*, it is an idea whose time has come. This idea represents a rather down-to-earth, straightforward, and common-sense approach of using student voice to guide school-improvement efforts. Yet this simple idea has the potential to transform classrooms and schooling. It might just change *your* conception of effective schooling in your community and district.

Occasionally in life, you see or experience something that seems so powerful, yet so simple, that you find yourself wondering, "Why didn't I think of that?" Remember when you first saw a carry-on bag rolling through an airport on tiny wheels? Next thing you knew, rolling luggage was everywhere, completely transforming the way we all travel. You are about to experience just such a moment.

This book lays out a new vision for public education based on a simple idea: *listening to students*. Authors Leigh Colburn and Linda Beggs present a vision they have designed, developed, tried, and tested. In this book, you'll see how all the pieces fit together into a replicable blueprint for excellence, a new vision of schooling tailor-made for our age. The lives of students growing up in the post-9/11 world have been increasingly filled with conflict, chaos, and violence. If you are serious about addressing the full-spectrum needs of students growing up in this world, you need to read this book. If you are determined to address the needs of students impacted by poverty, to help ensure that all students are learning effectively, coming to school regularly, and graduating, read this book. If you are serious about ensuring equity and supporting the success of your students, this book might just be what you have been waiting for. Read on.

Not long ago, I had heard of Leigh and Linda but had never met them. They had read *Building a Culture of Hope*, which I wrote with Emily Gibson, and came to see her speak at the 2019 National Youth-At-Risk Conference in Savannah, Georgia. Emily took my arm, and in a loud, crowded hotel lobby, she said, "Come over here, you need to meet these people."

I had no idea what I was in store for. Their energy and enthusiasm arrived like an emotional tsunami. As an old warhorse who has experienced several decades of battles over poverty and education, I am rarely impressed by the next new thing. I thought I had seen it all. I was about to discover how wrong I could be. In the middle of that busy hotel lobby, Leigh and Linda told me about their work. In a moment, the noisy distractions of the hotel disappeared, and I was totally engrossed. Before we had finished our conversation, I began to realize the power of what I was hearing. I interrupted our talk and said, "Hang on. Hang on. I need to make a call." I contacted my publisher, Douglas Rife of Solution Tree, who was also at the conference, and told him that I had some people he needed to meet. Douglas attended their next session, and that night he met Leigh and Linda for dinner. By the end of the evening, they were all talking about the possibility of doing a book. Today, you are holding that book in your hands. That is the power of this idea.

The idea, of course, sounds simple: seek out and respond to student voice. Yet, as is so often the case, this simple idea turns out to be powerful and infectious, opening up an entirely new world of possibilities and responsibilities. To see the effort at school improvement growing out of student voice is a sight to behold. What starts as an effort to understand the needs of students blossoms into a multifaceted wave transforming not only the schools but the communities surrounding them.

This book is not just the next neat thing. Instead, you'll find a distinctly different approach that recasts what we have typically come to think of as school improvement, what we even think of as school. It actually transforms our conception of the role and scope of public education. Rather than focusing on the academic needs of students and, separately, their social-emotional needs, Leigh and Linda have brought the entire world of schooling into a comprehensive whole child model that not only makes sense, but works. They have shown us how to be more effective at teaching and learning, and they have shown us how to help students find hope and act on optimism. They have shown us how we can help better prepare students for both school *and* life.

Out of the complexity and confusion surrounding school improvement, Leigh and Linda have provided a new gestalt of clarity and understanding. They have taken the research on effective schools, high-poverty and high-performing schools, social-emotional learning, interrupting poverty, community schools, cultures of hope, and resilient schools and woven it all together into a thing of beauty. They have developed a model of school improvement that encompasses and integrates all these widely divergent views in the scholarly universe of school improvement, and they have made it truly student centered. Quite humbly, they call it *The Wraparound Guide*, an essential resource for gathering student voice, building community partnerships, and cultivating hope.

By listening to student voice, Leigh and Linda have deconstructed the concept of social-emotional needs. Behind the rather placid, sometimes bored, and other times anxious faces of high school students sitting in class and responding to their teachers' prompts and questions, we now know more than ever before about the often raging emotions and anxieties going on in their lives. Through gathering student voice, we learn more about the concerns and confusion they have about sexual issues and gender identity and about the aftereffects of stress, family and community crisis, and trauma. We know more about their worries about their parents; addictions; domestic abuses; fear of unemployment, eviction, and homelessness; concerns about what to do after high school; feelings of insecurity and fear; and so much more than even the most dedicated experts might even imagine—which is all to say nothing of fears about pandemics, civil unrest, and global climate.

Expanding on concepts Emily and I explore in *Building a Culture of Hope*, Leigh and Linda have drilled down and unpacked concepts like optimism, belonging, self-worth, self-regulation, and purpose so that educators can develop specific supports and services that can address students' very distinctive needs. Their approach is not only about educating the whole student; it is about educating the whole child.

After meeting Leigh and Linda, I took time to consider how their work could change and improve schools. In reviewing the accounts retold in *The Wraparound Guide*, I was intrigued to see how quickly school leaders implementing their processes of school improvement have pivoted their focus to issues of respect and trust. I can imagine that in some small-group discussion of possibly disinterested students talking about teaching and learning, one young student might interrupt the discussion and ask a question that changes everything. She asks, "Are you really interested in our ideas? Do you *really* want to know about what is interfering with our schoolwork?"

Suddenly, the group of students seems to wake up and start nodding their heads and agreeing with the question. Together, I imagine the students asking themselves a silent question: "Can we trust you?" I believe at this moment that a new set of doors opens up with unexpected opportunities. Leigh Colburn and Linda Beggs can help you walk through these doors.

As trust and respect grows, a real conversation develops. Rather than discussing issues of teaching and learning, over time, the students begin sharing the things that fill up their lives with anxiety, concern, and confusion. Students *want* to talk about real issues that sometimes overwhelm their interest in school. These very personal issues trouble so many students, getting in the way of success in school . . . and life. For schools to take these needs seriously, one thing is obvious—it demands a completely different response than most schools have used in the past. The processes in this book will help you uncover what students are crying out for—a full range of personal assistance and support.

Most important, this can happen anywhere, and Leigh and Linda can show you how. In this book, they have laid out all of the pieces to help any school address the academic needs of students, the social-emotional needs of students, and the human needs of students and their families. In this new vision of educating the whole student, serious academic work is integrated with health services, emotional supports, and often even help with housing, food, and clothing. This book presents a brilliant, useful, and perhaps essential effort to improve the education of American youth. Leigh and Linda have shown that communities will respond to the voices of the children and youth in their neighborhoods, and those communities will step up and help. They have shown that the student services that they have come to provide fit perfectly with the rest of the school and that the better the support services, the more effective the learning. To paraphrase poverty and education expert Eric Jensen, regarding success in school and life, hope is more important than ability. For students surrounded by wraparound services, there is surely a new hope for a better future.

Oh yes, for those teachers who are so overworked and often overstressed in their efforts to address their students' needs, they too have new hope. They have an effective new group of professionals who have stepped up and joined them, a new group of professionals who can help. The lives of students and their families are better, the lives of teachers are better, and the world of public education is better.

Robert D. Barr is the author or coauthor of fifteen books on poverty and education, including with Emily Gibson, Building a Culture of Hope *and* Building the Resilient School.

INTRODUCTION

Our staff has been listening to the needs of students for years without the ability to truly serve not just the educational needs but the needs of the whole child. Now, I am proud to say that I know we are truly making a positive difference in the lives of our students and families.

—High school teacher

In the fall of 2015, Marietta High School in Georgia cut the ribbon on the Graduate Marietta Student Success Center (now the Marietta Student Life Center)—ten repurposed rooms to host wraparound services designed to address the needs of all the school's students. It included space for full-spectrum services, from a food pantry to community and clinical services. A community partners room, outfitted with open workspaces, hosted eight desks for embedded partners ranging from licensed therapists to bilingual parent and family liaisons. (For purposes of inclusivity, we refer to *family liaisons* in this book rather than *parent liaisons*.) Just months later, *the Center* (as students and staff refer to it) buzzed with an average of 150 students visiting every day to meet with the graduation coach, therapists, tutors, social workers, mentors, and college and military recruiters. When asked for feedback about the services available, one high school student said:

> I've taken the center up on its tutoring, mentoring support, therapy, and the college and career services. Personally, I think the tutoring is the most beneficial to the whole school, but I know that the therapists can also make a true difference. Every service provided is amazing and 100 percent trustworthy, which is what we all need. The center can truly change your life, and I'm proof of that. It is a trustworthy support system, and I believe with all of me that every school needs one.

As this statement avows, schools can be a protective, supportive, and trustworthy factor in the lives of their students. Without question, students come to school with a variety of talents and strengths; likewise, they come to school with a variety of barriers to health and learning. The purpose of this book is to assist schools in the creation of student-informed systems of support that are proactive, responsive, customizable, and solution-focused. During the creation of the Wraparound Center in Peoria, Illinois, wraparound director

Derrick Booth told his community, "We are not going to let the problem be bigger than the solution. There's hope in our wraparound center. There's hope when individuals utilize these services and supports, that there's light at the end of the tunnel. There's hope" (Peoria Public Schools, 2016).

We begin this introduction with words from Leigh Colburn, coauthor of this book and founder of the Graduate Marietta Student Success Center, who describes how student-informed wraparound services began in her school. With this story in mind, we explain the necessity of this book, who should read it, and how it's organized.

voices FROM THE FIELD

> Our center has created a closer connection between the community and the school itself. People from the community and our school are taking the time to listen, show up, and show an interest in us and our problems regarding school and life. This program has so many parts that no student should ever feel alone in the school or community for having a problem—especially a problem that is not their fault or that they cannot deal with by themselves. This program teaches us that we are not alone and that there are people in our community who can help us.
>
> —High school senior

How Our Wraparound Journey Began

By Leigh Colburn

For ten years, starting in 2005, I served as the principal at Marietta High School. In 2013, during my eighth year as principal, my superintendent, Emily Lembeck, and school board chair, Randy Weiner, asked me what we were going to do to continue the school's positive momentum and growth in graduation rates. As background, I am a graduate of this same school, and as such, I have firsthand experience with the demographic changes that have taken place since the 1980s. When I graduated in 1983, the school was majority white, and the student body represented predominantly middle-class families. By 2013, the small town had evolved into a small urban city in the suburbs of Atlanta. The majority of the residents were not homeowners but instead were renting in high-density housing that had developed within the city limits. The student population of the city's one high school was majority-minority and majority economically disadvantaged, including a rapidly growing population of students for whom English was their second language. Throughout this time, the support for and spirit of the school remained enthusiastic. The town showed up to display its Blue Devil pride at Friday night football, at alumni events, and at our annual homecoming parade.

When I took the helm in 2005, during the era of No Child Left Behind (NCLB, 2002), our school spirit was shining brighter than our academic achievement. Our football team was undefeated, but we struggled to make adequate yearly academic progress, and we teetered on the verge of a state takeover. With an all-hands-on-deck approach, our school offered a host of academic interventions, such as credit recovery, tutoring, support classes, test prep, dual enrollment, and an alternative education program. In 2006, not only did we avoid a state takeover, but we began to close achievement gaps. We initiated changes that yielded positive results in attendance, discipline, enrollment in rigorous coursework, and more.

For eight years, we did the heavy lifting in the areas of school improvement and school turnaround. We received awards and recognition, our test scores continued on an upward trajectory, and we pushed even harder. But our teachers struggled to keep up with each year's newest innovation, and our staff seemed to be suffering from initiative and compassion fatigue. Even great teachers who skillfully connected with students began to complain about student apathy and doubted their ability to make a measurable difference for their students. I had to face facts: yes, we had improved our results and measurables, but at what cost?

In 2011, our academic and graduation gains began to slow. Fast-forward to 2013, when I am standing in front of our board of education, and they are asking me how we will sustain what had been, until this point, dependable growth every year in our graduation rate. There was nothing wrong with their question, but I didn't have an answer. As principal, shouldn't my goal be to continue striving until 100 percent of my students are graduating? In all honesty, the question perturbed me because I was out of ideas for academic innovation. I didn't know what I could propose as the year's next new thing. Deep down, I suspected our academic interventions were not really addressing *all* our students' needs. I knew—or at least thought I did—the struggles many of my students faced, including transiency, poverty, trauma, and immigration problems. I also knew my school-improvement plan had nothing in it to address these complicated issues.

Following the board meeting, I discussed with my mathematics and English department chairs our possible next steps. One asked a question that fundamentally changed our approach: "What would our students say?" I decided to find out. Fortunately, my superintendent and school board supported me and gave me the time necessary to query students' thoughts and then follow their lead.

For the next two years, we conducted grassroots research within our school, interviewing and surveying thousands of current and former students and family members and asking them what we could do to help students move across the stage to graduation. What we *did not hear* was as important as what we heard. We did not hear about a need for more tutoring, and we did not hear about a need for more test prep. Tutoring and test prep went unmentioned not because those things are unimportant but because we already had them available for our students. What we did hear from our students who graduated—and from our students who dropped out—were the barriers they believed got in the way of their achievement. Figure I.1 (page 4) reflects not only the range of responses we heard but the potential impact of the stated factors on students' ability to graduate.

Consider the barriers shown in figure I.1. Within the structure and confines of a brick-and-mortar high school, leaders and staff typically do not have the resources, expertise, funding, policies, or mindset to address these barriers. Yet, our students were clear: they needed and wanted our school to be more than a place for academic preparation.

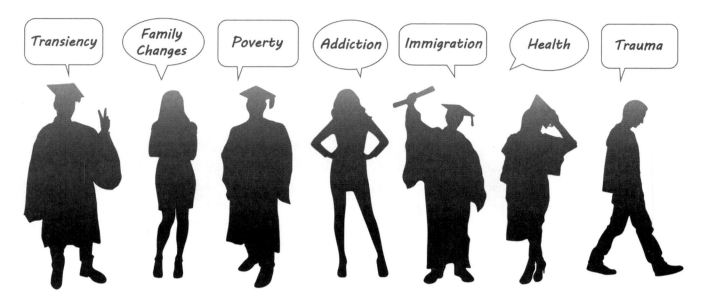

Source: © 2020 The Centergy Project.

Figure I.1: Student-identified barriers to learning and graduation.

As the stories, ideas, and truth of our students informed our next steps, our district leadership faced the hard reality that we must adjust our mindset about schooling and student support. As principal, I set out to develop a holistic, whole child support system customized to the needs of our students and our community. Armed with qualitative and quantitative data we gathered from students, I knew what types of partnerships, opportunities, experiences, and assistance we needed to make accessible to our students. In the summer of 2015, I stepped away from the principal's position to become the wraparound director of the Graduate Marietta Student Success Center, which is now the Marietta Student Life Center.

Augmenting a strong academic foundation with wraparound *worked*. From 2013 to 2017, our four-year graduation rate gained twelve points (18 percent), and our equivalent five-year graduation rate—which I believe is equally as important because it includes off-track students—rose seventeen points (26 percent). In our first year of offering wraparound services, with the support of the superintendent, school board, and community, we delivered over $1 million in resources and services to students and families in our community, and we did this by partnering with thirty-seven state agencies and nonprofit organizations. To ensure equitable access to services for our students and their families, we co-located staff from sixteen of those agencies on our high school campus. We accomplished this by listening to our students and then meeting their needs, building a culture of hope.

Staff feedback also told us the work of the Graduate Marietta Student Success Center during those years boosted teacher and staff morale. Instead of feeling helpless when learning about their students' problems, teachers and staff knew the school had built-in resources to help their students. One high school counselor shared:

> Essentially, I feel like our center is a one-stop shop because it helps address any number of issues. I have the ability to walk students in crisis to the center

where there are numerous activities (meditative coloring books, yoga balance balls, manipulatives, clinicians, and so on) to help calm their nerves in a safe and inviting environment. When my students are struggling academically or have missed several days of school, I refer them to our academic tutors who provide assistance, both during the day and after school, . . . everything from helping students make up missed assignments to editing research papers. I feel that the center has benefited our entire school community. (Betsy Alpert, personal communication, April 2017)

The work at Marietta High School garnered a great deal of positive attention from educators and media eager to learn how to respond to the varied needs of students. In 2017, I retired from my position as director of the Graduate Marietta Student Success Center and launched a consultancy along with my business partner, Linda Beggs. We named our firm the Centergy Project, a play on the words *center* and *synergy*. Together, we have worked in schools delivering the Centergy Cycle—a flexible, scalable, and replicable seven-step method to bring student-informed wraparound supports to schools anywhere. We wrote this book to provide schools with practical tools for gathering student voice, to inform the delivery of wraparound services, and to encourage schools in the endeavor of supporting the needs of the whole child.

My hope in advocating for this work is twofold. First, I want schools to discover the transformative power of student voice with regard to improving the school experience. Second, I hope our readers will gain from implementing wraparound services what I gained, a reconnection to why I became an educator in the first place. This work affords educators and schools the opportunity to make a truly positive difference in the lives of students. Ultimately, I want this book to have a positive impact on the way educators communicate with their students. As student voice experts Russell J. Quaglia and Michael J. Corso (2014) assert, we must thoughtfully consider when and how we engage in conversations with our students to position them as the potential rather than the problem.

Why This Book Is Needed

The world of school improvement is changing. Figure I.2 (page 6) is a graphic representation of the three waves of school improvement, which Dan W. Rea and Cordelia D. Zinskie (2017) describe in their article "Educating Students in Poverty: Building Equity and Capacity With a Holistic Framework and Community School Model."

The following list describes the core aspects of the three waves (Rea & Zinskie, 2017).

- **Wave 1:** The first wave of reform had a limited focus on cognitive growth and operationalized standards and accountability frameworks. This required schools to address the academic achievement of individual and disaggregated groups of students. It resulted in metrics-based legislation, such as NCLB (2002) in the United States.

- **Wave 2:** The second wave formed when schools began to acknowledge the critical importance of the relationship among the student, the teacher, and the school. Schools began responding to nonacademic data—statistics about

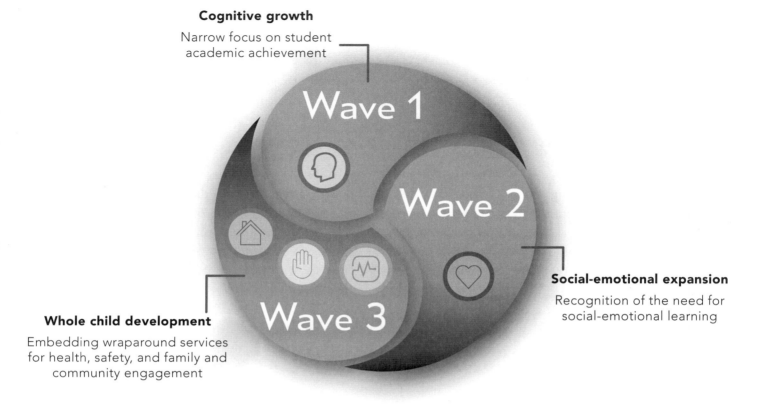

Cognitive growth
Narrow focus on student academic achievement

Social-emotional expansion
Recognition of the need for social-emotional learning

Whole child development
Embedding wraparound services for health, safety, and family and community engagement

Source: Adapted from Rea & Zinskie, 2017; © 2019 The Centergy Project.

Figure I.2: The three waves of educational reform.

disproportionality; student arrests at school; and escalating incidences of self-harm, anxiety, and substance use among their students. Tragic school shootings—such as those in Sandy Hook, Connecticut, and Parkland, Florida—increased focus on school safety and student mental health and highlighted the need to deepen the connection between students and their schools. Schools responded with social-emotional learning interventions and restorative practices seeking to promote social and emotional health in children and teens (Barr & Gibson, 2013).

- **Wave 3:** The third wave, whole child reform, sees school leaders understanding the kaleidoscope of factors that impact student achievement—many of which lie outside the classroom. Schools are looking for opportunities to partner with parents and communities to mitigate out-of-school factors that negatively impact in-school learning. Schools are also acknowledging their role and their potential to serve as a protective factor for their students.

Rea and Zinskie (2017) describe the third wave of school reform as a focus on whole child development that aligns with the Whole School, Whole Community, Whole Child (WSCC) approach from the Association for Supervision and Curriculum Development (ASCD, n.d.). Building on the second wave of reform and going beyond it, the whole child wave proposes a holistic and comprehensive framework to equitably address students' complex needs and capacities (Rea & Zinskie, 2017). In alignment with the whole child wave, schools are responding with initiatives to boost students' resilience, well-being, and self-regulation (Barr & Gibson, 2020).

As the third-wave work of whole child schools evolves, an interesting clarification is emerging. Rather than responding to cognitive (academic) and social-emotional learning as separate parts of a child's school experience, neuroscience is proving the interconnectedness of people's cognitive development and their social-emotional development (Darling-Hammond & Cook-Harvey, 2018). Separating cognitive growth from social-emotional growth simply doesn't make sense. Most of us don't need a scientist to tell us what our own experience has taught us: we learn best when we confidently possess safety, aspiration, agency, and love (Platt, 2019).

Social scientists use the term *social capital* to describe the informal bonds people have to family, friends, acquaintances, and neighbors. This community lens also includes involvement in religious institutions, athletic teams, civic organizations, clubs, and the like (Carney, 2019). Not surprisingly, communities with high social capital report high levels of happiness, optimism, and public safety in addition to a host of positive educational outcomes, such as academic achievement, economic success, and child welfare (Putnam, 2015).

In contrast to social scientists, educators look through the lens of individual students when considering both protective factors (such as safe neighborhoods and schools, positive and healthy friends, and positive adult relationships) and risk factors (such as transience, family changes, and substance use) to evaluate a student's likelihood of school success (Youth.gov, n.d.). Unfortunately, no society equally distributes social capital and protective factors, leaving many students at higher risk of adverse childhood experiences (ACEs), such as poverty and trauma. Without visionary leadership, conscientious execution, and collaborative community building, schools' efforts are frequently insufficient to fill the gaps, leaving teachers and administrators fatigued and disillusioned. And yet, as momentum builds for the whole child approach, schools are embracing their role as a protective factor, navigator, and builder of social capital while seeking to become a place where students believe their peers and adults care about them as individuals as well as about their learning. *This is hopeful work.*

A Word About Mental Health, Trauma, and ACEs

Joe Hendershott (2016), an expert on working with wounded students, explains, "Engaging with students and being more inclusive establishes a sense of community where empathic relationships can be practiced. However, failing to establish empathic connections with students can cause feelings of isolation for them" (pp. 44–45).

There is additional good news. Under the Every Student Succeeds Act (ESSA, 2015), federal funding previously restricted to academics-focused programming is available for interventions and support aimed at the development of the whole child (more on this in chapter 6, page 139). As we acknowledged earlier in this section, many of the barriers students face in life reside outside the school and are beyond the expertise and reach of educators. Even school leaders eager to collaboratively address these issues with community organizations don't know quite how to start. Many community partnerships in schools—frequently called *partners in education* (Southwest Educational Development Laboratory, 2013)—focus on transactional encounters, such as reading to classrooms, sponsoring athletic events, and participating in job fairs. A key component in schools providing wraparound services is achieving a different level of partnership—the hosting or co-locating of service providers and community services agencies within the school—that makes varied types of support equitably accessible to all students. There is even more good news—this book will provide you with coaching, processes, and tools for making school-based wraparound services a reality for your students and families.

Last, this book approaches the concepts of shared leadership, whole child learning, and wraparound services differently than other books by emphasizing a commonly overlooked element—student voice. In this book, you will learn how to harness student voice in an entirely new way, engaging students to design programs and interventions based on their experience, insight, and wisdom.

Who Should Read This Book

While the examples in this book are reflective of work in high schools, middle school administrators and staff can and should adapt our processes to suit their school culture while also being mindful of issues such as parental permission and the capabilities (maturity) of middle school students. We wrote this book for two audiences wanting to launch wraparound services: (1) decision makers and (2) implementers. *Decision makers* will learn the *why* behind gathering student voice to inform wraparound services. The decision makers include people in positions such as the following.

- Middle and high school principals

- Superintendents

- School board members

- District-level student-support staff (psychologists, grant specialists, and intervention leaders for services such as multitiered systems of supports [MTSS], response to intervention [RTI], and positive behavioral interventions and supports [PBIS])

In addition to addressing the *why*, those tasked with *implementing* wraparound services will find detailed information to address the *how*, which includes the entire process for establishing wraparound services, from having initial conversations with students to establishing partnerships to launching a wraparound center. In the implementers category, we include people in positions such as the following.

- School counselors
- Social workers
- Family liaisons
- Graduation coaches
- External service providers
- Teachers

Although we wrote the school processes in this book for secondary schools, once a wraparound service is established within a district, all K–12 schools can utilize the partnerships and services to support all families.

How This Book Is Structured

This book provides school and community leaders with a practical, flexible, and actionable framework—a how-to guide for the start-up and sustainability of wraparound services. This framework is grounded in our extensive experience as practitioners, and we include an anonymous sampling of voices from the thousands of students we've interviewed and surveyed—from urban to suburban to rural. We're confident you'll be impressed with the value of their contribution to the conversation of making schools better.

We organize this book's content into four parts that encompass the seven-step Centergy Cycle framework for implementing wraparound services (figure I.3). The following sections explore the role of each chapter in detailing this seven-step framework.

Source: © 2018 The Centergy Project.

Figure I.3: The Centergy Cycle—A framework for providing wraparound services grounded in student voice.

Part I: Laying the Foundation

Before you learn about the specific steps in the Centergy Cycle, we investigate the landscape of school improvement with regard to the whole child movement, student voice, and wraparound services. In chapter 1, we explore statistics related to child wellness in North America and the WSCC approach that ASCD (n.d.) and the Centers for Disease Control and Prevention (CDC, n.d.b) endorse. After providing an overview of the whole child approach, we introduce you to the value of gathering student voice. You will learn the fundamentals for building a culture of relational trust while exploring the cognitive *and* social-emotional needs of students and families. We also introduce the basics of our wraparound model and the seven steps you will take to create a wraparound school with programming based on student voice.

This chapter is an overview of the research and rationale related to the whole child approach, student voice, and wraparound services. It provides the baseline knowledge to support the how-to practitioner guidance found in subsequent chapters.

Part II: Gathering Student Voice

The first phase of creating a wraparound school begins with mining student voice through various processes in which students reveal their barriers as well as their ideas for effective school responses. Chapters 2 and 3 address the two steps that form this phase.

Chapter 2 focuses on identifying needs. Discovering student needs begins with intentional conversations with all types of students at your school, from high achievers to those who are significantly off track. You'll learn about three methods of gathering voice—(1) conversation circles, (2) off-track interviews, and (3) graduation stories—to reveal what students think about their school experience and the barriers they face to school and life success.

Chapter 3 is about establishing priorities. In this chapter, you will go on a deeper dive and learn about two more voice-gathering activities: (1) the Student Voice Needs Survey and (2) focused conversations. These processes, when utilized with individual students, groups of students, and the whole school, yield both quantitative and qualitative data for the purposes of prioritizing needs, identifying necessary partnerships, and projecting potential caseloads.

Part III: Building Your Infrastructure

This phase involves putting the pieces in place to launch steps 3–6 in the cycle. While we present these as steps, they are not strictly sequential, and a school may adapt the order to its circumstances. For example, hiring a director is covered as part of step 6 (create your structure) because staffing is explored as part of the wraparound center's organization. However, if your school hires a director at the inception of the initiative, you'll benefit from having leadership in place from the beginning to shepherd each of the other processes in this part. While each partnership follows the same steps, the pacing of partnership establishment will also vary. Some partnerships will come together easily, while partnerships of greater complexity will take longer to plan and launch.

Chapter 4 addresses identifying resources. Once you understand your needs and priorities, you'll want to assess your community's resources. These include volunteers, donors, and potential partners. We show you a tool called the Community Asset Map to help you develop a holistic understanding of the resources (agencies, nonprofits, and other organizations) delivering services in your community. Any or all of these may become an essential partner in delivering and sustaining wraparound services. Aligning the Community Asset Map with your identified needs and priorities reveals which partnerships your schools need most.

Chapter 5 focuses on the work of establishing partnerships. Creating partnerships between schools and community organizations begins the transformative process of bolstering protective factors for your students and families while growing the social capital of your community. In this chapter, we provide guidance on meeting with community organizations to explore your shared mission, examine data, establish goals, plan programming, and define the scope of your partnerships. Finally, we walk through the process of conducting a community strategic-planning meeting to pull your partnerships together.

Chapter 6 addresses funding. Many school leaders may express concern about the funding required to provide wraparound services to their students and families. This chapter looks at generating funds from a variety of sources (braided funding) to support full-spectrum programming. We start by examining ESSA (2015) flexibility regarding the whole child approach and wraparound services and then delve into potential funding sources from your community as well as grants. In addition, we explain the role the wraparound director plays in fundraising.

Chapter 7 addresses the structure of your wraparound center. It addresses four questions school and district leaders will ask. (1) What will we do? (2) How will we do it? (3) Where will we do it? and (4) Whom will we serve? We review student voice processes that wraparound staff utilize to develop programming. We also introduce a holistic, interconnected model capable of integrating current staff and programming with co-located service providers. Finally, we provide different space configurations designed to offer resources, services, and programming to the whole school, identified groups, and individual students.

Part IV: Launching and Sustaining Wraparound Services

The final phase in the Centergy Cycle involves pulling all the preceding steps together to connect students and families with services and to maintain the momentum established while carrying out this work. While the proverb "Well begun is half-done" is certainly apropos, continuing the work is what fulfills the mission. Sustainability involves anticipating and preparing for potential obstacles.

Chapter 8 details connecting students and families with services. We frame your thinking, planning, and measuring related to the wildly important goal of connecting students and families with the services they need. Additionally, we explore public relations strategies as well as friendly, low-barrier referral processes to facilitate easy access to services.

Because the efforts to build wraparound services mean nothing without sustainability, chapter 9 is about how to keep your center going. We share lessons learned on our journey working with schools to keep the whole child movement alive through maintaining voice processes, assessing progress, navigating leadership changes, developing inclusive programming, and managing funding. By following strategies in this chapter, you'll create a sustainable wraparound center capable of graduating resilient students while strengthening your school and building a healthier community.

Finally, an appendix walks through each step of the Centergy Cycle to model how schools can address an issue that affects virtually every community in the United States—substance use. We follow the entire Centergy Cycle in showing how a school might target and address this complex issue, from conducting conversation circles to delivering full-spectrum programming.

Throughout the book, and as you've already seen, we've included special feature boxes that will inspire your efforts or contextualize your understanding of the need for wraparound services. Voices From the Field boxes highlight a variety of quotations about students', parents', school staff's, and partner agencies' experiences related to wraparound services that we've gathered since 2015. Many of these quotes are necessarily anonymous, but all highlight the value of wraparound services. A Word About Mental Health, Trauma, and ACEs boxes offer published guidance from professionals in these fields to augment your knowledge about the impact of adverse experience on children and teens. While we cite a variety of published works and resources throughout this text, you will find several quotes from two books written by Joe Hendershott (2009, 2016), *Reaching the Wounded Student* and *7 Ways to Transform the Lives of Wounded Students*. We believe his work as an educator and his experience as a parent have informed his perspective in ways we find deeply authentic, credible, and hopeful. Joe's work has not only influenced the two of us, but it is also giving shape to the movement of creating trauma-informed classrooms and schools. We hope these diverse perspectives (student, parent, teacher, partner, researcher) will pique your curiosity and move you to listen to the voices in your school and community.

AND HOW ARE THE CHILDREN?

The Rev. Patrick O'Neill, retired of the First Unitarian Congregational Society of Brooklyn, New York, wrote the following passage to highlight the importance of children's well-being to the larger community. We replicate it here, with his permission, as a prelude to chapter 1:

Among the most accomplished and fabled tribes of Africa, no tribe was considered to have warriors more fearsome or more intelligent than the mighty Masai. It is perhaps surprising, then, to learn the traditional greeting that passed between Masai warriors: "Kasserian Ingera," one would always say to another. It means, "And how are the children?"

It is still the traditional greeting among the Masai, acknowledging the high value that the Masai always place on their children's well-being. Even warriors with no children of their own would always give the traditional answer, "All the children are well." Meaning, of course, that peace and safety prevail, that the priorities of protecting the young, the powerless, are in place. That Masai society has not forgotten its reason for being, its proper functions and responsibilities. "All the children are well" means that life is good. It means that the daily struggles for existence do not preclude proper caring for their young.

I wonder how it might affect our consciousness of our own children's welfare if in our culture we took to greeting each other with this daily question: "And how are the children?" I wonder if we heard that question and passed it along to each other a dozen times a day, if it would begin to make a difference in the reality of how children are thought of or cared about in our own country.

I wonder if every adult among us, parent and non-parent alike, felt an equal weight for the daily care and protection of all the children in our community, in our town, in our state, in our country . . . . I wonder if we could truly say without any hesitation, "The children are well, yes, all the children are well."

What would it be like . . . if the minister began every worship service by answering the question, "And how are the children?" If every town leader had to answer the question at the beginning of every meeting: "And how are the children? Are they all well?" Wouldn't it be interesting to hear their answers? What would it be like? I wonder . . .

Part I

LAYING THE FOUNDATION

Chapter 1

UNDERSTAND CORE CONCEPTS

The fabled Masai greeting inquires,
"And how are the children?"
As we thoughtfully consider our response,
I'd like to pose three additional questions.
1. "Do we care enough to ask the children themselves?"
2. "Are we wise enough to listen to what they say?"
3. "Are we bold enough to act?"

—Leigh Colburn

We've already introduced you to the core concepts behind the Centergy Cycle and why your school and, more importantly, its students and families will benefit from establishing a center for wraparound services. Before you learn about the Centergy Cycle's steps in more detail, you'll need comprehensive knowledge about three essential concepts underpinning any effort to offer full-spectrum services: (1) the whole child approach to learning, (2) the critical importance of building trust between school staff and students, and (3) the variety and types of wraparound services a school might offer. In this chapter, you will learn what you need to know about all three of these.

Whole Child Approach

We closed the introduction to this book with a passage highlighting the importance of children's well-being to the larger community. And so we begin here by asking its central question, "How are the children?"

The truth is, many are struggling. Just like our children, our schools are struggling as well as they attempt to meet the learning and health needs of their students in a holistic, equitable, and effective manner. Many nations, including the United States, stand at a crossroads as young people face complex challenges unique to this point in time. Changing norms related to technology, marriage and family, personal identity, community dynamics, social migrancy, and discourse are all colliding, making their world different and difficult to navigate. In short, students haven't changed, but the experience of growing up has. Consider the following.

- Anxiety and depression in children and teens are on the rise, and their occurrence "cuts across all demographics—suburban, urban and rural; those who are college bound and those who aren't" (Schrobsdorff, 2016).

- "Mental health disorders are the most common health issues faced by our nation's school-aged children. One in five children suffers from a mental health or learning disorder" (Child Mind Institute, 2016, p. 1).

- The suicide rate in the United States has soared to a near thirty-year high, and the suicide rate of girls ages ten to fourteen tripled between 1999 and 2014 (Curtin, Warner, & Hedegaard, 2016).

- Canada has the third-highest suicide rate in the industrialized world, and only one out of five children who need mental health services receive them (Youth Mental Health Canada, 2019).

- Self-harm is not universal among teens with depression and anxiety, but it does "appear to be the signature symptom of this generation's mental-health difficulties" (Schrobsdorff, 2016).

- According to the CDC, 52,404 U.S. citizens died from drug overdoses in 2015. "Once rare, these avoidable deaths are now more common than auto-accident fatalities or gun-inflicted homicides and suicides" ("The Great Opioid Epidemic," 2016).

- "The age group with the greatest past-year nonmedical use of opioids is young adults aged 18 to 25" (National Academies of Sciences, Engineering, and Medicine, 2017).

Adverse childhood experiences (ACEs) of abuse, household challenges, and neglect are taking a toll on both mental and physical health. The resources cited in the preceding list paint a dire picture—in addition to trauma and abuse, these data show that rising addiction, self-harm, and suicide threaten the lives of our youth and the well-being of our communities.

A Word About Mental Health, Trauma, and ACEs

As a leading expert in childhood trauma, Terry Wardle (as cited in Hendershott, 2016) has examined the following wounds and their causes.

- **Wounds of withholding:** When a child's caregiver fails to meet the child's physical or emotional needs

- **Wounds of aggression:** When a child's caregiver physically or emotionally abuses the child

- **Wounds of stressful events:** When a child experiences an uninvited event that is beyond what is considered normal in a child's life

- **Wounds of betrayal:** When a child's caregiver abuses or misuses power over the child

- **Wounds of long-term duress:** When a prolonged period of pressure or pain has a devastating effect on a child

These wounds typically result in the following cycle (Wardle, as cited in Hendershott, 2016).

- **Wounds:** A person experiences a traumatic event, leaving a profound impact on his or her life.
- **False beliefs:** The wound activates negative feelings in the person, leaving him or her in a state of discomfort.
- **Emotional upheaval:** The false beliefs following the wound lead to sadness, depression, shame, or other unsettled feelings.
- **Dysfunctional behavior:** The person copes with the pain in negative, unhealthy ways.
- **Life situations:** The wound leads to distortions or disorders that override the original wounding event.

Not surprisingly, students living lives of chaos and crisis struggle to achieve academically—further diminishing their hope for a brighter future. Poverty and trauma are known to impact student achievement (Jensen, 2019), but Janis Whitlock (as cited in Schrobsdorff, 2016), director of the Cornell Research Program on Self-Injury and Recovery, also attributes contemporary angst and depression among teens to hyperconnectedness (habitually using internet-connected devices), overexposure (receiving excessive exposure to constant stimuli), and competitiveness (constantly feeling compared to and in competition with peers). She states:

> If you wanted to create an environment to churn out really angsty people, we've done it. It's that they're in a cauldron of stimulus they can't get away from, or don't want to get away from, or don't know how to get away from. (as cited in Schrobsdorff, 2016)

Amid the disorder, few debate the truth that many students fail to meet their potential due to circumstances residing outside the school. Yet there is hope. As schools have realized the opportunity and potential in facilitating a student's or family's connection with much-needed support and service providers, leaders have also taken note. For example, in the United States, ESSA (2015) recognizes the need for holistic solutions to address the whole child. The Child Mind Institute's (2016) report on children's mental health concurs with this trend and further states that if educators, policymakers, parents, and mental health professionals come together to advocate for a sensible integration of approaches, schools may provide a stunning return on investment:

> Schools must continue to innovate and integrate approaches to school-based mental health—bringing the systemic focus of programs like PBIS into closer alignment with intensive individualized interventions while encouraging developmental awareness through early screening and progress monitoring. Schools must become the prime driver behind improving the mental health of America's children. (Child Mind Institute, 2016, p. 13)

These findings related to the whole child do not exist in isolation. In 2007, ASCD launched the Whole Child Initiative to broaden the conversation about education from a narrow definition of academic achievement to the promotion of children's long-term development and success (ASCD & CDC, 2014). In 2010, the CDC launched the Coordinated School Health (CSH) approach, which also addressed whole child aspects of education (Fisher et al., 2010). The WSCC model we first detailed in this book's introduction (page 6) incorporates elements of both these initiatives; it seeks to support schools in addressing students' academic, social, and emotional growth while also attending to the nonacademic needs of students and their families. The ASCD and the CDC developed this model in collaboration with leaders from various sectors to strengthen and unify their efforts to ensure "every young person in every school in every community is healthy, safe, engaged, supported, and challenged" (CDC, n.d.b).

Beyond combining the Whole Child Initiative with the CSH approach, the WSCC model also establishes two important objectives (CDC, n.d.b):

- It emphasizes the relationship between educational attainment and health, by putting the child at the center of a system designed to support both.

- It provides an update to the CSH approach to better align with the way schools function.

The official *Whole School, Whole Community, Whole Child* report further states, "Health and education affect individuals, society, and the economy and, as such, must work together whenever possible. Schools are a perfect setting for this collaboration" (ASCD & CDC, 2014, p. 2). In the same report, the ASCD and the CDC (2014) cite public health expert Lloyd J. Kolbe (2002):

> We call on communities—educators, parents, businesses, health and social service providers, arts professionals, recreation leaders, and policymakers at all levels—to forge a new compact with our young people to ensure their whole and healthy development. We ask communities to redefine learning to focus on the whole person. We ask schools and communities to lay aside perennial battles for resources and instead align those resources in support of the whole child. Policy, practice, and resources must be aligned to support not only academic learning for each child, but also the experiences encouraging development of a whole child—one who is knowledgeable, healthy, motivated, and engaged.

Kolbe (2002) affirms that schools need to coordinate and modernize their health programs as part of any effort toward overall educational reform. He argues that without this coordination to collectively improve education, health, and social outcomes, "we will forfeit one of the most appropriate and powerful means available to improve student performance" (Kolbe, 2002, p. 10).

These groups and experts understand that schools need to consider the whole child by including so-called *nonacademic* considerations in the learning effort. However, we think it's important to clarify that we find the descriptor *nonacademic* confusing as it relates to barriers to health and learning. Do we believe barriers to health and learning exist? And if so, do we believe these barriers described as *nonacademic* do, in fact, impact academics? According to Dawn Anderson-Butcher, Hal A. Lawson, Jerry Bean, Paul Flaspohler, Barbara Boone, and Amber Kwiatkowski (2008) in their article "Community Collaboration to Improve Schools," educators experience nonacademic barriers to learning that derive from students' exposure to developmental risk factors:

> Risk factors include emotional and behavioral problems, unmet basic needs for good nutrition, involvement with antisocial peers, unstable housing, inadequate family supports, and family conflict and related instabilities (Doll & Lyon, 1998; Early & Vonk, 2001; Lawson & Anderson-Butcher, 2001). These nonacademic barriers constrain optimal student success. Together they serve as reminders of the interdependence among academic learning and achievement, social development, and positive health and mental health. (p. 163)

We prefer the specificity of descriptors such as *developmental risk factors, nonschool environment, adverse childhood experiences,* and *protective factors* over the commonly used term *nonacademic factors*. Essentially, we suggest the language educators use intentionally align with the holistic view that a student's experiences, well-being, and learning are inseparable and should not be compartmentalized into descriptors such as *academic* or *nonacademic*.

Acknowledging and addressing experiences that have become barriers to learning requires schools to adjust their approach. Figure 1.1 (page 22) features a graphic representation of Rea and Zinskie's (2017) article on the 5H Holistic Framework (5HHF). Their 5HHF article identifies, defines, and organizes best educational practices to address equitable access and opportunity in an actionable manner. The risk factors explored and the protective factors Rea and Zinskie (2017) proffer "holistically address the educational needs and capacities of all students—especially students in poverty—for physical/mental health (Health), safety/ security (Hands), social-emotional care (Heart), cognitive development (Head), and family/ community support (Home)" (p. ii). Additionally, the article describes how ESSA (2015) supports their framework.

All these whole child efforts underscore a growing recognition of the need to create multifaceted, synergistic support systems inside and outside schools to promote the whole child's health and well-being. However, all the approaches we've discussed thus far lack opportunities to listen to those who understand students' lives best—the students themselves. We contend schools must build a foundation for their whole child efforts based on student voice.

When we refer to gathering student voice in this book, we are really asking that you consider the following questions.

- "Do we care enough to ask students themselves?"
- "Are we wise enough to listen to what they say?"

In reflecting on these questions, consider the words of freelance author Robert Brault (2014): "A child seldom needs a good talking-to as much as a good listening-to" (p. 106). Stephen M.

WHOLE CHILD HOLISTIC FRAMEWORK

5H HOLISTIC FACTORS (5HHF)

HEALTH | PHYSICAL & MENTAL **4**

Physical
- Healthy School Climate
- School Meals/Beverages
- Physical Education Program
- Health Education Program
- In-School Services
- Community Services
- Community & Family Partnerships
- Employee Wellness Program
- Qualified Health Educators

Mental
- Awareness Raising
- Stigma Removal
- Warning-Signs Recognition
- In-School Treatment
- Staff & Parent Education
- Trauma-Informed Practices
- Suicide Prevention
- Community Treatment

1 **HEAD | COGNITIVE DEVELOPMENT**
- School Size
- School Leadership
- Teacher Attributes
- Instructional Features
- Curriculum Characteristics
- Learning Time Opportunities
- Learning Strategies
- Learning Resources
- Advanced Courses
- Post-Secondary Preparation

HEART | SOCIAL-EMOTIONAL CARE **2**
- Unbiased Expectations
- Trusting Relationships
- Resilience Development
- Self-Esteem Enhancement
- Diversity Appreciation
- Emotion Management
- Relationship Skills
- Communication Skills
- Decision-Making Skills
- Growth Mindset
- Internal Motivation
- Leadership Styles
- Supportive School Climate

3 **HANDS | SAFETY & SECURITY**
- Equitable Discipline
- Preventable Discipline
- Instructional Approach
- Clear Expectations & Consequences
- Differential Reinforcement
- Restorative Justice
- Effective Interventions
- Authoritative Corrections
- Self-Discipline
- Minimize Classroom Removal
- In-School Suspension
- Bullying Prevention
- Safe School Climate

HOME | FAMILY & COMMUNITY ENGAGEMENT **5**

- Family Assessment
- Welcoming Schools
- Two-Way Communication
- Family Engagement
- Community Resources
- Family Knowledge
- Community Assessment
- Community Partnerships
- Community Mentors
- Community Advocates

Source: Adapted from Rea & Zinskie, 2017; © 2019 The Centergy Project.

Figure 1.1: The 5H Holistic Framework—5HHF.

Covey (2004), author of *The 7 Habits of Highly Effective People*, puts it another way when he implores readers, "Seek first to understand, then to be understood" (p. 235).

We find that schools rarely mine student voice concerning students' personal barriers to learning, the effectiveness of support systems in place, or the alignment of programming with students' needs and aspirations. To the degree that schools do gather student voice, they typically limit the scope and inquiry of such efforts to instructional improvement or the evaluation of school climate. Involving diverse students in focused conversations—both individual and group—about sensitive and complicated topics, policy creation or revision, and programming design is simply not a norm in many schools. We see this notion confirmed when we are consulting and conducting professional learning—whether at conferences or in school districts: educators invariably grab their phones and start snapping pictures of voice charts. We believe this must change to give our educational system a chance to fully meet the needs of the whole child. The WSCC fact sheet "Working With Students: Using Youth Voice to Promote Healthy Schools" affirms the importance of gathering student voice related to personal health and wellness: "Youth are the experts of their own experiences and are essential to making decisions about wellness policy, planning, and programs that really work" (Society for Public Health Education, 2019, p. 1). If educators are sincere in their efforts to support students academically, socially, and emotionally, it's almost impossible to exaggerate the power of listening with respect.

Trust

When seeking to gain the trust of your students, educators do *not* start with a blank slate. Students' experiences—inside and outside school, positive and negative—have influenced their propensity to trust people in positions of authority. Trust is a two-way street.

In *Reclaiming Youth at Risk*, trauma experts Larry K. Brendtro, Martin Brokenleg, and Steve Van Bockern (2019) characterize students' need for trusting relationships as being as basic as hunger or thirst. They note youth who experience trauma often display one of four pattern behaviors to convey their mistrust of adults: (1) *fight*, characterized by acting out; (2) *flight*, characterized by guarded behavior; (3) *fool*, characterized by the use of masking behavior; and (4) *follow*, characterized as youth who seek out like-minded peers for role models but not adults (Brendtro et al., 2019). Students who don't feel adults trust and respect them in their schools may simply refuse to engage, share, and learn (Barr & Gibson, 2020). However, adults who approach students with a genuine desire to listen and learn without judgment are more likely to be rewarded with deeper and stronger relationships with students.

Student voice advocates Russell J. Quaglia and Michael J. Corso (2014) encourage schools to lean into the wisdom of their students. They express student voice's importance and potential impact, stating:

> There are many ways in which student voice can have a positive impact on the educational challenges we face. When students believe their voices matter, they are more likely to be invested and engaged in their schools. When students believe teachers are listening to them, mutual trust and respect are likely

to flourish. When students believe they are being heard and influencing decisions, schools become more relevant to students' lives and are more likely to be seen as serving their needs. When adults and students partner, schools become laboratories for the multigenerational, collaborative, shared decision making that is part of most contemporary businesses, organizations, and companies. In addition, students' insights, creativity, energy, and confidence offer important perspectives that can help schools improve. (Quaglia & Corso, 2014, p. 3)

So how do you get students to trust their school enough to talk? Figure 1.2 provides valuable insight from the perspective of students in a conversation circle, a concept we explain in chapter 2 (page 38). Note this example and those we show in subsequent chapters are renderings of artifacts created during student voice sessions and accurately reflect comments of the participating students (grammatical nuances and all).

Building trust comes down to the intent to build trust and the leadership to pull it off. Covey (2018) identifies thirteen trust-building behaviors, of which we focus on four: (1) listen first, (2) talk straight, (3) demonstrate respect, and (4) extend trust. Brendtro and colleagues (2019) encourage educators to turn *toward* mistrustful youth, reacting positively to attention-seeking behavior, which they refer to as *bids for attention*, and communicating interest in students' lives. In *Trust First*, Pastor Bruce Deel and Sara Grace (2019) explain the importance of offering trust a little differently, stating that trust dynamics require people to cede or share control, which can be more complicated than extending other affirming qualities, such as compassion, empathy, and patience. As an example of this dynamic, they relate Deel's experience with a youth assigned to him as an alternative to jail for dealing drugs:

> I would welcome him warmly, then relax back in my chair. As much as I could, I let him do the talking. I listened. I kept my own demeanor calm, my gaze open. I kept my words and my thinking grounded in those three things I believe are foundational to trust: love, acceptance, and a nonjudgmental attitude. Would he start to trust me in that hour? Probably not. But I was creating the space for him to come to me next time a little less angry, a little more curious about who I was and what I might have to offer. (Deel & Grace, 2019, p. 23)

When students are speaking with a trusted member of the school staff, they share the unvarnished truth of their thoughts and their lives. Through intentional listening processes, staff learn from students what types of interventions would support them in addressing their barriers. Building trust between students and staff requires a deep, prolonged, and personal approach that includes the following actions.

- Gather student voice to create a culture where connecting with students is pervasive across the school.

- Strengthen relationships by facilitating connections among students, staff, parents, and partners.

- Cultivate hope by encouraging student agency, and grow the school staff's collective professional capacity by compassionately, responsibly, and creatively responding to student voice. When students see school leaders and faculty

I would trust my school enough to share my struggles if I could expect...

Empathy

No labelling, No stereotypes

Not to react to my appearance

For them to understand why I act the way I do

Trained therapists

Confidentiality

Staff not to take my mistakes personally

The teachers to not talk to eachother about my problems

For my family not to be blown up

No "pearl-clutching"

To understand I don't really know them well enough to trust them. I have all kinds of trust issues and building trust w/ me is going to take time and effort.

If I knew school staff could keep their emotions in check

Sincerity and Respect

Staff not to be afraid of me

for them to let me take it at my own pace w/o the pressure to go faster or deeper than I am comfortable going.

Access to people who have had the same experience or done the same thing

No fear of consequences and punishments. What I need is help but I can't tell you about "it" or you will give me punishment or quote policy to me.

The school to protect my reputation

Not to be taken away from my family

REAL listening and REAL talk

For them to not think 'I am just making excuses'

Them to use my experiences to help other kids

If I could receive the help I know they will recommend w/o my family being financially burdened.

them not to act like what I am going through is not important or that it is childish. It means something to me so it should mean something to them.

Compassion & Understanding

No judgement - less shame less blame

For adults not to interrupt me w/ their own stories

Not to start treating me differently

For them not to judge my family

If I knew they wouldn't yell at me or embarrass me

Them to try to understand my reasoning for certain situations (like absences)

them to help me toward an outcome, give me their opinion or some advice but then let me make the decisions since its my life

My school to have the resources & people I need to help out

Understanding that some kids act out due to what's going on on at home so when I've done something & I don't want my parents to find out, it's actually b/c it might actually make things worse at home

Source: © 2020 The Centergy Project.

Figure 1.2: Student voice chart on trust.

respond to their ideas, it buoys their hope with the following traits and beliefs (Barr & Gibson, 2013).

- ◆ *Optimism*—"Things can change."
- ◆ *Pride, self-esteem, and self-confidence*—"My opinion is valued."
- ◆ *Belonging*—"I matter here."
- ◆ *Purpose*—"I am making a difference now and in the future."

When students feel valued and heard, they feel more hopeful about the school and their place within it (Jensen, 2019). This is what makes gathering voice an essential part of the Centergy Cycle. The more intentional you are about gathering voice, the stronger the relationships you develop, the more hope you grow, and the more trust you build (see figure 1.3).

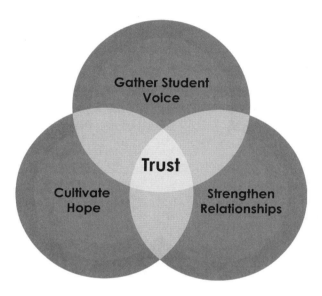

Source: © 2018 The Centergy Project.

Figure 1.3: Building trust.

The Community Schools Framework, published by the Institute for Educational Leadership (IEL) and the Coalition for Community Schools (CCS, 2017), provides excellent information regarding the interdependence of relational trust, equity, and school improvement, stating that relational trust is "the connective tissue that holds improving schools together. . . . It is built on four key attributes: respect, personal regard for others, competence, and integrity" (p. 12). IEL and CCS (2017) further state that the development of relational trust is "necessary to successfully maintain engagement of stakeholders whose support will ultimately help schools to thrive" (p. 12).

Although school improvement has traditionally taken place solely within the confines of the school district, Anderson-Butcher and colleagues (2008) explain the limitation of this approach:

Improvement planning is building-centered and "walled in." This walled-in improvement planning reflects traditional thinking about schools as stand-alone institutions focused exclusively on young people's learning and academic achievement, and it also reinforces the idea that educators are the school improvement experts. Of course, when improvement planning is walled in, external resources, opportunities, and assets are "walled out." (pp. 161–162)

We contend that avoiding a scenario in which school districts silo improvement, as Anderson-Butcher and colleagues (2008) describe, requires that schools predicate all whole child, student voice, and wraparound efforts on building relational trust and fostering collaboration. Figure 1.4 illustrates this concept. While the need for relational trust is simple to understand, the transition from siloed entities to associations of care is not easy for schools to achieve, which is where we arrive at the importance of wraparound services.

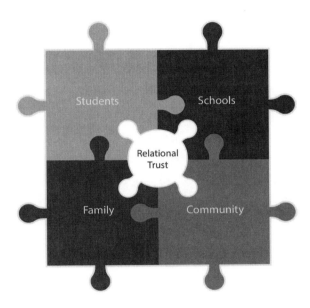

Source: © 2019 The Centergy Project.

Figure 1.4: Relational trust plays a key role in school improvement.

Wraparound Services

As schools consider the need to provide more than academic support, they discover they are uniquely positioned to address equity as it relates to a student's or family's access to services and opportunity. In "Cages of Their Own Design," author Fredrick Hess (2009) says school leaders demonstrating breakthrough and visionary leadership must learn to color outside the lines by recognizing "the difference between how business is usually done and how it could be done." To fully embrace a whole child philosophy and implement wraparound services, school leaders must challenge conventional wisdom, exercise flexibility, embrace possibility, and collaborate with noneducators. Such leaders must break the cage educators too often lock themselves inside to ensure they can better and more fully serve students, families, and communities. For this book, we group school- and community-based wraparound services into the following six categories.

1. **Health and wellness:** Access to embedded health clinics, mental health providers, and updated, relevant health curriculum addressing students' physical, mental, and social-emotional health

2. **Basic needs:** Access to fundamental resources such as adequate food, clothing, housing, school supplies, and transportation

3. **Community services:** Access to community-based programs—such as adult education, support for teen parents, mentoring, and support and recovery services related to domestic violence and sexual abuse—as well as immigration services

4. **Academic opportunity:** Access to programming and resources, such as technology, after-school tutoring, educational advocacy, alternative suspension programming, or credit recovery aimed at boosting academic achievement

5. **College and career transition:** Access to high-quality college and career transition assistance, including counseling, dual enrollment, college visits, job fairs, college application assistance and financial aid guidance, apprenticeships and job skills training, mentors, military recruitment, and aptitude, interests, and personality instrument.

6. **Safety and justice:** Access to information and services related to restorative practices, law enforcement, probation, legal rights, court proceedings, probation, personal and home safety, juvenile justice, and legal aid

Figure 1.5 depicts these six categories as part of our recommended wraparound model.

Source: © 2019 The Centergy Project.

Figure 1.5: The wraparound services model.

*Visit **go.SolutionTree.com/leadership** for a free reproducible version of this figure.*

A Word About Mental Health, Trauma, and ACEs

According to the Child Mind Institute (2016):

> Children struggling with mental health and learning disorders are at risk for poor outcomes in school and in life, and outdated approaches to discipline are only making matters worse. . . . A widely deployed, integrated system of evidence-supported, school-based mental health and preventive services is needed. If we want to help our children and our schools, we cannot wait. (p. 1)

Schools planning to focus on wraparound initiatives designed to benefit the whole child must develop shared beliefs, create a school atmosphere of trust and support, select a single but integrated schoolwide framework, and establish practices for schoolwide monitoring and evaluation (Barr & Gibson, 2020). This broadened mission will create challenges above and beyond the three Rs of *reading*, *writing*, and *arithmetic* to include a fourth R—*resilience*.

School leaders will need to build new and enduring community connections. Despite school leaders' desire to provide more than academic resources to students, they often lack the experience, expertise, and resources to effectively address nonschool factors impacting academic achievement. In *Investing in What Works*, Leigh Dingerson (2015) reports on the work of researchers Tina Trujillo and Michelle Renée (2013), stating, "An increasing body of research suggests that strengthening ties between schools and communities is a critical component of effective turnaround" (p. 17). As such, the report further states, "School leadership should focus intentionally on building community and parent ties, and ensuring that schools are welcoming and accessible, particularly to parents" (Dingerson, 2015, p. 17).

In wraparound schools, community agencies, nonprofits, and businesses become strategic collaborators with a shared mission to cooperatively deliver their services through embedded partnerships. A grant description by the CCS, Communities in Schools, and StriveTogether (n.d.) articulates an emerging, hopeful, and synergistic vision for student-centered learning:

> Our vision and key characteristics confront the false dichotomy between addressing academic or non-academic needs that has driven much of education reform until recently. Improving student academic performance and creating the opportunities and supports young people deserve are inextricably linked; both are essential if we are to create an ecosystem in which our young people can learn and thrive. In that ecosystem, the ideas behind the whole child, personalized learning, youth and family voice, and related strategies live together, reinforcing and strengthening one another.
>
> Creating a student-centered learning system requires that we permanently break down historic silos and build much stronger bridges between public schools and other agencies and organizations concerned with the well-being and development of children and youth. In addition, multiple local initiatives intended to improve results for children and youth—sometimes competing and colliding—must align their efforts and work toward common goals, especially when they are working in the same public schools. (p. 2)

This book provides a framework and processes for launching wraparound services in schools. You will notice we do not refer to these centers as *community schools*. This is intentional on our part. Although many organizations use the phrase *community schools* to describe schools with a deep degree of collaboration with community partners, we restrict the descriptor to those schools that utilize the full framework for community schools as defined in the *Community Schools Playbook* (Partnership for the Future of Learning, n.d.). This publication describes community schools as having "a foundation of powerful teaching that includes challenging academic content and supports students' mastery of 21st century skills and competencies" (Partnership for the Future of Learning, n.d., p. 3). The description continues with a comprehensive framework combining four key pillars (features) that establish the conditions students need in order to thrive (Partnership for the Future of Learning, n.d.).

1. Integrated student supports

2. Expanded and enriched learning time and opportunities

3. Active family and community engagement

4. Collaborative leadership and practices

While a wraparound initiative can touch on each of these pillars, its primary focuses are integrated student supports plus active family and community engagement.

Dingerson's (2015) report provides greater clarity on the concept of a wraparound initiative and its potential impact on equity. She states the availability of wraparound services to students and families is fundamental to school improvement in high-poverty communities: "Students cannot learn to their full potential when they are hungry, exhausted or ill, or when their parents cannot support them at home" (Dingerson, 2015, p. 17). The report also highlights efforts in Ohio and Kentucky schools to establish health and other services within the school building, including programs to support the broader community, including citizenship training for parents, English language services, job training, and more (Dingerson, 2015). Related to funding these services, the report states:

> Many of these programs are financially supported by redirecting funds from other agencies or services. For example, health clinics funded through state and federal programs can be relocated into school buildings, area social service agencies and non-profits can come together to offer programming in the school and to the school community using philanthropic and public dollars available to them. The key is creating the relationships, and establishing the school building as a hub for such community and student-centered services. (Dingerson, 2015, p. 17)

Robert D. Putnam's (2015) book *Our Kids* details the sad reality many students face—the erosion of the American Dream (the belief that all people can have a prosperous life through high-quality education and a strong work ethic). Putnam (2015) attributes this decline to shrinking social connections, which have historically opened up opportunities for prior generations, leaving a growing number of students without the support systems they need to thrive. The 2016 report titled *Community Schools: Transforming Struggling Schools Into*

Thriving Schools (Center for Popular Democracy, CCS, & Southern Education Foundation, 2016) stresses the importance of voice; collaboration among families, schools, and the community; and the provision of embedded wraparound services. We believe wraparound services have the potential to strengthen the four areas Putnam (2015) identifies as powerfully affecting how well children do in life: (1) families, (2) parenting, (3) schooling, and (4) community.

Conclusion

Schools are well positioned to become the hub of connection and opportunity in areas where societal and family protective factors—such as family connectedness, safe neighborhoods, and overall resilience—have eroded. As the third wave of whole child school reform comes ashore, educators need practical and actionable guidance for how to address equity by tapping into community resources and expertise. By following the steps depicted in the Centergy Cycle (figure I.3, page 9), school and community leaders can first identify and prioritize barriers to student success and then centralize community resources for the purpose of mitigating identified barriers to health and learning.

Even before the added stressors of a pandemic and civil unrest in 2020, students were already growing up in a different world than their parents and teachers did. Susanna Schrobsdorff (2016) writes:

> [Modern students] are the post-9/11 generation, raised in an era of economic and national insecurity. They've never known a time when terrorism and school shootings weren't the norm. They grew up watching their parents weather a severe recession, and, perhaps most important, they hit puberty at a time when technology and social media were transforming society.

In *Building a Culture of Hope*, Robert D. Barr and Emily L. Gibson (2013) advocate for schools to respond to this reality with intentional and integrated support systems—systems capable of cultivating and enhancing hope and resilience by growing optimism, belonging, self-worth, purpose, and self-regulation. Using the Centergy's Cycle's respectful, collaborative, and actionable framework, your school and district can deliver on-site, full-spectrum wraparound services for your students and families. The approach is scalable and built on a foundation of relational trust and collaboration. Students, parents, community members, and educators can work together to address a wide range of school and student needs in a coordinated, hopeful, cost-effective fashion. By leveraging the expertise and resources within your community, you'll be poised to do the following.

- Respond to your students' self-identified needs in a respectful, compassionate, motivational, and effective manner.

- Create a synergistic system of interconnected support initiatives and opportunities.

- Afford equity of access and opportunity to all students and families.

- Strengthen relationships among school staff, students, and families.

- Build social capital by deepening connectivity among your school, your students and families, and your community.

Following Leigh's proposal to her school board, she asked to resign the principal position she had loved for ten years so that she could facilitate the launch of the district's wraparound center. This was going to be meaningful work. This was going to be hopeful work. *This could truly make a difference.*

Part II

GATHERING STUDENT VOICE

Chapter 2

IDENTIFY NEEDS

If people want schools to improve, they need to ask the students how to improve them. We know a lot about schools, and our experiences and ideas could really help adults have a deeper understanding of what we need and what is working and what is not.

—High school student

The first step of the Centergy Cycle (identify needs) begins with gathering student voice about the barriers beyond the classroom that interfere with students' academic achievement and social-emotional health. Author and management consultant Margaret Wheatley (2011) writes, "Be brave enough to start a conversation that matters." To that purpose, the big *why* of gathering student voice is to transform school from something done *to* or *for* students and families to something done *with* students and families. Figure 2.1 (page 36) captures student responses to an essential question, "Why is it important for schools to gather student voice?"

Done well, processes of deep, authentic engagement with students not only promote a culture of trust but also inform and drive programming as well as school improvement. Quaglia and Corso (2014) state clearly that students are a school's potential, not the problem:

> We believe student voice should be instrumental to any educational reform agenda. Our theme, therefore, is *Listen, Learn,* and *Lead.* We must not only ask young people their thoughts, but we must truly listen. We must learn from what they are saying by asking important questions and discovering why they feel as they do. And finally, we must utilize what we learn to be effective educators. (p. xiv)

Author and expert on the effects of poverty on students Eric Jensen (2019) further asserts that the simple act of listening to students affirms their worth and importance and gives them the feeling of being appreciated and respected. Moreover, offering students a voice in class gives them a greater sense of control and self-confidence in their learning and leads to greater engagement: "The class becomes *our class* instead of only the teacher's class" (Jensen, 2019, p. 103). While listening has a positive impact on students' classroom performance,

Why is it important for schools to gather student voice?

Because it makes us feel heard, safe, relieved, worth it, cared for, smart, acknowledged, gratified, trusted, wanted, validated, and understood, like I'm valued as a human. It makes me feel like I can trust our school.

NO ONE understands the experience of schools better than the students who are living it — we know what's wrong for us and what isn't.

It is important to listen to our voice but it is also important to follow up on what we say so we know you listened, cared, thought about our ideas, and didn't waste our time.

We want to feel like a family — not just a student.

Because our parents and the school staff experienced school in a different time.

It will increase our motivation to come to school.

Because it is nice to be treated like a colleague or a trusted source.

We want to talk about policies that affect us — phone, dress code, PDA, technology, tardy, bathroom, having water, transition time, use of lockers — all kinds of policies.

So we can make our school better and then be able to brag all the stuff that is going on.

It is our school and our school experience. Students should be listened to so you can understand our experiences and really understand what is going on and what we need.

We are kind of the center of what it's all about.

So we have the chance to tell the truth about what is going on.

Because students in school don't usually have a voice about most anything that happens in school. School happens TO us.

So you can understand what is really going on and what we are thinking — what is affecting our learning — what we need and then you can get ideas about the right steps you can take to help us address our issues.

Students know what is really going on in classrooms, in the bathrooms, in the hallways, and on the buses, so ask us.

Listening just increases everybody's understanding.

Source: © 2020 The Centergy Project.

Figure 2.1: Student voice chart on the importance of gathering student voice.

school staff can also deepen students' connection with their school by involving them in the process of planning student support or school improvement around the students' own needs and priorities.

A Word About Mental Health, Trauma, and ACEs

Sometimes, educators are better talkers than listeners; they tend to interrupt, explain, correct, or expand on students' thoughts. Hendershott (2016) explains that giving educators space to listen to wounded students forms the foundation for gaining these students' trust. He emphasizes the value of providing wounded students the opportunity to tell their stories so their wounds can surface. Quoting brain researcher Daniel J. Siegel, Hendershott (2016) adds:

> Healing from a difficult experience emerges when the left side [of the brain] works with the right to tell our life stories. When children learn to pay attention to and share their own stories, they can respond in healthy ways to everything from a scraped elbow to a major loss or trauma. (p. 33)

Wounded students' stories don't have to define them; the way they learn to process their stories will.

Beyond enhancing school climate and culture, student voice processes yield valuable content capable of increasing the effectiveness of schools. The student voice processes we describe in this chapter and chapter 3 (page 63) will yield qualitative and quantitative information your school can use in the areas of school improvement, student and family engagement, partnership planning, professional development, parent and community education, and grant proposals.

Gathering student voice to identify needs requires knowing *how* to gather it. Depending on a variety of factors, a single staff member might facilitate these processes, while in others, it's best to have a team involved. For example, a counselor may conduct all interviews with off-track students while a principal might pull together the senior class to set the stage for graduation stories. Whatever the case, underlying all these processes is the desire to strengthen relationships through a facilitative approach akin to *motivational interviewing*, which is a form of "arranging conversations so that people talk themselves into change, based on their own values and interests" (Miller & Rollnick, 2013, p. 4). Empathy is at the heart of motivational interviewing (North, 2017), requiring the interviewer to shift from a prescriptive approach, where he or she is the expert giving advice, to a collaborative approach, where he or she treats students as partners with a shared mission of positive change (Naar-King & Suarez, 2011). In our experience, students overwhelmingly validate a motivational approach to gathering their voice; this tells us that objective inquiry and a lack of judgment are critical to gaining their trust.

Table 2.1 (page 38) shows an overview of the student voice processes used in the first step of the Centergy Cycle: identify needs. This chapter presents three processes for achieving this step: (1) conversation circles, (2) off-track interviews, and (3) graduation stories. These processes focus on accumulating qualitative data to identify categories of needs (such as transience, mental health, and immigration). The next chapter features step 2 processes related to establishing priorities based on the needs you identify.

Table 2.1: Student Voice Processes—Step 1

	Process	Purpose
Step 1: Identify Needs	Conversation circles	Gather broad information about academic achievement, social-emotional wellness, and family engagement.
	Off-track interviews	Conduct personal conversations with off-track students to learn about barriers and develop action plans when appropriate.
	Graduation stories	Gather reflective feedback from graduates on their school experiences.

Conversation Circles

Gathering student voice begins with engaging students in guided conversations. These conversations occur between student groups and staff facilitators (typically one staff member to facilitate the conversation and one to take notes). We use the term *circles* figuratively to reflect a sense of inclusion and equality rather than a prescribed room arrangement. You can tailor conversation circles to serve a variety of purposes, such as the following.

- **Inquiry:** Includes identifying student needs and barriers to learning, clarifying perceptions, and exploring ideas or concerns related to instruction, climate, or safety

- **Brainstorming:** Includes generating ideas for carrying out items such as grade-level spirit activities, increasing participation in school activities, and event planning

- **Problem solving:** Includes addressing or troubleshooting problems such as littering on campus or cell phone use during class

- **Improvement:** This includes refining or fine-tuning common practices such as arrival and dismissal processes; pep rallies; and programming, process, and policy development

These purposeful conversations produce tangible ideas for school programming and improvement while also affirming and engaging students. In our experience, involving students in the process of school improvement is not the norm in most schools. In such schools, on those few occasions where staff members do gather student voice, they often limit the scope and perspective of that voice to highly engaged and high-achieving students—those who staff perceive to be leaders. Therefore, staff members are more likely to value these students' opinions. Likewise, staff and parents often monopolize or gatekeep core topics such as culture, achievement, programming, student support, and barriers to learning. Schools willing to convene more diverse groups of students—not just the high achievers—to discuss critical issues often find students can make incredibly valuable contributions to the collective perspective.

This discussion must be just that—a discussion. When schools conduct activities to gather mass information—such as administering schoolwide surveys on which students check boxes to express their engagement—rather than deeply and authentically engage with a broad base of students, they may find themselves in possession of unactionable data that lack the context student voice provides. We find intentionally gathering student voice an essential and strategic step in the transformational work of becoming a school focused on whole child development.

voices
FROM THE FIELD

Is anyone going to really do anything with this information? We've taken a lot of surveys with no follow-through. I don't want to waste my time.

—High school senior leader

Figure 2.2 provides an overview of conversation circles, conducted to determine barriers and opportunities related to academic achievement, social-emotional wellness, and family engagement. Through these conversations, schools can uncover what students desire and value as part of their school experience as well as discover academic and nonacademic concerns that students identify as getting in the way of their success and overall wellness.

Objectives	Identify academic and social-emotional barriers to achievement.
	Identify family needs.
	Socialize the concept of wraparound services.
	Build a culture of trust.
Suggested time frame	Sixty to ninety minutes
Facilitators	One facilitator to lead the discussion
	One notetaker (optional)
Number of students per session	Ten to twenty students
Number of sessions	A variety, to include a cross section of students, such as:
	• High-achieving students
	• Average, engaged students
	• Disengaged students
	• English learners
	• Off-track students (students with discipline issues, truancy problems, and so on)
	• Grade repeaters (such as retained ninth graders)
Materials	Flip chart and markers; tape, if needed, to hang flip chart paper; sticky notes
Location	A private area conducive to conversation and group movement

Figure 2.2: Conversation circle planning guide.

Like all people, students want someone to understand them, listen to them, and believe they have something worthwhile to say (Brendtro et al., 2019; Rice & Dolgin, 2008). As such, and because conversation circles are exploratory in nature, your display of empathy and acceptance is critical to uncovering the narratives and perspectives of your students (Naar-King & Suarez, 2011). Further, students who have struggled in school expect direction and correction from school conversations rather than consultation. By specifically requesting their input, you may even find these previously disengaged students wanting to take a public role in idea generation as well as process and program development. Additionally, these conversations have the potential to awaken loyalty and purpose in students if facilitators approach the circles with genuine curiosity and nonjudgment. It's almost impossible to exaggerate the power of simply listening with respect.

Ultimately, conversation circles yield qualitative data for the construction of a Student Voice Needs Survey, which makes it possible to gather the quantitative data necessary to identify priorities for services and partnerships (see chapter 3, page 63). For example, if the need for food and clothing surfaces in conversation circles, you might use the survey to log the specific numbers of students interested in care closets providing food and clothing. Clarifying the extent of the need informs the level of service that partners (like a nonprofit food bank) might provide as well as the space required to deliver the service (for example, a school food pantry). We expand on this work throughout the book.

voices
FROM THE FIELD

We remember holding a series of conversation circles with a group of students who helped write the Student Voice Needs Survey. When the time came to discuss the process for rolling out the survey to the student body, students suggested they should take the lead by facilitating grade-level meetings to explain the purpose and encourage their peers to take the assignment seriously because, as they said, "This survey really matters." One quiet girl suffering from social anxiety raised her hand to volunteer, noting this effort was important enough to her to overcome her public-speaking fears.

—Leigh Colburn and Linda Beggs

The following sections contain ideas for rolling out conversation circles—what to do before conducting conversation circles, what to do during them, and some additional uses you may find for the information they generate. However, it's important to note that these ideas are not set in stone. Adapt them as necessary while keeping in mind the most essential aspect of conversation circles is to keep the experience *relational* and *personal*. Developing a culture of trust begins with listening; thus, conversation circles are a critical first step toward intentionally gathering student voice, strengthening relationships, and cultivating hope.

Before the Conversation Circle

Before you conduct any conversation circles, you must complete a few essential tasks, such as determining who to invite among both students and staff. For staff, we find it's helpful to have two faculty or staff members—one to facilitate discussion and one to take notes.

When choosing a facilitator, a person's attributes and skills matter much more than his or her title, especially his or her ability to do the following.

- Quickly establish rapport with students.
- Listen without judgment (verbal or nonverbal).

A small number of adults (usually fewer than four) may observe for training or other purposes, such as developing subject-matter expertise related to the conversation topic. To foster transparency, any time observers attend, introduce them and explain to students why they are attending.

As we noted in the introduction to this book, we advise that schools implement conversation circles specifically with middle or high school students. We recommend seeking input from these students (as opposed to elementary students) because many older students have the maturity and ability to reflect on their life and school experiences thus far. For example, an eighth- or ninth-grade student struggling with anxiety is in a better position to objectively reflect on events and experiences that escalated his or her anxiety during elementary school.

To make students as comfortable as possible, meet with student groups that are homogenous in design but still representative of the school as a whole. (Refer to figure 2.2, page 39.) You may also decide to further subdivide the groups by gender when you think it's appropriate to the topic or school's dynamics.

The following sections suggest two additional actions you can take before conducting a conversation circle to ensure participation and a productive process: (1) send personal invitations and (2) prepare flip charts and the conversation circle space.

Send Personal Invitations

Invitations to conversation circles, such as the example in figure 2.3 (page 42), present you with an opportunity to create a high-touch culture in your school and connect with students as individuals. Students you select should receive a personal invitation, either face-to-face or with a printed invitation, rather than an email, text, or general announcement. Don't require attendance—allow students to decline the invitation.

Prepare Flip Charts and the Conversation Circle Space

Effective conversation circles require the use of several flip charts. Table 2.2 (page 42) provides a guide for preparing sets of these flip charts to set expectations, break the ice, and identify student needs. Rather than starting from scratch with each meeting, the facilitator or notetaker adds to these same flip charts with each group. As a new group comes in, the notetaker should change the color of the marker he or she is using to indicate which groups came up with different ideas. Having all groups' ideas recorded on the same page increases transparency and assures students you are not singling them out for some hidden agenda. Additionally, having ideas already in place on each chart ensures that later groups must dig beyond the surface-level ideas and issues previous groups identified to get to deeper topics.

You're Invited to a Conversation Circle!

"Once you choose HOPE, anything is possible."

—Christopher Reeve

Our school wants to find out from you—our students—how to make our school a better place for you and your families. We are holding a series of conversation circles to listen to what you have to say about how the school can support you academically and in other areas of your life.

Date: January 9, 2020

Time: 12:30–2:00 p.m.

Location: Wraparound Group Conference Room

I hope you will join us!

Sincerely,

Ms. Greene, Counselor

_____

Please drop this form off to Ms. Greene in the counseling office and let us know if you will be coming on January 9 so we can notify your teacher to excuse you from class.

Student Name: _____ Cell Number: _____

	Yes, I will attend the conversation circle.
	I might attend the conversation circle, but would like to talk to you to learn more.
	No, I will not attend the conversation circle.

Figure 2.3: Sample invitation to a conversation circle.

Table 2.2: Flip Chart Preparation

Purpose	Flip Chart Heading
Set expectations	Group norms
Break the ice	What do you care about?
	What gives you hope?
	What helps you come back from something difficult?
Identify student needs	Academic, college, and career services
	Behavior and life skills
	Community partnerships
	Family needs

In addition to preparing flip charts, consider the best place to hold your conversation circles. Choose a relatively private space where students face the flip charts and the facilitators. To limit side conversations, avoid having students face each other. A half-circle works well for this purpose. Also, prepare hall passes for students returning to class after the meeting and offer snacks, water, or other refreshments if you're able.

During the Conversation Circle

While conducting conversation circles, staff facilitators may expect to see some groups of students dramatically increase their engagement throughout several meetings—especially quiet, disengaged students or students who either are off track in their learning or frequently receive discipline referrals (or both). But at a first meeting, facilitators should expect students who are not typically asked their opinions to enter with visible skepticism and doubt—crossed arms, furrowed brows, cocked heads. Some may even ask if they're in trouble. Once facilitators establish rapport and students trust the inquiry is a sincere attempt to gather their honest feedback without judgment, expect the mood to lift as students more readily and substantively share their experiences and ideas.

Approach this task with a spirit of curiosity and a lack of judgment. You are likely to hear things that you disagree with or that are demonstrably false; that's OK. Your goal is to listen rather than correct so students leave feeling heard and valued. During the discussion, you may need to redirect or remind students regarding agreed-on norms in some situations, but this is not a time for facilitators to debate the opinions, experiences, or feelings students express. Simply listen.

The following sections explain how you carry out the phases of a conversation circle, which include explaining the purpose, setting group norms, using icebreakers, gathering information on needs and barriers, and concluding the conversation circle.

Explain the Purpose

Introduce yourself plus any other adults present, and explain your and their roles. If other staff members are present to observe, explain they are here to listen, not to participate. You might reinforce this with any adult observers before the meeting because they can instantly change the conversation circle's dynamics with an innocent yet ill-advised comment. For example, we remember a principal directing a student who was slouching in his chair to sit up during a conversation circle about substance use. (Note that we write in detail about substance abuse and the Centergy Cycle in the appendix, page 227.) The principal wasn't rude or too authoritarian. Nevertheless, the notion that this was a safe space for self-expression evaporated, and all students shut down.

After introductions, thank the students for agreeing to join this conversation circle. Explain you have invited them because their opinions and ideas are important to you, the school, and the district. Encourage them to speak not only for themselves but also from the experiences of friends and other students who may not be present. Introduce the concept of wraparound services using the wraparound services model illustrated in figure I.3 (page 9), if you think it will support your explanation.

Explain what will happen with the information you gather. Include the following in your explanation.

- Staff will create a Student Voice Needs Survey.
- Students will take the survey.

- Staff will use the survey data to prioritize services and external partners based on need.
- Staff will hold focus groups with students to gather more voice about potential programming.
- The school will offer targeted services to students and their families.

Set Group Norms

Once you've set the tone of the conversation by introducing yourself, any staff present, and the concept of wraparound services, have students develop a set of group norms that will establish guiding principles for the conversation. For example, start the conversation circle by saying something like the following:

> I am meeting with you today to explore how we can collectively improve the experience of school by better meeting the needs of our students and families. This experience may be different from other meetings you have had with school staff because I am not here to talk to you about changes you need to make, nor am I here to make any recommendations at all. I am here to find out as much as possible about the lives of students in our school and the type of support you believe would make the greatest positive impact for our students. As you can see from the charts, we have some topics we are going to explore, but I would like to agree on some group norms first. How can we make sure we get the most out of our time together?

Record students' answers on the Group Norms flip chart for reference. Expect a list of basic good manners—*speak one at a time, be respectful, put phones away,* and so on. Emphasize that a critical part of respecting others is to maintain the confidentiality of all those involved in the circle. If students do not ask to include the following, add these to the list of norms: *tell the truth for yourself and others* and *listen to and respect the truth of others.* Last, add *be loyal to those absent.* This last item is especially important. Covey (2004) puts it like this:

> One of the most important ways to manifest integrity is to be *loyal to those who are not present.* In doing so, we build the trust of those who are present. When you defend those who are absent, you retain the trust of those present. (p. 196)

Explain to students that they should respect people outside the room and not criticize others, both peers and staff. This is particularly critical to gaining the trust and support of teachers. The initiative of gathering student voice will quickly derail if conversation circles become gripe sessions about the faculty or staff. If a teacher's name comes up as an exemplar of effective behavior, feel free to pause and have the notetaker record the positive feedback to share privately with the teacher.

As subsequent groups come in, you may simply review these group norms and ask if anyone wants to add to them. Likewise, as gathering student voice becomes a habit at your school, a quick reminder of group norms will suffice.

Use Icebreakers

As an icebreaking activity, display the flip charts with questions (What do you care about? What gives you hope? and What helps you come back from something difficult?) and ask students to contribute their thoughts. This helps students get comfortable talking about themselves and the day-to-day challenges they face. Help facilitate the ensuing conversation as necessary, and record their answers. If some students prefer not to answer aloud, permit them to write their responses on sticky notes they can place on the charts before leaving. Should you encounter students who don't want to participate, respectfully thank them for coming and give them a pass to leave. In addition to getting students talking, this activity gives you and other staff, when they read the charts, an opportunity to connect with the students and tap into their hopes, values, and experiences.

Gather Information on Needs and Barriers

The real gathering of student voice begins as you address needs and barriers to learning. Begin with the Academic, College, and Career Services flip chart, asking students, "What types of support do students need in the areas of academics and college or career preparation?" Start the post-icebreaker conversation with this topic because it's both expected and nonthreatening to talk about. Students generally feel safe talking about issues such as SAT prep, tutoring, and internships, and opening with this line of inquiry allows you to establish rapport before moving to the more sensitive areas of social-emotional needs. Figure 2.4 (page 46) features an example flip chart with the kind of student feedback you are likely to receive.

Continue with the Behavior and Life Skills, Community Partnerships, and Family Needs charts, examples of each of which are pictured in figures 2.5 (page 47), 2.6 (page 48), and 2.7 (page 49). In *Motivational Interviewing With Adolescents and Young Adults*, Sylvie Naar-King and Mariann Suarez (2011) provide a couple of tips to help you keep the environment nonthreatening, which is especially important when moving into these more delicate issues. First, keep your pronouns in the third person to avoid making students feel personally put on the spot. Likewise, the word *problem* suggests a label, decreases students' agency to change their behavior, and may result in a student becoming defensive. For example, when discussing substance use as a barrier, a question such as "Do you use drugs or alcohol?" is likely to put students on the defensive. Instead, try, "We've mentioned substance use. What are some of the things affecting students that might result in alcohol or drug use?" (Naar-King & Suarez, 2011).

Conclude the Conversation Circle

As the conversation circle begins to wrap up (usually after about sixty to ninety minutes), thank students for their willingness to share their thoughts and ideas. Explain any next steps you have planned, such as the possibility of subsequent meetings or when you expect to roll out the Student Voice Needs Survey.

Additional Uses of Conversation Circle Results

The primary artifacts of your conversation circles are your flip charts. Use these to interject student voice into school culture and the community in a variety of ways. Think of every interaction with a teacher, administrator, potential partner, or volunteer as an opportunity

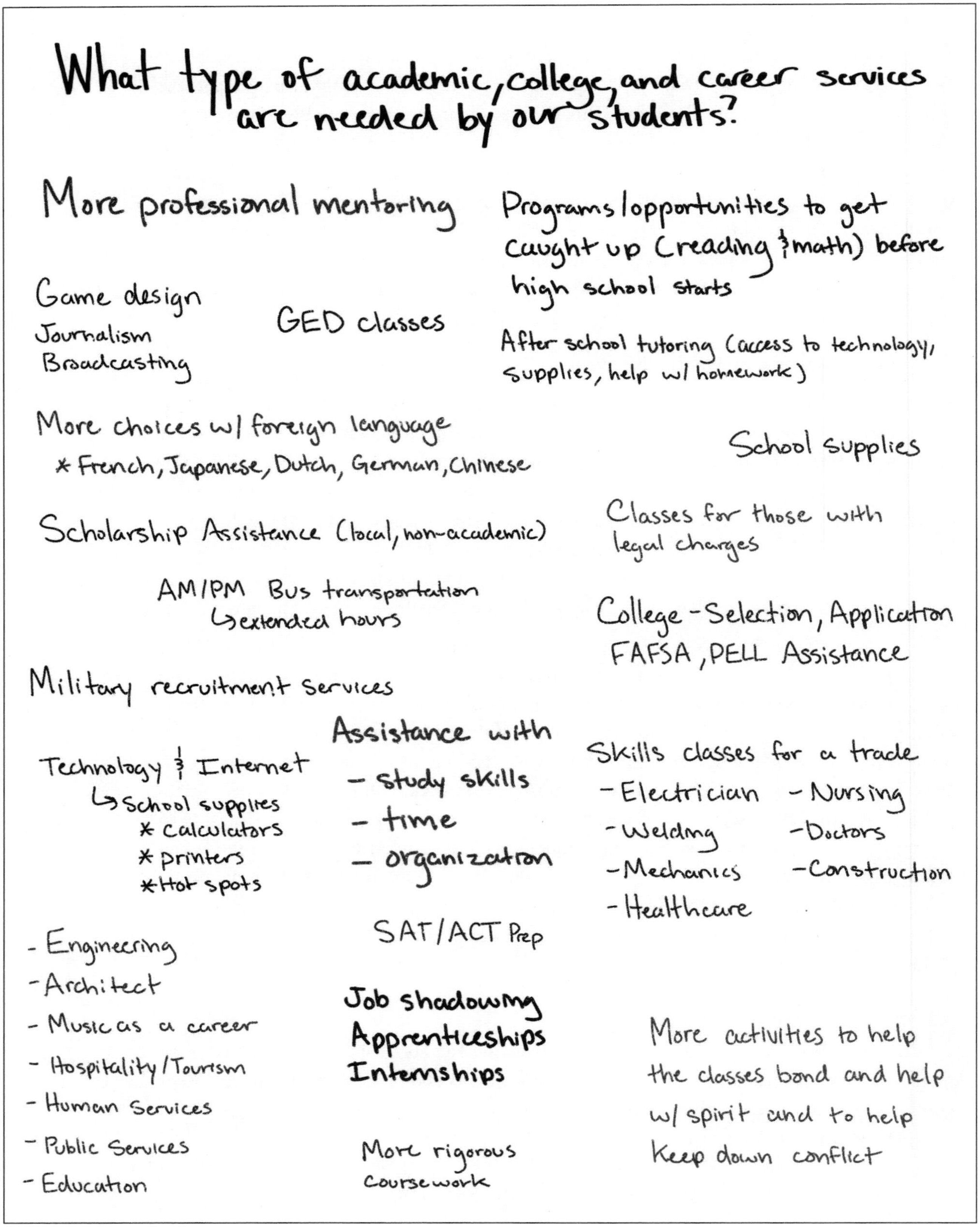

What type of academic, college, and career services are needed by our students?

More professional mentoring

Programs/opportunities to get caught up (reading ¿math) before high school starts

After school tutoring (access to technology, supplies, help w/ homework)

Game design
Journalism
Broadcasting

GED classes

More choices w/ foreign language
* French, Japanese, Dutch, German, Chinese

School supplies

Scholarship Assistance (local, non-academic)

Classes for those with legal charges

AM/PM Bus transportation
↳ extended hours

College - Selection, Application
FAFSA, PELL Assistance

Military recruitment services

Technology ¿ Internet
↳ School supplies
   * calculators
   * printers
   * Hot spots

Assistance with
— study skills
— time
— organization

Skills classes for a trade
- Electrician   - Nursing
- Welding   - Doctors
- Mechanics   - Construction
- Healthcare

- Engineering
- Architect
- Music as a career
- Hospitality/Tourism
- Human Services
- Public Services
- Education

SAT/ACT Prep

Job shadowing
Apprenticeships
Internships

More rigorous Coursework

More activities to help the classes bond and help w/ spirit and to help keep down conflict

Source: © 2020 The Centergy Project.

Figure 2.4: Academic, College, and Career Services flip chart with feedback.

What types of behavior and life skills assistance are needed by our students?

More exposure/experience with diverse people (special needs, Faith, Races, careers, culture)

Driver's Ed

Building healthy relationships

Financial literacy (Entrepreneurship)

Ending toxic relationships

A class for teaching Social/emotional skills

Self-management of technology (social media, etc.)

Public speaking Presentation skills

First Aid/Response/CPR

Self Defense – Personal/Home Safety

Interviewing skills, Resume writing

Yoga/Meditation

Conflict Resolution/Mediation
↳ Student to student
Student to teacher
Athlete to coach

Nutrition and Wellness

Source: © 2020 The Centergy Project.

Figure 2.5: Behavior and Life Skills flip chart with feedback.

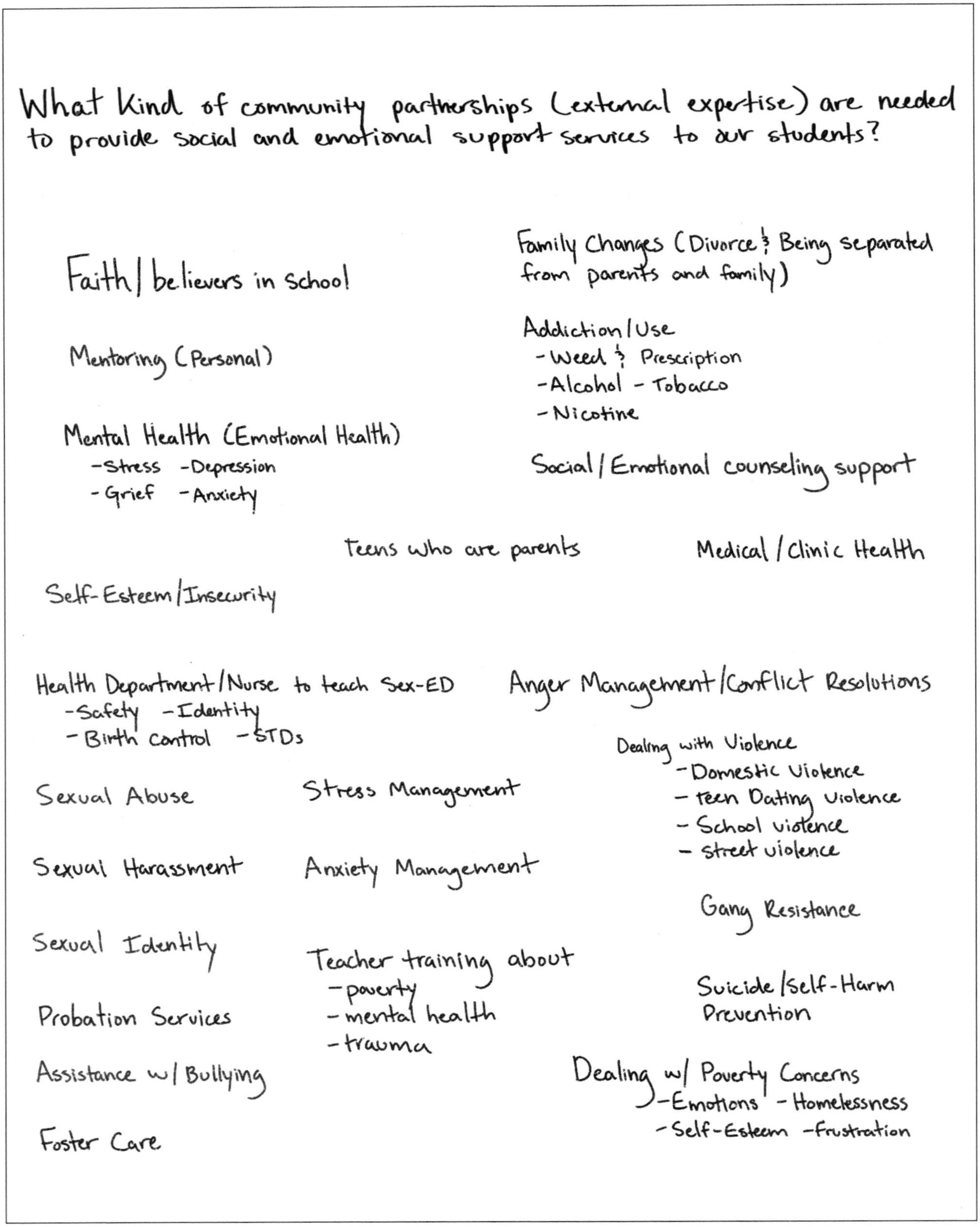
What Kind of community partnerships (external expertise) are needed to provide social and emotional support services to our students?
Faith / believers in school
Family Changes (Divorce & Being separated from parents and family)
Mentoring (Personal)
Addiction / Use
-Weed & Prescription
-Alcohol -Tobacco
-Nicotine
Mental Health (Emotional Health)
-Stress -Depression
-Grief -Anxiety
Social / Emotional counseling support
Teens who are parents
Medical / Clinic Health
Self-Esteem / Insecurity
Health Department / Nurse to teach Sex-ED
-Safety -Identity
-Birth control -STDs
Anger Management / Conflict Resolutions
Dealing with Violence
-Domestic Violence
-teen Dating Violence
-School violence
-street violence
Sexual Abuse
Stress Management
Sexual Harassment
Anxiety Management
Gang Resistance
Sexual Identity
Teacher training about
-poverty
-mental health
-trauma
Suicide / Self-Harm Prevention
Probation Services
Assistance w/ Bullying
Dealing w/ Poverty Concerns
-Emotions -Homelessness
-Self-Esteem -Frustration
Foster Care

Source: © 2020 The Centergy Project.

Figure 2.6: Community Partnerships flip chart with feedback.

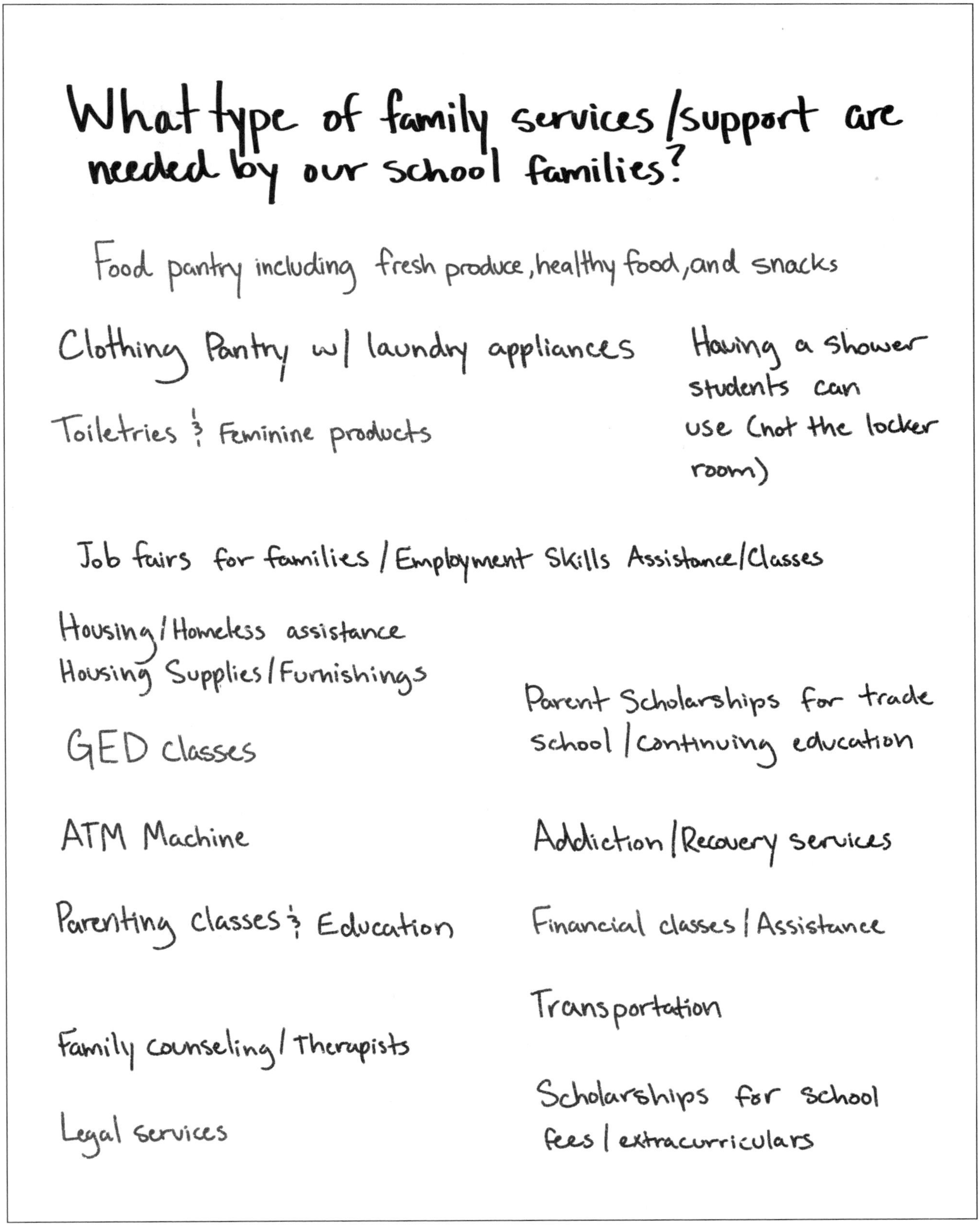

What type of family services/support are needed by our school families?

Food pantry including fresh produce, healthy food, and snacks

Clothing Pantry w/ laundry appliances

Toiletries & Feminine products

Having a shower students can use (not the locker room)

Job fairs for families / Employment Skills Assistance/Classes

Housing/Homeless assistance
Housing Supplies/Furnishings

GED classes

Parent Scholarships for trade school/continuing education

ATM Machine

Addiction/Recovery services

Parenting classes & Education

Financial classes/Assistance

Transportation

Family counseling/Therapists

Legal services

Scholarships for school fees/extracurriculars

Source: © 2020 The Centergy Project.

Figure 2.7: Family Needs flip chart with feedback.

to share your students' voices. Begin with your faculty. Understanding the barriers students face can open teachers' minds by giving context to the academic and behavioral challenges that surface in the classroom. At a faculty meeting, conduct a carousel walk activity where teachers and staff circulate and read the charts, then facilitate a discussion about what the charts reveal. Debrief with the following questions.

- "What affirms your thinking?"
- "What surprises you?"
- "Is there something missing?"
- "How does this information influence your approach to students?"

Similarly, you may share this information with potential donors and volunteers as well as school district leaders. The bottom line is that you have to champion the communication of your students' experiences and ideas. It will have a profound impact on your school when all stakeholders take the time to listen.

voices
FROM THE FIELD

However an administration chooses to deliver the results of the student voice they have gathered (such as conversation circles), it is absolutely paramount that the delivery of the information be spot-on. If you want the information to be meaningful, it has to be conveyed to the faculty in such a manner that they fully grasp what they are reading as if their health, future, and life depend on it.

—Daniel Marshall, high school counselor

Off-Track Interviews

Off-track interviews are designed for school staff to personally touch base with students who are not on track for graduation, such as students with projected or prior failure of required courses coupled with high absences. The goal is to respectfully listen to each student's story and facilitate next steps—for the student and the school—when possible. As you will learn in this section, the goal is not to fix anything during this meeting. An off-track interview is about gathering information, strengthening relationships, and determining how to move forward.

The primary purpose of off-track interviews is for you to understand the main reasons students in your school fail to matriculate or graduate on time. With these data, you can build proactive support services into your wraparound strategy. Sometimes, an interview prompts a productive, goal-oriented conversation to help the student determine practical next steps. When Leigh conducted off-track interviews at her school, in just one week, she received the following responses to the question, "When did it begin to go off track for you?"

- "I am autistic, so school is very hard for me."
- "An affair my dad had nearly destroyed my family."
- "Not living with my family because I just couldn't, so I had to live with my uncle's family, and I haven't seen my parents in a long time."
- "Overcoming an eating disorder."
- "I got pregnant."
- "I started smoking pot. At least, that is where it started."
- "We've been homeless most of my life."
- "My father's continual unemployment."
- "My mother's cancer."
- "My father's suicide."
- "My mother's incarceration for stealing from the school."
- "Coming to terms with and dealing with my homosexuality."
- "My parents' divorce."
- "My best friend's death."
- "Our family has very little money and no transportation."
- "Being bisexual."
- "My mother's drug habit and our homelessness because of it, all the different men in her life, working two jobs while I was in high school, and taking all honors classes."
- "My cancer."
- "My father's death."

Off-track interviews may be spur of the moment or part of scheduled touch-base meetings. You or staff (such as a counselor or a graduation coach) might hold these meetings at the end of a semester, before a retention conference or decision, as part of student transition or goal-setting meetings, or when a student is withdrawing or you suspect the student may not return for the next school year. For students not planning to return, don't miss the chance to elicit and learn from them as well as give them the dignity and respect of listening to them before they fully withdraw, transition to an alternative setting, or permanently leave your school. Otherwise, set yourself a goal of conducting periodic off-track interviews with students who meet defined criteria, such as students who are more than one year off track for on-time graduation or students who are significantly at risk of failing or dropping out.

The following sections address how you prepare for an off-track interview and how you manage the interview itself.

Before the Off-Track Interview

As with conversation circles, we recommend two staff members be present for the interview. It is wise to thoughtfully consider the personality and responsibilities of each potential facilitator. Choose someone who is skilled in building rapport or has an existing positive relationship with the student. For instance, it might be prudent to avoid tasking administrators who are primarily school disciplinarians with this responsibility. To set the student at ease, conduct the interview in a neutral room, such as a library or conference room, rather than an administrator's office. Keep in mind any special needs the students might have; for example, if the student is an English learner, there should be a translator present. Before the interview, review and have available the following student records (when possible).

- Attendance record
- Current schedule and grades
- Discipline record
- Transcript (if applicable)

These records will help staff familiarize themselves with the student as well as provide clarifying information to the student who may not fully understand his or her situation regarding credits earned or the impact of attendance policies.

A Word About Mental Health, Trauma, and ACEs

Hendershott (2016) writes:

> In a YouTube interview with Father Gregory Boyle, author of *Tattoos on the Heart*, Father Gregory stated that kids "can't see their way clear to transform their pain, so they continue to transmit it" (Tippett & Boyle, 2012). This is a powerful statement as we consider the importance of giving our wounded students time and space for communicating their fears, their needs, their hurts, their weaknesses, and their stumbling blocks. The willingness to listen and hear where a wounded student is coming from may just open the door to that student having hope. (pp. 60–61)

During the Off-Track Interview

The off-track interview is not a scripted process. Depending on the student, the interview could take a few minutes to an hour (or more). You want the tone to be warm, respectful, and safe. To facilitate this, begin the meeting by reassuring the student that he or she is not in trouble and the purpose of the meeting is to get his or her feedback and to discuss his or her academic progress and future plans. Instead of a script, figure 2.8 offers a structured guide to conducting the interview, and it will help you navigate difficult conversations with students facing overwhelming challenges.

Although answering the questions in figure 2.8 will help you compile information to help you identify barriers your students face, don't hesitate to broaden the conversation with the student should it seem appropriate. Also, before taking notes using this figure, make sure you ask permission of the student to do so. If the student doesn't give permission, respect the decision, and put away the form. By doing so, you are demonstrating the collaborative spirit you're trying to create (Naar-King & Suarez, 2011).

Be prepared for some students to inaccurately answer "Yes" to the question, "Are you on track to graduate?" When that happens, take the time to walk through their transcript, current grades, and graduation requirements to clarify their standing toward graduation. When stating these clarifications, avoid offering unsolicited advice, attempting to help the student, or trying to fix other problems uncovered during the off-track interview. Called the *righting reflex,* this human tendency often presents itself as premature problem solving

Date: _____ Student: _____

Facilitators: _____ Location: _____

Materials:

☐ Attendance record   ☐ Current schedule and grades

☐ Discipline record   ☐ Transcript

☐ Other:

Set the Stage

Begin the meeting by reassuring the student that he or she is not in trouble and explaining the purpose of the meeting is to get his or her feedback and to discuss his or her academic progress and future plans.

Seek to Understand

Say, "Please tell me about your experiences in school."

Ask, "Are you on track to graduate?" (Circle the answer you receive.)

No	Ask, "When did it begin to go off track for you? What was going on in your life at that time? What happened?"
Yes	Review the student's progress against graduation requirements for the purpose of clarifying the student's current status. Follow that with "When did it begin to go off track for you?"

Notes:

Ask, "Do you see yourself as a high school graduate?"

Ask, "What could we have done differently, or what could we do differently now, to help you address any concerns that are getting in the way of your graduation?"

Ask, "Is there one person on campus with whom you have a strong relationship?"

Determine Next Steps

Ask, "What do you see as your next steps?"

Additional Notes:

Figure 2.8: Off-track interview guide and facilitator notes page.

*Visit **go.SolutionTree.com/leadership** for a free reproducible version of this figure.*

and advice, which prevents students from being actively involved in the interview and actually places them in a passive role, stifling their autonomy (Naar-King & Suarez, 2011). If students show an interest in changing their circumstances, position yourself as a sounding board or coach rather than a director or leader. If a student seems motivated, rather than telling him or her what to do next, offer assistance (or access to specialized assistance) in developing a plan.

Committing to Off-Track Interview Practices

Implementing off-track interviews can be a significant undertaking depending on the number of students struggling with achievement. However, over time, your school can systemically embed this process to proactively plan interventions, respond to students' academic and social-emotional needs, connect students and families with services, and detect and address trends students identify.

Graduation Stories

Graduation stories are reflective narratives your graduating students write to describe their personal experience with schools. The weeks leading up to graduation give you a perfect opportunity to gather real talk from students preparing to transition out of your school. Because students whose graduation is approaching usually feel triumphant, they are primed to be their most reflective and transparent. These stories can come in many forms—essays, poems, videos, or art. Figure 2.9 illustrates an example of a written graduation story.

To discover the mosaic of student experiences within your school, invite all your seniors to participate in this activity. No one knows your school better than your graduating seniors, so don't miss the chance to hear in their own words what they think is great about your school, what struggles they experienced, and when they had victories. Daniel H. Pink (2018) explores the significance of endings in his book *When*. He notes the following research surveying Stanford seniors on graduation day:

> At the core of meaningful endings is one of the most complex emotions humans experience: poignancy, a mix of happiness and sadness. For graduates and everyone else, the most powerful endings deliver poignancy because poignancy delivers significance. One reason we overlook poignancy is that it operates by an upside-down form of emotional physics. Adding a small component of sadness to an otherwise happy moment *elevates* that moment rather than diminishes it. "Poignancy," the researchers write, "seems to be particular to the experience of endings." The best endings don't leave us happy. Instead, they produce something richer—a rush of unexpected insight, a fleeting moment of transcendence, the possibility that by discarding what we wanted we've gotten what we needed. (Pink, 2018, p. 164)

My biggest challenge was definitely staying in school after my baby was born when I was fifteen. It was a long, hard road, but that just goes to show that anything is possible if you try hard. I have to say, I'm very proud of myself for finishing my classes nine months before my intended graduation date.

There were many things I liked and did not like about high school. My favorite part, however, was the traditions and school spirit. The pep rallies, football games, and the school band playing friday mornings on game days were so much fun.

I'll be starting at technical college in June. Then I'm planning to transfer to college in January, where I'll become an ultrasound technician. Hopefully in five years I'll have a steady career at our local hospital.

Today we went to speak to kids in elementary and middle school. I wasn't planning on going, but I decided to sign up at the end. Everyone was going to elementary schools, but honestly, the sixth grade needed to be inspired more than the little kids. I'm thankful that I did go to speak to them because I really felt like I motivated some of them at least a little bit. I told them about how I've struggled in the past four years with household issues, being a teenage mom, and with staying in school. Basically my point was to show them that no matter what your struggles are in life, there is no reason not to graduate and become successful. It made me feel pretty good (and proud), and I just wanted to thank you for that experience.

Figure 2.9: A graduation story.

Source: © 2020 The Centergy Project.

To have success with this activity, you must find the magic moment—the *when*. Do it before or during testing, and you'll get graduation stories that reflect the mindset of students distracted by the whirlwind of test preparations and the last weeks of school. Ideally, find a time after all tests and before graduation. You may combine this with other end-of-year senior processes or celebrations, such as senior night, graduation practice, senior class pictures, or cap and gown distribution.

The following sections address the key points you should plan for when collecting graduation stories: setting the hook and purpose, establishing the graduation story process, exploring additional uses of the results, and understanding dos and don'ts of graduation stories.

Set the Hook and Purpose

The success or failure of this activity hinges on the way the person collecting graduation stories presents the process to students. You are asking students to share their experiences—good and bad—with you *as a favor* to help you improve the school. Establish a hook and purpose by acknowledging their unique position of knowing the school like no one else. Let them know their voice is valuable to you. Make your appeal personal. To accomplish this, choose someone who students trust—ideally, the principal—to fully explain the activity's purpose to them. If the principal is not the best choice, select a teacher, an administrator, a counselor, an advisor, or other students to facilitate the activity. (In any case, the principal should read the stories.) Avoid assigning the facilitation of the activity to a large group of people (like all homeroom advisors) because the more diffused the responsibility of rolling out this activity, the higher the chance of inconsistent results.

It is important for the activity facilitators to inform students and teachers who will read the stories and how the school will use them. Consider including at least the following messages to set the context for students, expanding as appropriate for your school.

- "You have a chance to leave a legacy. School leaders will read all the stories to better understand the lives of students, and we will use this understanding to improve the school."
- "This may be the most meaningful assignment you've ever had. Don't leave without your voice counting."
- "You will receive completion credit only for your effort—no letter grade. We are not grading for grammar or spelling. We want you to tell us about your experiences in your authentic voice." (Try this if the graduation story is an assignment.)
- "You may remain anonymous if you wish."

Finally, keep in mind that a student may disclose information requiring intervention from school leaders. For example, a student may include his or her name and reveal something requiring mandatory reporting, such as abuse. Therefore, the individual tasked with collecting these stories must read them immediately and be prepared to respond according to established protocols when appropriate.

Establish the Graduation Story Process

When collecting graduation stories, the *how* matters. You have *one chance* to gather the voice of your graduates. Once they are out the door, it's too late, so this activity is worth the thought, collaboration, and deliberation required to get it right. Do it with intention, and you will be rewarded with rich, invaluable feedback that can enlighten your leaders and staff to make transformational changes to your school.

Provide maximum flexibility and allow artistic license regarding the product students produce—video, essay, or art. Your goal is to unleash each student's unique voice; encourage students to express their individuality, tell their stories, and provide academic and nonacademic information. As one option to help students understand what they should produce, you might offer them a sheet like the one in figure 2.10.

What's Your Graduation Story?

Name: _____ (optional, but transparency is appreciated)

Congratulations on your pending graduation! This is your final writing assignment as a high school student. You will receive completion credit for your response. Your work will not be graded and may be anonymous if you so choose.

We want to become a better school for our students, and we believe we can learn from your experiences.

Please tell us your graduation story. Here, you'll see nine questions. Please choose at least five questions, and respond to them with a one- to two-page (or more) essay, video, or piece of art—your voice, your choice. Thank you for your honest feedback.

1. What was your greatest challenge to learning and graduating?
2. When times were tough, who or what gave you hope?
3. What kept you engaged in school?
4. Was there something that was important for us to understand about your life, but we never knew it? If so, could you tell us about it and how we could have better supported you?
5. Do you have a suggestion for improving the student experience or the way we support students at our high school? If so, what is it?
6. Did you ever consider dropping out? If so, what changed your mind?
7. What is your favorite memory from high school?
8. What do you consider your greatest accomplishment so far?
9. What are your plans next, and where do you see yourself in five years?

Figure 2.10: Graduation story template.

Visit **go.SolutionTree.com/leadership** for a free reproducible version of this figure.

Leaders often want to streamline the process by creating a graduation questionnaire solely on an electronic platform, such as Google Docs. *Resist this urge!* A generic survey may be efficient, but efficiency is the enemy of effectiveness, especially when you are trying to get people to share their experiences, feelings, and dreams. By all means, allow electronic submissions, but don't make an electronic, standardized response format the primary means of creating or collecting graduation stories. For example, you might:

- Have a representative go into each advisement class to explain graduation stories and have the students return them to the principal (via hard copy or email)

- Hold a senior meeting to introduce graduation stories and return them via email or to a centrally located box

- Introduce the activity at the first graduation practice and invite seniors to return their stories to subsequent practices or at the graduation ceremony

A variety of methods are advisable, so long as you ensure the method of collection is transparent and protects the privacy of all students to safeguard against non-anonymous stories circulating throughout your school.

Explore Uses of the Results

After collecting as many stories as possible, the principal and school leadership team (the structure of which varies from school to school) should read them with open hearts and minds—looking for trends to fuel school improvement. Delegating the primary task of reading graduation stories to those without decision-making responsibilities risks diminishing the impact because it creates the perception that the activity is a lower priority within the school.

Treat the stories you collect respectfully and with a *high degree of confidentiality*. Create a set of stories (with names removed) to use as your primary source for schoolwide activities. Redact any negative comments aimed at individuals, whether students or adults. Teachers, parents, and families will not appreciate their personal information becoming part of the public narrative of your school.

Once the principal or leadership team fully distills the feedback from graduation stories and discerns any trends, consider the following activities to act on what you have learned from your students.

- Bring in experts to educate staff on identified issues impacting students (such as anxiety, grief, poverty, trauma, mental health challenges, and parental deployment).

- Select stories to share with faculty.

- Privately share any comments from students who specifically name a teacher or staff member. Those receiving positive mentions from their students will be gratified to know they have had a positive impact on students. Likewise, any receiving negative comments deserve to know that as well.

- Use students' positive comments in newsletters, press releases, and other promotional materials.

- Incorporate feedback into school improvement or professional development plans.

- Use student narratives in grant applications to obtain funding for interventions and projects sparked by student feedback.

To help guide your own efforts, consider the following example of how Butler High School in Richmond County, Georgia, conducted its graduation story activities. In 2018, Principal Stacey Mabray (personal communication, July 20, 2020) called a senior meeting several weeks before graduation to introduce the activity to her seniors.

She explained the purpose of a graduation story, emphasizing the importance of their voice, and she encouraged them to produce a video, write an essay, create a piece of art, or use any other format they wanted. She also set up an online link for students who preferred using technology for the creation and submission of their response. Every student who turned in a graduation story received a save-the-date wristband with the graduation date. The wristbands became coveted senior bling—and a not-so-subtle reminder to complete the assignment! Mabray was also able to personally thank students when she saw their wristbands.

Mabray's efforts were not in vain. She received an outpouring of stories—essays, letters, and videos—from her students as they said goodbye to the school. This effort also bore fruit in future years. Because her method was public, the juniors kept an eye out to know what to expect for their senior year.

Mabray continued in the following years, explaining, "It has become a three-year tradition at Butler High. We have a team each year that culls through these stories, and we utilize the students' voices to help shape and refine policy and practice at Butler High. It has been a great way to connect with those 'less vocal' kids and hear about their experiences" (personal communication, July 20, 2020).

Give this effort similar focus and attention at your school, and we predict graduation stories will become a valued tradition within just a few years.

Understand Dos and Don'ts of Graduation Stories

Table 2.3 provides a list of dos and don'ts that you can use as reminders when you are planning the graduation stories activity.

Table 2.3: Dos and Don'ts of Graduation Stories

Do	Don't
Make a personal appeal; explain the purpose.	Rely on mass communication—emails, announcements, and so on—to solicit responses.
Allow students autonomy as to their final product—handwritten or typed essay, emailed or hand-delivered video, artwork, and so on.	Turn this activity into a standardized online questionnaire; the more analytical this assignment feels, the less likely students will view it as an authentic means of listening.
Time the activity near year-end ceremonies.	Assign the activity during high-stakes testing.
Devote time to read every story.	Delay reading or delegate it to others.

The most important *do* of all is to make graduation stories part of your school's tradition and to not make them a one-and-done event. By intentionally and regularly seeking the perspective of your graduates, you'll learn much about your school culture's strengths and areas that need your attention. Done well, the graduation story process provides qualitative information you can use to improve your school, truly respond to your students' needs, and create a school culture that produces resilient graduates filled with optimism, belonging, self-worth, purpose, and self-regulation and equipped for life success (Barr & Gibson, 2020). It will also reconnect you to why you're an educator—to make a positive difference in the lives of students.

voices FROM THE FIELD

"

I was in my eighth year as a high school principal at a Title I high school when I decided to begin asking students to share their graduation stories with me. After implementing a myriad of academic interventions, about a quarter of our students were still failing to walk across the graduation stage. I knew our school needed to do something more, and I wanted to know the feedback and ideas of my students. What would our students say?

While I always considered myself a highly relational leader with a close read on my students, I was surprised at the impact reading their stories had on me—as an educator, as a leader, and as a person. It's one thing to know demographics of the student population and personal details of many students; it is an entirely different thing to sit down and digest almost four hundred personal narratives. What I learned transformed the way I approached almost every aspect of my job.

I remember one particular student who was always a bright spot in my day—happy, bubbly, engaged, and ranked in the top 5 percent of her class. She seemed like she was thriving personally and in school. I knew her mother battled cancer when she was a freshman, her dad suffered a financial crisis when she was a sophomore, and her parents divorced when she was a junior. Nevertheless, she showed up at school eager and delightful.

I remember reading the opening line of her graduation story: "You never knew a smiling face could hide so much."

That sentence convinced me as to the severity of the changes this young woman had navigated throughout high school. I had seen her academic achievement as a sign that she was thriving in spite of the challenging changes in her life.

As I read the graduation stories, I learned about our students' lives, but I also learned what they valued. They told me that our efforts in creating memorable student experiences (like rocking pep rallies, field trips, homecoming parades, and class-specific and senior experiences) were well spent. I read about school staff who connected with students in meaningful and significant ways. I learned what programs and efforts the students believed were making a positive difference. I learned what we were doing well and where we needed to improve, and I learned more about the barriers our students said were negatively impacting their ability to learn, graduate, and thrive. Mostly, I learned what types of partnerships, opportunities, experiences, and assistance we needed to make accessible to our students. I knew I wanted our school to be more than a place for academic preparation, and our students blessed me with their stories, and their truth informed my next steps for creating a holistic, wraparound, whole child support system customized to the needs of our students and our community.

—Leigh Colburn

"

Conclusion

How can educators and schools address concerns such as mobility, poverty, family changes, immigration, addiction, health, and trauma? Teachers, principals, and parents know these barriers and more are hindering student learning and future success, but they are unsure regarding the roles schools can play in creating a culture of hope and future success. While adults may be uncertain how to address these concerns, students have a great deal to say regarding the preferred response and potential impact of schools. Identifying needs through student voice provides school staff the opportunity to make authentic connections with students and to develop innovative programming that is tailored to the needs of their students and families.

Whether you talk with groups of student leaders or you meet individually with off-track students, slowing down to listen will deepen understanding of students' struggles, hopes, and dreams as well as cultivate hope. Don't rush this process. As pictured in figure 1.3 (page 26), gathering student voice, strengthening relationships, and cultivating hope are all facets of trust, and trust is the keystone in creating a wraparound support system customized to the needs of all your students and your community.

Chapter 3

ESTABLISH PRIORITIES

The reason our school knew how to create this program is because they asked us, the students, what we needed. We answered and helped design it. . . . We are surrounded by community members who provide services from many different organizations. I believe the most important result from our center is that our students are becoming more motivated to take initiative to strive for success within school and their personal life. Our center has created a closer connection between our community, our staff, our students, and their families.

—High school junior

You should expect some outcomes of gathering student voice to bring uncomfortable realities to the surface and challenge some superficial feel-good climate data that some leaders might prefer to push out. Truly listening to your students is no small endeavor, as you delve into the reality—the truth—of their lives. We heard Lyle Wells (2018) from the Flippen Group explain it this way:

> Authentically seeking the truth takes time and energy, but it's worth it. To be brave and lead in challenging times as a leader, you must *seek* the truth, *speak* the truth, and *stretch* yourself to confront the *but* [meaning the fears and constructs that keep you from acting], for the opportunity to truly and meaningfully *serve* others.

Some school leaders may fear issues revealed from activities like conversation circles, off-track interviews, and graduation stories will be labeled by the community or in the local newspaper as *school problems* rather than *community problems*. Fortunately, our experiences tell us student voice grabs people's attention and awakens their desire to respond because students' needs become too hard to ignore. When school leaders widely share student voice, they position the school as a vital part of the community's response to real issues, such as mental health challenges or substance abuse.

The challenge then becomes to amass the data identifying needs as a means to establish priorities for next steps. In step 1 of the Centergy Cycle, you identified students' needs by acquiring rich narrative and qualitative data describing the breadth of the challenges they face. When sifting through these data, it's sometimes hard to know where to start. What you need at this stage are quantitative data to point you in the direction of the most pressing student needs, followed by a deeper dive into students' feedback about those needs. To facilitate this establishing of priorities, this chapter details step 2 of the Centergy Cycle, which involves two key areas of focus: (1) the Student Voice Needs Survey and (2) focus groups and individual focused conversations. Table 3.1 depicts step 2 in the process.

Table 3.1: Student Voice Processes—Step 2

	Process	Purpose
Step 2: Establish Priorities	Student Voice Needs Survey	Anonymous (large group and aggregate): Quantify student needs to establish priorities and project potential caseloads. Individual (personal and identifiable): Connect individual students with services.
	Focus groups and individual focused conversations	Delve into specific barriers to understand student perspectives and elicit programming suggestions.

Together, step 1 and step 2 processes provide a school district with the unfiltered *why* for implementing wraparound services that will support what students most need. Simon Sinek (2011) developed the Golden Circle to encourage leaders to start with *why* before they get to *how* or *what* because *why* keeps people focused on the purpose. Student voice provides a vehicle to attract allies who will work with "blood and sweat and tears" (Sinek, 2011) because a shared belief that communities can help students thrive inspires them.

The barriers your students identify reflect greater issues in your community, not just your school. For example, if your students are struggling with homelessness, domestic violence, or addiction, so is your community. However, because student voice is remarkably compelling, individuals and organizations almost always recognize the truth in the narratives and respond with "How can we help?" The data you collect from the Student Voice Needs Survey, focus groups, and individual focused conversations will help you answer this question.

A Word About Mental Health, Trauma, and ACEs

In their article titled "Going Deeper," Michael Fullan, Mag Gardner, and Max Drummy (2019) write:

> It is important for educators to look at the broader landscape of the world and acknowledge that the forces that are wracking society have made their way into schools. And today's schools, which continue to operate in the early 20th century mode in which they were created, are not doing what they can to counter these trends. (p. 64)

Student Voice Needs Survey

The Student Voice Needs Survey quantifies electronically the qualitative data gathered from step 1 processes, which your school will use to establish priorities and project potential caseloads. Due to its length and scope, we include a sample of this survey as a reproducible at the end of this chapter (see page 82). This represents just one form your survey might take, and we recommend reviewing it to get a sense of its structure and content and then continuing to develop it relative to your school's specific needs and available resources. For example, you might prefer a printed and written survey, or you might prefer to re-create it using an online program or platform, such as Google Docs or SurveyMonkey. Let's consider some of the factors that go into tailoring a Student Voice Needs Survey to the needs of your students, school, and community.

Qualitative information gleaned through conversation circles and off-track interviews (plus graduation stories, if available) forms the basis of the Student Voice Needs Survey, which we divide into four categories from key flip charts of the conversation circles in chapter 2 (page 35).

1. Academic, college, and career services

2. Behavior and life skills

3. Community partnerships

4. Family needs

These are the voice of your students, which Jensen (2019) sums up as "the right-now expression of feelings, opinions, and narratives" (p. 103). When you involve students in developing your Student Voice Needs Survey—from design through execution—they give you this essential information using clear, authentic language to get actionable results.

voices
FROM THE FIELD

On one survey, we began with the word *cutting* as a concern students identified in conversation circle discussion about behavior and life skills. When students reviewed the survey prior to administration, one asked, "Do you mean cutting class or cutting yourself?" Good question! With their help, we changed the question to instead refer to *cutting or self-harm*, improving the survey's clarity. Not coincidentally, the students left those meetings with a greater sense of agency and engagement.

—Leigh Colburn

As with the processes associated with identifying needs, surveying students should be continual; it is the snapshot of your student body, and it is prone to change. Think of administering an annual anonymous schoolwide Student Voice Needs Survey as checking the pulse of your students' needs. To support you in developing your school's Student Voice Needs Survey, the following sections address key aspects of this process: surveying freshmen, launching the survey, reviewing survey results, following up on the results, dealing with the *big four* (self-harm, suicide, abuse, and domestic violence), and conducting annual surveys.

Surveying Freshmen

The sample survey provided within this chapter is a reflection of grade 10–12 student conversations, meaning many of the academic, college, and career topics queried are more relevant to high school–age students in the upper classes. High schools wanting to survey incoming freshmen should consider customizing the Academic, College, and Career Services section (page 82) with details relevant to the freshman experience or opportunities. One suggestion is to conduct conversation circles with ninth-grade students about the transition from middle school and use this information to create a customized section addressing freshman transition, orientation, or class-specific activities. Alternatively, hold a conversation circle with fall-semester sophomores to gather voice regarding their ninth-grade experiences, and use this information to create a ninth-grade version of the Academic, College, and Career Services section.

Launching the Survey

The first time a school conducts a Student Voice Needs Survey, the objective is to gather timely and anonymous aggregate data for planning purposes. Schools use this survey to accomplish the following.

- Introduce the purpose of a wraparound center to students and staff.
- Normalize school inquiry and communication regarding nonschool concerns.
- Involve students in the design of the wraparound center.
- Clarify how the school will use the data it gathers.
- Project potential future caseloads for services.

As you read through the sample survey at the end of this chapter (page 91), notice the future focus of the questions. Further, the rating scale clarifies that the services on the survey may be offered in the future; therefore, the completion of the survey is not a request for immediate services. To help make this focus clear for students, figure 3.1 provides a sample introduction explaining for students the purpose of the Student Voice Needs Survey. Or you might invite your students to write the directions, as in figure 3.2. When presenting the survey, schools should always include instructions for reporting concerns about students' own or others' safety.

Upon reviewing the reproducible survey in this book, you might be tempted to jump over step 1 in this process (identify needs) and administer the sample survey as is. *Resist this urge!* To be effective, your survey *must* reflect the specific issues your students identify. Additionally, the process of genuinely involving your students through conversation circles, off-track interviews, and graduation stories creates an environment where students don't see this as "one more survey," having little to no real impact on their lives. Student voice is the secret sauce for earning your students' trust and gaining their buy-in to the wraparound initiative. The process of gathering voice and the collaborative creation of the survey is just as important to the totality of the initiative as the data the survey collects.

Thank you for taking the time to complete our survey!

At our school, we understand many different factors impact academic and life success. Your voice is very important to our planning process, and your answers to the questions on this anonymous survey will let us know which support services our students most need. After all, no one knows more about student life and your own personal challenges to learning than you.

In the coming weeks and months, we will continue to seek the input of students on necessary programs and services. You may be invited to participate in focus groups in the future to discuss specific topics. If so, we hope you'll come share more about your experience and your ideas to make our school better.

For urgent matters related to your personal safety or the safety of others, please contact your counselor immediately.

Figure 3.1: Sample introduction to explain to students the Student Voice Needs Survey.

The survey is completely anonymous, so please be *honest*. Students helped create this survey so our school can better understand and support our unique needs. Our principals, the superintendent, and a group of community members are asking *us* about our learning and experiences, and this survey is one way to let our voices be heard.

Thank you!

For urgent matters related to your personal safety or the safety of others, please contact your school counselor immediately.

Figure 3.2: Student-written example to explain the Student Voice Needs Survey.

Reviewing Survey Results

Once students have completed the survey, prepare aggregate data to review. Depending on the platform you used to have students fill out the survey, you can often accomplish this by exporting the data from its source into a spreadsheet, such as Microsoft Excel. However, the options available to you will vary depending on the format of your survey and the data-analysis tools available to you. With the aggregate information, it's time to see what the data communicate about student voice in your school. Use the guide in figure 3.3 (page 68), which we refer to as a *data dig*, to analyze the survey's anonymous data with an eye toward accomplishing the following.

- Identify needs around critical issues that must take priority (the big four discussed on page 68).

- Choose a couple of services that will be relatively straightforward to implement or that will produce quick wins based on already established services leadership can tweak for improved effectiveness.

- Establish priorities for partnerships with established organizations in the community based on potential caseloads.

Student Voice Needs Survey Data Dig
1. What about the data affirms my thinking?
2. What surprises me?
3. What do I perceive as positive?
4. What is concerning to me?
5. Are there data that substantiate a change in how we are supporting our students? What suggestions do I have for improving our provision of three support services we already offer so that they address services our students request?
6. What is a requested service that would be relatively straightforward to implement?
7. What critically important need are we ethically compelled to respond to by partnering with an external agency or organization to provide the needed expertise or support? In other words, what incredibly important need is outside our expertise? (This need represents a prioritized partnership opportunity.)
8. What pieces of data spur further inquiry?
9. Where do I see opportunities for restorative discipline or justice? Where might we respond with services rather than consequences?
10. What need groupings, if any, have emerged that could be addressed together in a clustered approach?

Figure 3.3: Guide to review results of the Student Voice Needs Survey.

Visit go.SolutionTree.com/leadership for a free reproducible version of this figure.

Following Up on the Results

With a thorough review of the results complete, the next step is to establish your priorities for initial services. For example, your school may decide to concentrate on mentoring and mental health. You could then conduct a series of focus groups (page 70) to gather student voice around your priorities. Figure 3.4 shows example Student Voice Needs Survey data for the Community Partnerships category, question 6, in a survey consisting of 1,139 total responses.

School leaders reviewing the complete survey results will likely find categories where they feel they can respond in highly competent ways, especially those categories in the academic areas. While they still face practical challenges of logistics and funding, leaders are essentially working in their comfort zone. On the other hand, leaders will undoubtedly feel some trepidation in the areas outside educators' expertise, such as those related to the big four (see the next section), incarcerated loved ones, eating disorders, or mental health.

Dealing With the Big Four

When engaging in conversation circles in high school, students commonly suggest services related to four barriers: (1) self-harm, (2) suicide prevention, (3) abuse (physical, sexual, mental, and emotional abuse and neglect), and (4) domestic violence. When schools include these topics on their survey, affirmative responses in one or more of these categories should elicit a response—*not* an overreaction. Remember, these personal, family, and societal issues occur across all demographic groups and in every community.

6. Please review the following items that can interfere with emotional and mental health. Services may be available at school from external partners to provide students with **social and emotional support** with regard to prevention, education, restoration, and recovery. Please check any item indicating those services you would use, the services you might use, and the services you would not use.

	Would Use		Might Use		Interested Students		Would Not Use		Did Not Answer	
Anger management	234	20.54%	242	21.25%	476	41.79%	647	56.80%	16	1.40%
Eating disorders	154	13.52%	263	23.09%	417	36.61%	705	61.90%	17	1.49%
Gang resistance	124	10.89%	176	15.45%	300	26.34%	818	71.82%	21	1.84%
Sexual activity	269	23.62%	279	24.50%	548	48.11%	570	50.04%	21	1.84%
Grief	162	14.22%	289	25.37%	451	39.60%	663	58.21%	25	2.19%
Pornography habits	446	39.16%	404	35.47%	850	74.63%	277	24.32%	12	1.05%
Divorce	126	11.06%	197	17.30%	323	28.36%	797	69.97%	19	1.67%
Family changes (changes in responsibilities, culture, and choices)	196	17.21%	299	26.25%	495	43.46%	624	54.78%	20	1.76%
Substance use (tobacco, drugs, alcohol)	183	16.07%	215	18.88%	398	34.94%	717	62.95%	24	2.11%
Sexual identity (LGBTQPIA)	121	10.62%	180	15.80%	301	26.43%	819	71.91%	19	1.67%
Mental health	269	23.62%	279	24.50%	548	48.11%	570	50.04%	21	1.84%
Depression	287	25.20%	292	25.64%	579	50.83%	541	47.50%	19	1.67%
Self-esteem	305	26.78%	326	28.62%	631	55.40%	488	42.84%	20	1.76%
Anxiety	328	28.80%	335	29.41%	663	58.21%	457	40.12%	19	1.67%
Family counseling	154	13.52%	235	20.63%	389	34.15%	730	64.09%	20	1.76%
Suicide prevention	188	16.51%	226	19.84%	414	36.35%	702	61.63%	23	2.02%
Cutting or self-harm	165	14.49%	197	17.30%	362	31.78%	757	66.46%	20	1.76%
Sexual abuse	120	10.54%	166	14.57%	286	25.11%	827	72.61%	26	2.28%
Childhood trauma	199	17.47%	222	19.49%	421	36.96%	694	60.93%	24	2.11%
Domestic violence or violence at home	126	11.06%	171	15.01%	297	26.08%	816	71.64%	26	2.28%
Dating violence	125	10.97%	192	16.86%	317	27.83%	793	69.62%	29	2.55%
Toxic relationships	262	23.00%	287	25.20%	549	48.20%	579	50.83%	11	0.97%
Foster care or living apart from family	150	13.17%	245	21.51%	395	34.68%	723	63.48%	21	1.84%
Family members battling substance abuse	143	12.55%	211	18.53%	354	31.08%	762	66.90%	23	2.02%
Family members facing concerns related to mental, emotional, or physical health	162	14.22%	256	22.48%	418	36.70%	693	60.84%	28	2.46%
Family members who are incarcerated (in prison or jail)	142	12.47%	213	18.70%	355	31.17%	763	66.99%	21	1.84%

Figure 3.4: Survey results for the Community Partnerships category.

With regard to student responses to a question about abuse, a school might include a menu or breakout section citing different types of abuse or list the types separately if there is a need to disaggregate data by type of abuse. A school might also include *physical abuse* with a descriptor of domestic violence or add *neglect* to a descriptor dealing with basic needs. In any case, regarding concerns related to mandatory reporting, the survey's wording deliberately doesn't say, "I need help with," and the anonymous, large-group survey doesn't include personally identifying information. For example, a student's indication that he would most likely participate in services related to suicide prevention does not necessarily signify the student is suicidal. An affirmative response to services related to suicide prevention could also indicate concern for a loved one, a vocational interest in psychology or social service, or a personal experience with a suicide that has occurred.

When a cohort of students relate an interest in or need for services associated with the big four, it should serve as a call to action for school systems and service agencies to provide information and services to students and educational information to parents. Note that the sample survey introductions we showed in figure 3.1 (page 67) and figure 3.2 (page 67) instruct students to immediately contact a school counselor should they be aware of a personal safety situation threatening themselves or any other student. This language is intended to safeguard students and clarify staff's need to respond in a timely manner to reports of students who are in harm's way. In a situation where you do use the large-group survey with an individual student in a non-anonymous situation, the student may reveal information requiring mandatory reporting. In this situation, staff must adhere to the processes and required timelines their school already has in place.

Conducting Annual Surveys

In chapters 4 (page 103) and 5 (page 119), you will begin to learn about the importance of having outside resources support wraparound efforts. Once you have these partnerships and services in place, conducting the Student Voice Needs Survey annually will keep your data current and relevant as you seek to maintain these partnerships and a suite of services that remain consistent with students' needs.

Within the first few weeks of each school year, current students should review the anonymous Student Voice Needs Survey and provide feedback to staff to make any needed updates before it is readministered. These annually refreshed data points will serve to assess any changes needed to current services as well as identify underutilized programming. For example, a survey may show a cluster of students, well beyond current participation in an established anger-management support group, who are requesting programming on anger management. You can then seek student input to determine the best approaches to boost participation. Likewise, you may find the need to drop programming based on decreased demand.

Focus Groups and Individual Focused Conversations

With data on student voice gathered and analyzed in the form of the Student Voice Needs Survey, the next step is to conduct focus groups and individual focused conversations with those in the best position to brainstorm the most effective school responses to specific needs—your students. Unlike the Student Voice Needs Survey, focus groups and individual focused conversations are collaborative experiences between staff and students. They provide opportunities to build rapport and trust, grow self-efficacy, encourage reflection, generate ideas, normalize the sharing of information, and provide an opportunity for the analysis of related data. Specifically, they give students a platform to provide deeper perspectives on their barriers to learning as well as input into programming capable of addressing their specific needs. By listening to students without judgment, you'll tap into new possibilities for your school to approach challenges your students face. As writer Brenda Ueland (1993) explains:

> Listening is a magnetic and strange thing, a creative force. . . When we are listened to, it creates us, makes us unfold and expand. Ideas actually begin to grow within us and come to life . . . and it is this little creative fountain inside us that begins to spring and cast up new thoughts and unexpected laughter and wisdom. (p. 205)

As with conversation circles, consider having two trusted and skilled facilitators present during focus groups. One adult should serve as the primary group facilitator while the second adult participates as an observer and a notetaker. Focus group facilitators should use off-track interviews, discipline data, staff referrals, and student self-identification to gain insight as to which students are facing specific barriers and might be productive members of a focus group. Group size and makeup can vary according to the topic—meaning groups could be homogenous or heterogeneous, depending on need. However, in general, a focus group should not exceed fifteen participants. Figure 3.5 provides an at-a-glance overview of focus groups.

Objectives	Build a culture of trust.
	Explore student perspectives.
	Gather programming suggestions.
	Support students facing barriers.
Facilitators	One facilitator to lead discussion
	One notetaker (optional)
Suggested time frame	Sixty to ninety minutes
Number of students	Twelve to fifteen
Materials	Flip chart
	Personal Reflection Notes document (page 87)
	Student Voice Needs Survey results
	Markers
	Medium and large sticky notes
	Pens
	Tissues
Location	A private area conducive to conversation and group movement

Figure 3.5: Focus group planning guide.

Similar to the temptation to skip identifying needs in favor of going right to the Student Voice Needs Survey, leaders eager to begin establishing partnerships and launching services frequently want to skip the step of conducting focus groups. They seek to leave decisions regarding curriculum, programming, and services to the expertise of outside providers. As you will learn in part III (page 101), the counsel of partners is important to consider, but it comes after you have explored the perspective, wisdom, and creativity of your students.

In conversation circles, students regularly express the need for their teachers to care about them more as individuals rather than just as students (Parker, 2019). Focus group discussions provide an opportunity to put that student feedback into practice and approach students *as people first*. Ironically, when you do this, you'll have a better chance of moving the needle on their academic performance. According to the Quaglia Institute for School Voice and Aspirations (2016), which specializes in supporting student voice, students are seven times more academically motivated when they believe they have a voice and teachers are willing to listen and learn from them. What a beautiful way to show students school is theirs—a place of belonging where students matter.

The following sections offer ideas for rolling out a focus group, including what to do before the session, during the session, and after the session. You may adapt this process and its questions as necessary, keeping in mind your goal is making the experience nonjudgmental, relational, and exploratory. Next, we look more specifically at individual focused conversations and additional uses of both focus groups and these conversations.

Before the Focus Group

Before conducting focus groups, prepare the following.

- Personal invitations (figure 3.6)
- Personal Reflection Notes packets (page 87)
- Discussion prompt
- Flip charts with headings from the Personal Reflection Notes document

Similar to conducting conversation circles, students are more likely to participate if they receive a personal invitation, rather than seeing or hearing a general announcement. While you may use an electronic platform to send these invitations, you will likely get a higher participation rate if you invite students face-to-face or deliver printed invitations to them. As you work to determine whom to invite for a focus group, for now, avoid inviting potentially disruptive students who may affect the group dynamic. Their input is valuable, but use your individual focused conversations to meet one-on-one to obtain their ideas. Regardless of your preferred way to share invitations, make sure the tone is friendly, respectful, and hopeful. Also, consider offering students light snacks and refreshments at focus group sessions, specifically mentioning that in the invitation. In our experience, if you feed them, they will come.

Students will use the Personal Reflection Notes pages to reflect on questions related to the focus group topic. Customize the template on page 87 based on the topic of the focus group. Print a copy for each student.

Let's Talk: Anger and Its Effect on Our Students and Families

"Feelings are something you have, not something you are."

—Shannon L. Alder

On our Student Voice Needs Survey, students indicated a need for more support in the area of anger. We would like to invite you to participate a small focus group to help us better understand what support, programming, and changes our current school practices need to better support our students. Your participation is voluntary but would be greatly appreciated.

When: January 30, 2020 in

Time: 8:30–10:30 a.m.

Where: Classroom 125

On January 30, you are invited to meet with other students and a facilitator to discuss anger and its effect on our students and families and how we as a school can better respond. All the information gathered will be kept anonymous and will only be used to improve our school and other schools. We would love to know your thoughts and learn more about your personal experience and ideas.

Sincerely,

Ms. Greene, Counselor

Please drop this form off for Ms. Greene in the counselors' office and let us know if you will be coming at 8:30 a.m. on January 30 so we can notify your teacher to excuse you from class.

Student Name: _____ Cell Number: _____

	Yes, I will attend the "Let's Talk" focus group.
	I might attend the "Let's Talk" focus group, but would like to talk to you to learn more.
	No, I will not attend the "Let's Talk" focus group.

Figure 3.6: Example of a focus group invitation for a session on anger.

It's also important that focus group facilitators establish discussion prompts ahead of time to get the conversation started. Prepare a chart defining the topic of the focus group, such as anxiety, depression, and grief. Figure 3.7 (page 74) shows documentation of a focus group on anger, which started with a simple prompt defining anger to which students added additional layers during the session. Finally, prepare flip charts for a large-group discussion. Your flip chart set should include prompts such as the following.

- What impact has _____ had on me, my friends, my family, my schooling? (See After the Focus Group, page 76, for an example.)
- When my _____ peaks at school, others might see . . .
- How can the school or school staff assist you in positively addressing or handling _____ when it occurs at school?

Anger — a strong feeling of annoyance, displeasure, or hostility

Long term negative impacts of uncontrolled or unhealthy anger — loss of opportunity, freedom, relationships, high blood pressure, stroke, anxiety...

Anger can be a positive, useful, protective emotion if it is expressed positively, appropriately

Other words used to describe anger: frustration, mad, defiant, out of control, "crazy", emotional, defiant, oppositional, "short fuse"

Family Counseling - 160   Stress release - 339

Building healthy relationships - 350

Leadership + Decision making - 365
                    ↳ React / Respond

Peer meditation / Conflict Resolution - 307

School Staff / Student Conflict resolution + meditation - 314

Yoga, meditation, tai chi - 270   Anxiety - 250

Toxic relationships - 169   Dating violence - 134

Abuse - 119   Violence at home - 115

Source: © 2020 The Centergy Project.

Figure 3.7: Notes from a focus group on anger.

- What school situations, experiences, or times escalate or trigger _____ in a manner that impacts your life?

- What would you want teachers or school staff to know or understand about a teen's struggle to manage _____ ?

- What types of information, activities, events, staffing, support, and programming related to _____ do you think would benefit students?

- If you really knew me, you would know . . . .

During the Focus Group

Simply stated, the agenda of a focus group is to accomplish the following.

- Introduce the purpose of the meeting.

- Allow personal reflection time.

- Explore students' ideas of an effective school response to the barrier.

Focus groups should be friendly in tone and true to their purpose: to explain the concept of wraparound services, destigmatize the conversation, explore student perspective on an identified topic, and gather ideas for potential support programming. Thank those in the group for their willingness to share their thoughts and experiences and to be advocates and allies for students struggling with the topic of discussion. If necessary, assure students that you invited them to the group because someone in the school's leadership thought their insight would be important, not because they are in any kind of trouble or labeled as a problem. Affirm that you, as a facilitator, believe they will give honest and forthcoming feedback and provide valuable insights to benefit all students and the school as a whole.

Introduce the topic with your discussion prompt flip chart, and begin the focus group by generating group norms as you did for conversation circles. Alternatively, use an existing norms artifact as a reminder. In the focus group introduction captured in figure 3.7, the facilitator began by defining anger and inquired whether anger could be a positive emotion. If appropriate, you may choose to extend the introduction with more topic-specific information by having students generate a collective list of words or phrases they use to describe the topic. While the primary purpose of a focus group is to gather information, the conversations that result from this introduction will allow you to gauge students' understanding of a topic and provide some education.

Provide participants with a copy of the schoolwide Student Voice Needs Survey results. Invite students to review the survey results and find all the indicators they believe could, in some way, be associated with the identified topic. As a group, record the number of students on the survey who responded with interest in using services on the identified topic. Figure 3.4 (page 69) shows the Student Voice Needs Survey indicators that students identified as related to anger. Notice the arrow connecting *Leadership and Decision Making* to the text *React/Respond* in figure 3.7. This resulted from an organic conversation prompted by a student suggesting the topic of leadership and decision making is related to anger. When the facilitator answered with "Tell me more about your thinking," the student stated not being able to manage one's anger could cause someone to react rather than respond. It was a very insightful comment and worth noting, so the facilitator documented the statement. By exhibiting transparency and involving students in the process of planning the school's response to the data, you show students the school is truly listening to and responding to their voices.

Once you have introduced the purpose and topic, distribute the Personal Reflection Notes document and allow approximately thirty to forty-five minutes for students to privately complete the document. See page 87 for a reproducible Personal Reflection Notes template. Note that we designed the list in this template for the barrier of *anger*. Tailor the template by replacing its list items with manifestations consistent with your identified barrier. For example, grief may include items such as difficulty focusing, crying, difficulty sleeping, weight loss, weight gain, loss of motivation, and so on. When giving students the Personal Reflection Notes document, instruct them that the group will reconvene to answer specific questions directly related to the school and topic. In the example template, we marked seven questions with a star to demonstrate how you might flag specific questions to students. (This is also a good time for you to prepare the flip charts if you haven't already.)

Following the group members' completion of the Personal Reflection Notes document, facilitate a discussion about the seven flip chart prompts by gathering responses aloud and recording the responses on the charts. Invite students to write responses on sticky notes if they would rather not speak aloud. As the discussion continues, prepare yourself for silent moments. Articulating thoughts about the topics you'll be exploring is probably a new experience for many students, so they may take time to get into a flow. If your group gets stuck on a question, offer a couple of choices, and ask their opinion, taking care not to tip your hand if you have a preference. Some students may also want to give you the "right" answer, so they will look for cues from you for safe answers, especially if your school culture is very structured. If that happens, play devil's advocate and ask an open-ended question, such as "Why might someone have a different opinion?" Keep in mind your objective is to evoke ideas from your students, not direct their outcomes.

In general, a well-facilitated focus group could last sixty to ninety minutes, but it could be shorter or longer. The time frame depends on the number of students involved, group dynamics, and the topic. Continue the conversation as long as comments are fruitful, and draw the conversation to a close when a natural ending point arrives or seems prudent. Thank students for their willingness to share their thoughts and ideas. Explain any next steps you have planned, such as the possibility of a subsequent meeting to gather further input. As an exit ticket, invite them to use one or several sticky notes to confidentially respond to a specific prompt, such as the one we suggest: If my teachers (school) really knew me, they would know . . . . Invite the students to place any additional or unspoken comments on sticky notes on any of the charts and collect the Personal Reflection Notes documents from students as they leave.

After the Focus Group

After students depart, consolidate unrecorded student feedback onto the flip charts so your charts will represent the totality of student responses to the discussion questions. To do this, add the following to the flip charts.

- Unrecorded comments about the seven starred prompts from the Personal Reflection Notes

- Comments from sticky notes

Figures 3.8 (page 78), 3.9 (page 79), and 3.10 (page 80) show examples of completed charts from the focus group on anger.

As a follow-up to the focus group, prepare a document that compiles all student comments from the charts and the Personal Reflection Notes documents. You'll find uses for this narrative later, such as for grant proposals, conversations with partners, refining student support processes, or professional learning for faculty. We provide more about these items in subsequent chapters.

Individual Focused Conversations

In some cases, and due to a variety of factors, you will want to work individually with certain students. Such factors might include concerns regarding group dynamics, a need for a deeper level of information about an individual student, and topic sensitivity (the big four and others). Additionally, you should consider having one-on-one conversations in the following situations.

- When a student is returning from a suspension or extended absence from class due to an event or hospitalization

- When your advocacy on behalf of an individual student is needed regarding the barriers the student identifies and the support he or she believes would be beneficial

- To gather student voice for the purpose of informing or preparing for a 504 plan or and individualized education plan (IEP) meeting

- For the purpose of connecting individual students and their families with services

When sitting down with a student one-on-one, have him or her fill out the Personal Reflection Notes document (page 87) to use for a structured conversation about a barrier he or she faces. Be mindful to explain the purpose of the conversation is to get the student's ideas about ways the school can support him or her as well as other students who are struggling. Have a copy of the Student Voice Needs Survey results to review with the student to alleviate any feelings of isolation the student may have. For example, if the student mentions having an incarcerated parent, share the number of other students who responded to that item on the survey.

You can capture in your notes any information gathered during individual focused conversations, the student's responses to an individual student voice survey, and the student's responses on Personal Reflection Notes.

This meeting may last for twenty minutes or an hour (or more) based on the student. If you find the student uncooperative, conclude the meeting with a thank-you and an invitation to re-engage in the future if or when the student is interested in meeting. Otherwise, use this as an opportunity to connect with the student and listen to his or her ideas.

Me

Fights   Headaches   Getting in trouble

The way I express my anger is I say really harsh things to people but I don't shout

Anxiety - I don't always know how I'll react to things

It makes me want to react physically

Blaming others   Substance abuse   YDC/Jail

I isolate myself   Vaping

My adrenaline rush causes blackouts

Hating things and hurting myself breaking my hand, ankle, foot

I'm bipolar

My Family

I'm mad at them a lot

Heated family altercations

Loss of family relationships

Substance use

Violence in my home/abuse

Fights

Hurting others

I get in bad fights with my siblings and parents

Stress/Health problems

What impact has anger had on...

My Friends

Loss of friends and others who were important to me

Substance use

Fighting/dating violence

The impact my anger has on my friends is them leaving me

My friends worry about me & the reactions I will have when people make me angry

They see the changes in me, and the effects of my anger and bipolar

My Schooling

Being labelled

When I am angry, it's not a good time for schooling b/c what I am angry about is in the front of my brain

Getting suspended/arrested

Substance use - weed/vaping

It's bad. It caused me to hit staff and break my hand

It's had the biggest impact on my schooling

Poor relationships with my teachers which makes it harder to learn

Source: © 2020 The Centergy Project.

Figure 3.8: Focus group notes on the impact of anger.

Is there a way the school or school staff can assist you in addressing/handling your anger when it arises? Is there a positive way the school could assist in conflict resolution?

Giving students choices/control

Training staff in conflict resolution, calming techniques

Having PE classes teach physical release skills
↳ yoga, exercise, tai chi, martial arts

Having the ability to walk it out or get the energy and adrenaline out

Having real talk, straight talk, involving students in the solutions

Adults need to respond & learn what is really going on w/o punishing, reacting, just giving out "policy"

Keeping confidentiality and not telling my business

Asking "what" questions instead of "why" questions, finding out about me not just judging what I did

Source: © 2020 The Centergy Project.

Figure 3.9: Focus group notes on how a school could help students manage anger.

Are there certain school situations, experiences, or times that escalate or "trigger" anger in a manner that impacts your life in a negative way?

Other students

Students who run their mouths

Social media

Social bullies / drama queens

Students who pick on my brothers/sisters

Comparing me to my brothers and sisters

Gossip

"Snitching"

Suspending

Adults who hold grudges and keep bringing up something you've done wrong in the past or just keep talking about your past

When teachers... yell, are disrespectful, have different rules for different students, have different rules from the rest of the school, teachers who stereotype, teachers who hate their job. Teachers who are moody and snap but expect students not to.

Taking away all my choices, control, my power in a situation

Source: © 2020 The Centergy Project.

Figure 3.10: Focus group notes on situations that trigger anger.

Additional Uses of Focus Group and Individual Focused Conversation Results

These planned encounters, designed to help you establish priorities, provide school staff the opportunity to listen with intent to their students' voices. Often, you'll walk away not only with a deeper understanding of their perspectives but also with fresh ideas to pursue.

Use the compilation documents resulting from your focus groups and individual focused conversations to inject student voice into your culture in a variety of ways. For example, share this deep dive into specific barriers with your faculty. Just as you did with conversation circles, hang the charts at a faculty meeting. Encourage a carousel walk where teachers and staff circulate and read the charts and then discuss new and affirmed perspectives as well as best practices to support students. Facilitate large- or small-group conversations with teachers and the school leadership team to discuss potential changes to practices, programming, and possibly even policy.

Similarly, sharing compelling information from this work can help you tell your story to the community. For example, use the charts and compilation documents with potential partners as you establish partnerships and begin to work together to design services and programming responding to the voices you have gathered. Also, you can include cogent comments in newsletters, while being sensitive to honor rather than exploit students' experiences as well as support grant applications with student comments about the need for or efficacy of wraparound services.

Conclusion

The information gleaned from step 1 and step 2 of the Centergy Cycle builds a wealth of knowledge about student voice that will inform next steps regarding individual or group follow-up as well as wraparound program design and development. Follow the lead of your students, allowing them every opportunity to fully participate in this real-talk experience and to guide the school's next steps.

At this point, you'll be prepared to look to your community for the resources your students have identified as priorities.

Student Voice Needs Survey—High School

Thank you for taking the time to complete our survey!

At our school, we understand many different factors impact academic and life success. Your voice is very important to our planning process, and your answers to the questions on this anonymous survey will let us know which support services our students need most. After all, no one knows more about student life and your own personal challenges to learning than you.

In the coming weeks and months, we will continue to seek the input of students on necessary programs and services. You may be invited to participate in focus groups in the future to discuss specific topics. If so, we hope you'll come share more about your experience and your ideas to make our school better.

For urgent matters related to your personal safety or the safety of others, please contact your counselor immediately.

Date: _____

1. Have you attended other high schools?

   ☐ Yes

   ☐ No

2. Please select your grade level.

   ☐ Freshman (ninth grade)

   ☐ Sophomore (tenth grade)

   ☐ Junior (eleventh grade)

   ☐ Senior (twelfth grade)

3. Please check all barriers preventing you from participating in school activities outside school hours.

   ☐ Transportation

   ☐ Caring for siblings or other family members

   ☐ Work

   ☐ Other (please specify)

Academic, College, and Career Services

4. The following services may be available to provide students with **academic, college, and career services**. In an effort to identify what students want most, please check the services you would use, the services you might use, and the services you would not use.

	Would use	Might use	Would not use
More choices for challenging coursework (such as advanced placement, foreign language, dual enrollment, and online courses)			
Access to school materials			
Access to technology after school, on weekends (at school), or both			
Help with study skills, time management, and organization			
Instructional support outside school hours (such as a writing lab, tutoring, technology access, or a quiet place to study)			
Assistance with internet access at home			

	Would use	Might use	Would not use
Self-assessment tools regarding personality, aptitudes, emotional intelligence, or career exploration			
Mentoring programs			
Military recruitment services			
Test preparation for the Armed Services Vocational Aptitude Battery (ASVAB)			
College admissions test preparation (SAT or ACT)			
College selection assistance			
College application and scholarship assistance (including for Pell Grants and FAFSA)			
GED (high school equivalency) test preparation			
Expansion of career pathway courses and training opportunities			
Career talks with local tradespeople and professionals			
Career shadowing			
Access to jobs and apprenticeships with those seeking to hire or provide internships to high school students			

What other programs or services do you need for your academic, college, or career preparation?

Behavioral and Life Skills Support

5. The following services may be available to provide students with **behavioral and life skills support**. In an effort to identify what students want most, please check the services you would use, the services you might use, and the services you would not use.

	Would use	Might use	Would not use
Help resisting bullying and harassment, including sexual harassment and cyberbullying			
School staff-to-student mediation or conflict resolution			
Student-to-student mediation or conflict resolution			
Help building healthy relationships			
Yoga and meditation classes			
Stress-release assistance			
Personal and home safety assistance (including CPR, first-aid, and self-defense training)			

continued ▶

	Would use	Might use	Would not use
Support for teens who are parents of young children			
Job-readiness assistance (interview skills, presentation skills, public speaking, résumé writing, and so on)			
Professional skills assistance (guidance on dress codes, dining, manners, and so on)			
Technology-management assistance (such as for social media use and screen time)			
Wellness and nutrition services (including cooking and meal planning)			
Probation services			
Driver's education			
Cultural diversity awareness and sensitivity (including religious, economic, and racial diversity awareness)			
Financial-planning assistance (for everyday-life needs such as choosing to buy or lease, managing credit, and filing taxes)			

What other behavioral or life skills support programs or services do you need?

Community Partnerships

6. Please review the following items that can interfere with emotional and mental health. Services may be available at school from external partners to provide students with social and emotional support with regard to prevention, education, restoration, and recovery. Please check any item indicating those services you would use, the services you might use, and the services you would not use.

	Would use	Might use	Would not use
Anger management			
Eating disorders			
Gang resistance			
Sexual activity			
Grief			
Pornography habits			
Divorce			
Family changes (changes in responsibilities, culture, and choices)			
Substance abuse (tobacco, drugs, or alcohol)			
Sexual identity (LGBTQPIA)			
Mental health			

	Would use	Might use	Would not use
Depression			
Self-esteem			
Anxiety			
Family counseling			
Suicide prevention			
Cutting or self-harm			
Sexual abuse			
Childhood trauma			
Domestic violence or violence at home			
Dating violence			
Toxic relationships			
Foster care or living apart from family			
Family members battling substance abuse			
Family members facing concerns related to mental, emotional, or physical health			
Family members who are incarcerated (in prison or jail)			

What other social or emotional support services or programs do you need?

Family Support Services

7. The following services may be available to provide students with **family support services**. In an effort to identify what students want most, please check the services you would most likely use, the services you would possibly use, and the services you would not use.

	Would use	Might use	Would not use
Help with personal health concerns (insurance, medical, dental, and vision concerns)			
On-site health clinic			
Financial education (information on home ownership; debt management; student loans; and renting, owning, and leasing decisions)			
Transportation services			
Legal assistance (on family law, emancipation, and juvenile charges)			
Job fairs for students and families			

continued ▶

The Wraparound Guide © 2021 Solution Tree Press • SolutionTree.com
Visit **go.SolutionTree.com/leadership** to download this free reproducible.

	Would use	Might use	Would not use
Food pantry			
Teen pregnancy and teen parenting support (supplies, mentoring, and classes)			
Childcare for students with children			
Hygiene products and support (feminine products, toiletries, and showers)			
Laundry facilities			
Clothes closet			
Homelessness assistance			
GED (high school equivalency) classes for parents			
Financial workshops on paying for college			
Parenting seminars for parents of teens			

What other family support services or programs do you need?

What need do you have that has not been identified in this survey?

The Wraparound Guide © 2021 Solution Tree Press • SolutionTree.com
Visit **go.SolutionTree.com/leadership** to download this free reproducible.

Personal Reflection Notes Template

Thank you for attending today's discussion to help us plan how our school can best support students regarding _____ so they can positively cope with school and in life. We need your thoughts and experiences to help us develop new resources in our school for students, including you and your friends.

We want your voices to guide this process!

Personal Reflection

Within the last year and related to _____, I have experienced the following. (Please check all that apply.)

☐ Verbal outbursts	☐ Suspension	☐ Harm to self	☐ Increased anxiety
☐ Headaches	☐ Fights	☐ Harm to others	☐ Depression
☐ Tingling	☐ Probation	☐ Insomnia	☐ Self-isolation
☐ Heated family altercations	☐ Blaming of others	☐ Loss of friends	☐ Eating or digestion problems

With these selections in mind, please answer the following questions about the barrier _____.

1. I've been known to express _____ negatively. (Please circle one.)

   Strongly disagree   Disagree   Not sure   Agree   Strongly agree

2. _____ has affected my day-to-day life in a negative way. (Please circle one.)

   Strongly disagree   Disagree   Not sure   Agree   Strongly agree

3. How likely is it that I would attend individual or small-group sessions focused on _____ _____? (Please circle one.)

   Never   Not likely   Undecided   Likely   Always

4. How likely is it that I would recommend or invite a friend to individual or small-group sessions focused on _____? (Please circle one.)

   Never   Not likely   Undecided   Likely   Always

5. What impact has _____ had on me, my friends, my family, and my schooling?

Getting to Know You

6. What change would I like to see for myself?

7. Something else you might want to know about me is . . .

8. What do I care about, or what is important to me?

9. What gives me hope?

10. What helps me come back from something difficult?

★11. If you really knew me, you would know . . .

Questions to Increase the Knowledge and Understanding of Others

12. What one thing would you want others to know about students who are dealing with _____ in their lives? What works for you?

13. Do you have successful strategies for coping with _____? If so, what are they?

14. When _____ peaks at school, others might see . . . (List examples of personal behaviors, such as fidgeting, crying, or shutting down.)

15. How could the school or school staff assist you in positively addressing or handling _____ when it arises?

16. What school situations, experiences, or times escalate or trigger _____ in a manner that negatively impacts your life?

17. What would you want teachers or school staff to understand about a teen's struggle with _____?

Questions to Develop Programs

18. What could we do or provide to make school a safe place for you to talk about or seek help related to _____?

19. Do you think it is important that we have an informational or support group for students struggling with _____ who want to learn strategies to positively cope with it? Why or why not?

20. If we started a student informational or support group on _____, what would keep you coming back?

21. If we started a student informational or support group on _____, what could get in the way and keep it from being successful?

22. What types of information, activities, events, staffing, support, and programming related to _____ do you think would benefit students?

23. How do you think we should go about inviting others to this group or getting the word out that we are going to have a group like this for our students?

24. What group name do you suggest for an informational or support group for students struggling with _____?

25. When you think about this struggle with _____, what gives you hope?

26. If you could meet with a young adult who struggled with _____ as a teen but is now doing well, what would you ask him or her?

27. Please share anything else you would like to tell us.

Name (optional): _____

Preferred method of contact: _____

The Wraparound Guide © 2021 Solution Tree Press • SolutionTree.com
Visit **go.SolutionTree.com/leadership** to download this free reproducible.

Sample Compilation of Student Voice on Anger

The following data combines notes from focus groups and student-submitted Personal Reflection Notes on the topic of anger.

Personal Reflection

Students answered specific questions about their anger as follows.

1. **I've been known to express anger negatively.**

Strongly disagree	Disagree	Not sure	Agree	Strongly agree
(5%)	(10%)	(10%)	(60%)	(15%)

2. **Anger has affected my day-to-day life in a negative way.**

Strongly disagree	Disagree	Not sure	Agree	Strongly agree
(18%)	(19%)	(27%)	(27%)	(9%)

3. **How likely is it that I would attend individual or small-group sessions focused on gaining anger-management and conflict-resolution skills?**

Never	Not likely	Undecided	Likely	Always
(0%)	(11%)	(22%)	(34%)	(33%)

4. **How likely is it that I would recommend or invite a friend to individual or small-group sessions focused on anger management?**

Never	Not likely	Undecided	Likely	Always
(14%)	(14%)	(29%)	(43%)	(0%)

5. **What impact has anger had on me, my friends, my family, and my schooling?**

   Note: The following results are a compilation of the focus group discussion flip chart shown in figure 3.7 (page 74) and responses to the Personal Reflection Notes. Numbers in parentheses indicate repeat responses.

Me	**My Family**
Headaches (6)	Heated family altercations (5)
Verbal outbursts (7)	Hurting others
Fights (6)	Loss of family relationships
Blaming others (3)	Stress or health problems
Harm to self (2)	Substance use
Harm to others (3)	Violence at home and abuse
Depression (3)	I have gotten into fights with my siblings.
Blackouts (2)	The impact my anger has had on my family is bad.
Self-isolation (2)	
Anxiety (2)	**My Friends**
Eating or digestion problems (2)	
It makes me want to react physically.	Anger from bipolar disorder has impacted my relationships.
Sometimes, it makes me want to shut down.	Loss of friends (4)
My anger makes me mad at people.	Substance use
I'm bipolar.	Fighting
The way I express my anger is I say really harsh words but I don't really shout.	Dating violence
I have strong emotions about a lot of things.	I have lost friends because I have gotten into fights with them.
Getting in trouble	
Youth development center or jail	

continued ▶

The Wraparound Guide © 2021 Solution Tree Press • SolutionTree.com
Visit **go.SolutionTree.com/leadership** to download this free reproducible.

Me	My Friends
Hitting things, hurting myself, and breaking my hand, ankle, and foot Substance use (marijuana, alcohol, or liquor), smoking, or vaping Past trauma has had an impact on me, so it has had an impact on all my friends, family, and schooling. Tingling Probation Insomnia	The impact my anger has had on my friends is they have left me. My friends worry about me and the reactions I will have toward people who make me angry.

My Schooling

When I am angry, it's not a good time for learning because what I am angry about is in the front of my brain.

Sometimes, you figure out that fighting is not worth it and you realize education and grades are more important, and then you realize it is better to fight outside school because you are missing days and have to double up on your work after having to repeat assignments, grades, and classes. And also as you get older, there can be bigger consequences, like you can get arrested or you can lose your life.

Getting suspended (2)

Being labeled

Substance use at school (drugs and vaping)

I have poor relationships with teachers, and that makes it harder to learn.

I was kicked off athletic teams.

I have gotten in trouble and missed classes, and now I am failing two classes.

My grades have gone down.

It's had the most impact on my schooling.

The impact that my anger has had on me is bad. It has caused me to hit staff and break my hands.

I don't like school anyway, but when I am angry, I don't do anything.

Getting to Know You

6. **What change would I like to see for myself?**

I want to stop fighting with people when I'm mad.

I want the chance to talk to people about my problems.

I want to change my attitude and my tone toward people.

I would like to see myself handle problems more safely.

I want my PTSD gone, my anger gone.

I would like to learn to stay calm.

I want to be able to take stuff that upsets me and just ignore it and move on.

I would like to be less angry.

7. **Something else you might want to know about me is . . .**

I don't like people.

I am inspirational.

I'm very understanding.

I like to work and I work fast.

I work good with my hands.

I would rather be at work and make money than be at school.

I work better with friends.

I have been abused all my life. That's why I have PTSD and I get flashbacks all the time.

Even though I can get mad easy, I can calm down fast.

I have mental and emotional problems.

I normally don't get crazy unless someone does certain things that really tick me off.

8. **What do you care about or what is important to you?**

My life, my brothers, and my sisters

My education

Myself and my money

My family

My brother and sisters

My friends and going to college

My mom and dad and siblings

My family and friends

My family, my friends, and my girlfriend

My future, work, friends, and family

9. **What gives you hope?**

My grandma

I don't know.

My mother, my teachers, and my brain

People trusting me

Nothing

My family

Anything that has great accomplishments that are possible for me

Money

10. **What helps you come back from something difficult?**

Music

Listening to my music and being by myself

Music I like

Just sitting and thinking

Music or drawing

Music and games

Walking away from the problem

Just to relax and do things to forget the situation

Time alone

11. **If you really knew me, you would know . . .**

I'm good if you don't make me mad.

I love money, and certain things get to me.

I am a leap-year baby.

I am silly.

I hate school.

I like to fish and hunt. I like dogs.

I feel depressed all the time because of abusive parents who have a lack of care for me.

About my life and how I have been treated and you would know about my anxiety.

I get mad easy but I am talkative and a jokester.

I'm really easy to get along with, and usually I don't hate or get upset unless something happens that I don't like.

I hate this school.

Questions to Increase the Knowledge and Understanding of Others

12. **What one thing would you want others to know about students who are dealing with anger in their lives?**

    Note: This question is also a group-discussion question. In this case, the facilitator asked the students to categorize "others" during the discussion.

    i. **I would want other students and my friends to know . . .**

    Give me my space and don't talk to me. Don't ask me a lot of questions.

    You don't always have to fight or have altercations.

    Think positive.

    You are not the only ones.

    Just walk away and breathe and try to think of something positive.

    It gets easier.

    ii. **I would want my family to know . . .**

    Give me alone time and space when I am angry.

    We have real life issues too.

    iii. **I would want school staff to know . . .**

    It is not a good time for a lot of questions.

    When I am angry, don't touch me. Give me space. Give me some time to think.

    Teenagers go through stuff too.

    Music and headphones can be helpful.

    Most of the time, it's not about you.

    Sometimes I am just having a terrible day.

    iv. **I would want everyone to know . . .**

    Give us some space or privacy.

    Sometimes it is not about you.

    Let it go after it is done. Don't keep bringing it back up.

    Don't ask me a lot of questions when I am mad. It makes me angrier when an adult keeps asking me the same questions.

    Understand that teens can have a lot of stuff or stress going on.

    Music and headphones can be helpful.

    Sometimes when I am angry, I shut down or try to go to sleep. I isolate. I listen to music and try to breathe.

    Sometimes I cuss, smoke, eat, or exercise.

    Sometimes we wear something on our head—a hood or a cap—so we don't have to make eye contact with people. Eye contact can make things more intense.

    I punch stuff when I get mad, so having a punching bag at school would help.

    I have tried punching a wall and a tree. It wasn't a good choice, so try punching something that won't break your hand.

    Sometimes, I think all people's problems can't be solved, and other times I think maybe they can be.

13. **Do you have successful strategies for coping with anger? If so, what are they?**

Yes, I try to manage and slow my breathing.

No, I just see red and then I don't really hear anything.

I walk it out.

No, but I would like some help in getting some.

Yes, I have at least two successful strategies.

No, I feel out of control.

Yes, once I get it all out, I can generally calm myself down.

Listening to music with my headphones on is really helpful.

Yes, getting some exercise or shooting baskets.

Just try not to think about it. Get your mind distracted.

Not really

14. **When my anger peaks at school, others might see me . . . (List personal behaviors, such as fidgeting.)**

Yelling

Hitting things

Fighting

Using profanity

Vaping or smoking

Zoning out

Being disrespectful

Losing it

Shutting down

Skipping class

Trying to go home

Not making eye contact

Wanting to be in a place that is dark and quiet because I get headaches

Wanting to be alone

Needing to get the negative energy out (I need to move—not just be told to sit down and listen or talk to somebody.)

15. **How can the school or school staff assist you in positively addressing or handling your anger when it arises?**

Sometimes it's stuff that happens outside school but then it comes into school.

Just simply talk with me.

Give students choices and control.

Train staff in conflict resolution and calming techniques.

Have gym classes that teach physical-release skills—yoga, exercise, tai chi, and martial arts.

Give students the ability to walk it out or get the energy or adrenaline out.

Have real talk, or straight talk, involving students in the solution.

Adults need to respond and learn what is really going on without punishing, reacting, and just giving out "policy."

Keep confidentiality, and don't tell my business.

Stop asking *what* questions and start asking *why* questions. Find out about me instead of just judging me for what I did.

Let me leave the room and walk.

Let me fight. Stop trying to stop the fight.

Yes, they could read about how to stay calm and not yell at students.

Try to understand the reasons behind or the cause of students' anger.

Yes, I need to be able to get away from who or what I am angry with.

16. **What school situations, experiences, or times escalate or trigger anger in a manner that negatively impacts your life?**

When the teachers talk badly about me

Middle school was negative for me.

Other students

Students who run their mouths

Teachers who compare me to my brothers and sisters

Students who pick on my brothers or sisters

Social bullies and drama queens

Gossip

Social media

Snitching

Suspensions

When teachers take action in class based on a suspension that had noting to do with their class

Students or adults who hold grudges and keep bringing up something I've done wrong in the past or just keep talking about my past

When teachers yell, are disrespectful, have different rules for different students, have different rules from the rest of the school, stereotype, or hate their job; teachers who are moody and snap but expect students not to

Taking away all my choices, control, and my power in a situation

Teachers yelling and messing with kids

When someone messes with my little brothers and sisters

Getting yelled at all the time

Teachers who are rude and bipolar acting

When others start acting different around important people

When I am angry in class, it impacts my learning and my time in that class.

17. **What would you want teachers or school staff to know or understand about a teen's struggle to manage anger?**

It would help if they would leave me alone when I am angry.

Leave me alone when I am mad. Give me some privacy to calm myself down.

Anger does impact how I am doing in school, and teachers should know angry kids may get abused at home and at school.

They just need to find a good, calm way to resolve the situation besides punishment.

When it comes to me, I don't do my work when I am angry and I'm a smart-ass.

I want them to know there is always something behind anger and usually it is related to pain or being hurt.

Questions to Develop Programs

18. **What could we do or provide to make school a safe place for you to talk about or seek help related to anger management or conflict resolution?**

Have metal detectors.

Provide a good environment for students.

Take the time to get to know your students and especially the ones with anger problems—find out what upsets them.

Give me someone I know I can talk to, not an administrator.

Offer assurance of no judgment.

Have older students who could serve as mentors or mediators.

Ensure I know I can get help.

Offer me access to someone who listens.

Have rules and procedures for keeping things confidential.

Offer accountability partners.

Offer access to someone who can do a wellness check, and ensure knowledge there is someone we can find to check in with.

19. **Do you think it is important that we have an informational or support group for students struggling with anger who want to learn strategies to positively cope with it? Why or why not?**

Yes, to help me or us learn to control anger

Yes, because it may help those in need of help

Yes, it is good to talk about it and get it out and figure out how to handle it.

I think so, because if you can help someone, I am sure that person would try to make it worth it and change.

Yes, some students definitely need it.

20. **If we started a student informational or support group on anger management and conflict resolution, what would keep you coming back?**

Having help with anxiety and depression

Offering food and candy

Knowing I can access it when I need help or when I have a question

Getting along with the people in the group

Having a leader share first, or someone else who has similar experiences share first

Being in a group with people with common concerns or ideas

Having a choice about gender-specific groups or mixed groups

Having groups divide by different grade levels since they are sometimes facing different concerns (I really think it would be good to have a group that is only ninth graders.)

Getting to know the people in the group quickly

Having one-on-one counseling available for times I want to talk to the group leader or therapist privately

Enforcing no-electronics rules for confidentiality and to keep people involved

Having trust among the group

Providing food (and changing it up with different foods)!

Continuing to be interactive

Having someone who understands what goes on outside school

Learning skills to do in the moment when you are mad

Offering physical activities that you can do when you are dealing with anger

Feeling welcomed

Establishing relevant and different topics for conversation (conflict in family, conflict due to social media, and more)

Feeling safe and not judged

Receiving positive reactions from other people in the group when a person shares (no laughing or making disrespectful comments) because others' reactions can affect the choice to share in the future

Feeling like I'm making an improvement

Having encouraging and positive attitudes around me

Meeting in different areas

Providing community-service activities

Playing music

Having a help line that you can call or text when outside the group and feeling anger (like a crisis line)

Using GroupMe to communicate about group meetings and helpful information

21. **If we started a student informational or support group on anger management and conflict resolution, what could get in the way and keep it from being successful?**

People who have conflicts with each other and don't like each other

If it is not helping people

Certain kids, and especially those with no respect for others

Lack of confidentiality or privacy

People coming into the group who think it won't help

Negativity, because negativity is contagious.

The size of the group. If groups are bigger than eight to twelve members, it may be hard to share if there are too many people. Having at least six to eight will be helpful in sharing similar experiences.

Judgment

Having groups during the day when there will be class conflicts or after school if there is no transportation provided

Having someone there you have a current conflict with (Let the group leader know so that he or she can have a mediation and resolve it before the group begins.)

Too many adults, because adults can be intimidating

Not being good listeners and talking over others

Just being mad and agitated during the group

Saying stuff outside the group or on social media but not saying it to the group

Language barriers (with English learners)

Having to talk about my family

22. **What types of information, activities, events, staffing, support, and programming related to managing anger, coping with change, resolving conflict, or mediating do you think would benefit students?**

Having a place to chill out—sofas, low lighting, low stimulation, headphones allowed, music playing

Somebody present in the "chill out" room who talks to us (real talk that is normal and straight-up), who gives us something to do with or about our anger, who keeps our confidence or confidentiality, and who listens but doesn't bring it back up over and over again

Having someone trained in conflict resolution whose full-time job is to assist students in conflict and who can focus on us and what we need

Having a place to calm down without judgment and without someone trying to control us; being able to listen to music; and having something to fidget with or do with our hands, like puzzles to do and paper to draw on or fold

Having someone trained in conflict resolution, meditation, and emotional or mental health—someone who is trained in listening, calming down, and in not lecturing

Therapists who can mediate, run support groups, and do individual counseling

Art and music classes or therapy

Having fun activities to ease the mind and manage the pain (Most people who are angry are in pain.)

Well, a cigarette break, but that probably isn't going to happen

Assistance in dealing with conflict with parents and family group

Knowing how to handle my own issues

Help dealing with being bullied and harassment

Help dealing with negative social media

Help dealing with teachers (teacher and student mediation)

Information on depression and how it relates to anger and the feeling of hopelessness

Help dealing with self-anger

Training for peer mediators

A group for students who have had physical fights

A group just for athletes

Something physical to do at school (something to hit?) to get out aggression

Stress balls

Games

Bonding at the beginning in school, classes, and groups

Things to do with our hands while in class, counseling sessions, offices, and groups to help stop the adrenaline or to deal with fidgeting

Art, journaling, sculpture, music, movement, yoga, tai chi, and weight lifting for people who aren't athletes

Something fun to do that will bring people together—even people who have discipline issues

One-on-one mentors

Anger-release games and activities (yoga, meditation, coloring books, and the ability to ask for mediation)

23. **How do you think we should go about inviting others to this group or getting the word out that we are going to have a group like this for our students?**

Look up students' discipline or violence history, and invite those who need it to come.

Just invite the angry students and then start talking about it in a way that helps them.

Find the students who are struggling, and ask them.

Whatever you decide to do, do it in private.

24. **What group name do you suggest for an informational or support group for students struggling with anger and in need of strategies related to conflict resolution and mediation?**

The Wisdom Over Anger (WOA) group

Number the groups instead of giving them a name.

25. **When you think about this struggle with anger management or conflict in your life, what gives you hope?**

The fact that I can control the circle of people I'm around and then change the way I act

Learning how to bite my tongue and control it

Nothing gives me hope when I am angry.

I don't get hope much.

My good friends and family

People who care enough to help you solve your problems

The fact that I know people care

26. **If you could meet with a young adult who struggled with anger or conflict as a teen but is now doing well, what would you ask him or her?**

How do you control your anger?

What got your anger up and running, and how did you learn to handle it?

What was going on in your home and in your school?

What helped you get over it?

What did you do to get help?

27. **Is there anything else you would like to tell us?**

No responses

The Wraparound Guide © 2021 Solution Tree Press • SolutionTree.com
Visit **go.SolutionTree.com/leadership** to download this free reproducible.

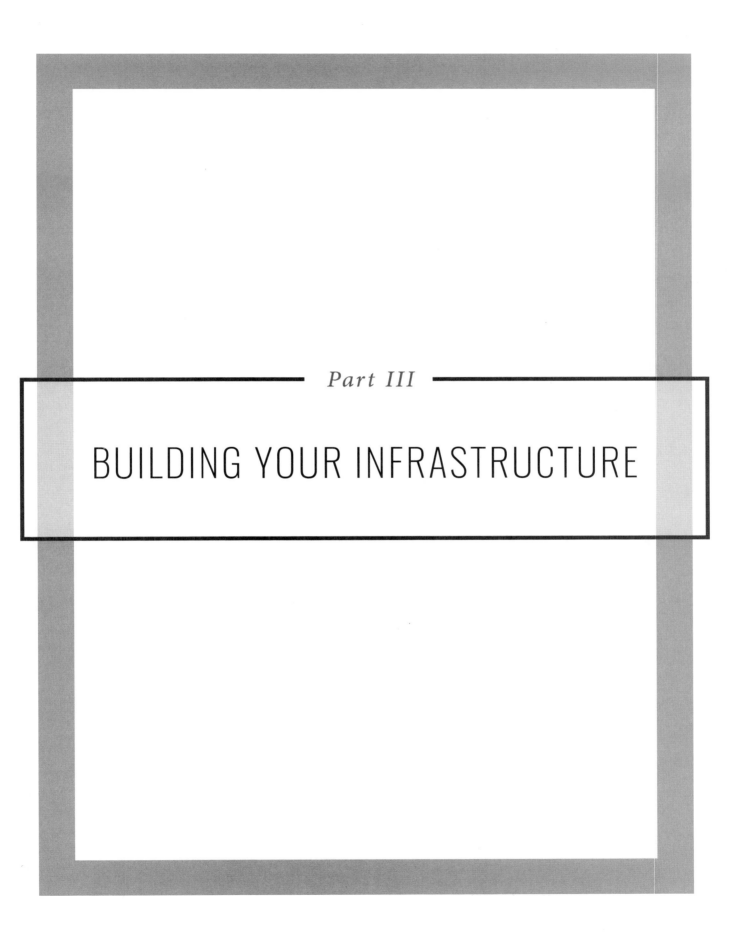

Part III

BUILDING YOUR INFRASTRUCTURE

Chapter 4

IDENTIFY RESOURCES

Before our wraparound center opened, students and teachers were
unprepared to deal with the wide range of complexities and issues
that many students faced—often alone—on an ongoing basis, issues
such as homelessness, lack of food at home, an inability to deal with
emotional distress, or help applying for college. The wraparound
approach understands that it takes a village to raise a child, and it
teaches something valuable to our students—that they are not alone
in the world.

—Adam Russell, high school teacher

Once you've identified needs and established priorities, step 3 in the Centergy Cycle involves identifying resources. For this step, you'll want to look to your community to connect with agencies, nonprofits, and other organizations working in the arenas important to your students and families. Your school likely has existing relationships with local businesses and organizations, but those connections can strengthen and broaden. "What teachers and schools need is for the whole community to see education as its job," observes Amanda Sappa (2019), chief executive officer of Communities in Schools of the Twin Cities. She adds:

> Then, schools can become hubs where trained professional staff . . . connect children and their families to everything the community offers: food, emergency housing, clothing, health care and social services, as well as academic supports like tutoring, mentoring and goal-setting. (Sappa, 2019)

A wraparound center creates the opportunity for your school to invite the community to join you in the mission of graduating healthy young adults. Table 4.1 (page 104) gives an overview of the processes used to identify which community resources might be a part of your school's hub of services

Table 4.1: Start-Up Processes—Step 3

	Process	Purpose
Step 3: Identify Resources	Types of resources	Identify sources of labor, funding, and in-kind donations as volunteers, donors, or partners.
	Full-spectrum programming	Explore four stages of full-spectrum programming: 1. Prevention 2. Education 3. Support (intervention) 4. Sustainability (recovery)
	Community asset mapping	Work with the following groups to identify community resources: • Student-support staff • Faculty • School and district staff • Community Choose an approach.

This chapter defines the different types of resources that may be available to your school and explores the reach of full-spectrum programming. It also outlines methods to map community assets by identifying community resources and potential partnerships. This knowledge will help you develop a holistic understanding of the services available in your community. Don't worry if you are unaware of or overwhelmed with the many organizations and community services beneficial to your students and families. You will be able to pace your onboarding of partnerships to suit your school's capacity. Although some schools may launch integrated services from the beginning, others start small with uncomplicated offerings to earn some quick wins while planning more complex partnerships.

Types of Resources

When starting your wraparound initiative, you'll need to find sources of labor, funding, and in-kind donations as well as organizations with the expertise and capacity to provide services to your students and families. Your aim is to marshal the community's resources to supply the nonacademic aspects of wraparound services, not to add more strain to your school system's stretched budget. For example, when outfitting the physical spaces of your wraparound center, you might find a nearby furniture store willing to provide your school with essential items such as sofas, lamps, and tables. Likewise, a local food bank may locate a food pantry on-site at one of your schools.

In the following sections, we describe these sources of labor, funding, and in-kind donations as *volunteers*, *donors*, and *partners*. Chapter 5 (page 119) will outline how to move from identifying potential partners to formalizing partnerships.

Volunteers

As in other contexts, volunteers are helpers who contribute their time and energy to a school but don't get compensation. Schools can engage volunteers to staff various activities. For example, you might feature a local fraternity alumni association at an etiquette seminar for boys before prom or have the association help organize a college trip. For situations involving unsupervised one-on-one interaction with students—such as mentoring—you'll need to perform your due diligence by requiring background checks and obtaining parental permission.

Donors

Like volunteers, donors do not receive compensation for their donation. Unlike volunteers, donors usually provide funds or donate goods rather than their time. Donors come in many forms—individuals, civic organizations, corporations, faith-based organizations, and foundations. Some may provide funding for specific purposes, like sponsoring students for field trips or senior activities, or endowing a space in your wraparound center. Others may donate to a school fund, local foundation, or nonprofit to supplement nonacademic needs the school budget does not traditionally provide for. You may also find corporate donors for in-kind resources such as career-shadowing experiences, interview-skills coaching, or laptops and internet access for low-income students.

Partners

Partners come in several forms, and you will learn much more about them in chapter 5 (page 119). In general, a school's relationship with a partner is more prolonged, intimate, and complex than with a volunteer or donor. Some partners commit to providing goods, such as food or school supplies, over a specified time frame. Other partners provide services, frequently on-site, and often require a *memorandum of understanding* (MOU), which is a formal document establishing the framework of the partnership with details such as the following.

- Data sharing
- Co-location of people
- Unsupervised, direct involvement with students
- Specialized expertise
- Collaborative funding

Volunteers, donors, and partners can be resources for the same need. For example, a volunteer may provide a lunch-and-learn seminar for students on using desk yoga to reduce stress before high-stakes testing. A donor may sponsor an on-site yoga instructor to give weekly yoga classes for students seeking assistance with emotional wellness. A partner, on the other hand, may provide one-on-one counseling for students struggling with anxiety.

Some organizations start as volunteers or donors and then transition to on-site partners over time. For example, a sorority alumni chapter may begin by providing clothing, cosmetics, and toiletries for a care closet and then grow into a mentoring partner with one-on-one mentor-student matches. The agreed-on level of oversight and formality will naturally increase in relation to the extensiveness of the connections between the partner and the student, the family, and the school.

Full-Spectrum Programming

For your wraparound initiative to be effective, you must intentionally create programs to serve *all* students—those excelling as well as those faltering. Ensure you are serving all students by developing *full-spectrum programming*, composed of the following four stages.

1. **Prevention:** "Is our school system doing anything internally to proactively impact the barrier?"

   Schools can look at their practices that promote positive social-emotional health and wellness, such as establishing positive, relational classroom management; engaging students in a schoolwide antibullying curriculum; hosting prescription drug information and take-back events to prompt parents to clean out their medicine cabinets; and providing personal-safety training related to social media, toxic relationships, and human trafficking.

2. **Education:** "How can we increase awareness and information about this barrier with our students, faculty, and community?"

   Think about educating and raising awareness within the classroom and beyond. Include school faculty, parents, and the broader community in planned activities such as the following.

   - Ensuring your health curricula is up-to-date, relevant, and engaging as well as inclusive of the latest data and research regarding mental health, substance use, sexual activity, and other issues

   - Providing professional learning for staff on the impact of poverty, mental health, the science of addiction, restorative practices, and trauma-informed practices on student learning

   - Weaving social-emotional topics into your parent-teacher association (PTA) nights—for example, showing the anxiety-focused movie *Angst* (Skerritt, 2017) with a panel of clinicians for a question-and-answer session

   - Hosting community forums around relevant local topics, such as homelessness, mental health challenges, addiction, or suicide.

3. **Support:** "Related to _____ (an identified specific barrier to learning), how can we intervene or best support students in a productive manner?"

   Support, including intervention, may occur if a student is referred for assistance or if a disciplinary infraction or episode requires staff intervention. Intervention actions and services may offset suspension time or aim to improve a student's well-being or restore a student's relationship with another person or the school. For example, school administration might require students who fought on school grounds to participate in a professionally facilitated mediation and offer them the opportunity to offset suspension time by coming to the wraparound center to participate in an anger-management support group. Alternatively, once services are implemented and well received, students may self-refer when seeking mediation to de-escalate an impending altercation. Staff might give the students ongoing support through services, such as an adult-student mentoring group or stress-management support group services, or your school might offer yoga and meditation as a part of physical education. As an ongoing example of support, a school may provide students the opportunity to participate in a program such as Sources of Strength (https://sourcesofstrength.org), which provides a framework and process for creating peer-led student support groups.

4. **Sustainability:** "How can we support students in a manner that empowers recovery or sustainability?"

When students transition out of situations requiring the close contact of intervention and support, aim to help them develop self-regulation skills to sustain their progress. You might customize a myriad of services, resources, and approaches to the student, barrier, or situation. Some may be informal, such as peer mentoring or as-needed check-ins and check-outs to touch base with a staff member. Others may be formal, such as ongoing individual therapy, job-placement and workforce-development assistance, or family assistance with finding affordable and sustainable housing opportunities.

Assisting students in attaining a level of aspiration, self-confidence, and self-regulation that empowers recovery and sustainability requires a variety of services, resources, and approaches that your wraparound center customizes to the student, the barrier, and the situation.

Although not every barrier lends itself to all four stages of programming, approach each barrier with an exploratory mindset, asking students to brainstorm strategies related to each stage. For example, schools cannot prevent a student from experiencing grief, nor are they able to provide programming to declare someone recovered from grief; however, they can increase awareness, provide support, and assist students in pushing forward after loss. Likewise, schools cannot prevent trauma from entering students' lives; but they can provide prevention programming related to making healthy life choices, and they can provide education and services related to harm reduction in the areas of personal safety, addiction, and sexuality. These can decrease a student's likelihood of experiencing trauma in the future.

After conducting focus groups or focused individual conversations with students, staff continue these conversations by connecting with parents, other staff, partners, and other individuals who have faced the identified barrier to further flesh out the school's full-spectrum approach. By having these real conversations with students and other individuals with shared life experiences, you'll discover opportunities for a broad and multifaceted approach to programming while also creating a culture where real conversations are destigmatized and students learn to self-advocate.

Figure 4.1 (page 108) shows a flip chart artifact from a focus group's discussion of stress and anxiety. It features ideas for each stage of full-spectrum programming. Notice how comprehensively students approached this topic. Some suggestions were classroom strategies that teachers could easily implement, such as asking students to complete a form labeled

What types of services, programming, staffing, events, and activities related to stress, anxiety, and emotional wellness do you think would benefit our students?

PREVENTION

Having more choice in classes about having to participate in debates, make whole class presentations, or lessons that involve "forced" conflict

Having a "do not call my name over the intercom" list

I think it's great when teachers give us the chance to tell them "10 Things you should know about me."

Having clubs that are chill—reading, board games, chess, art, music, knitting, crocheting

Yoga, meditation, Tai Chi classes as a PE course

Therapy dog

Please don't YELL or fuss at the whole class about something only a few students are doing

Pop tests are awful and real "triggers"—just know it

EDUCATION

Parent and teacher education about stress + anxiety

Community screening of the movie "Angst" with a Q+A with therapists

The health curriculum REALLY needs to be updated with information about social and emotional and mental health—not just physical health.

    1) Signs of...
    2) Successful coping ... unsuccessful coping
    3) How to know when it is time to get help
    4) How to be a good friend to someone who has...

Having a place students can get info about emotional health, strategies for calming down, and letting students know who they can go see about different issues.

Training all staff in de-escalation techniques

SUPPORT

Having a "safe" and comfortable room where we can chill, calm down, and process without consequences

Really good information in advance w/ reminders about assignments and tests is really helpful

Having a place to post thoughts and get information about available support

1:1 Therapy

Alternatives to suspension when you have screwed up in handling your emotions

Support groups (Peer or friend or therapist led)

Being able to talk to an adult who had anxiety as a teen and who is getting along well as an adult

Having a place to go when social anxiety peaks, like during lunch, a "crazy" transition time (if there was a fight, during pep rallies or something)

Art + Music Therapy options

I need more encouragement than other students and it's helpful when teachers know that

Being in a mentoring program

Listening to music and having headphones in even if I am not listening to anything helps during class change or in loud activities

SUSTAINABILITY

1:1 Therapy   Support Groups

Having a school climate that decreases stigma

A lot of kids w/ anxiety have big issues w/ self-esteem, self-doubt, and overthinking. It may sound silly, but having positive quotes in the classroom and around the building and hearing positive words can help a lot.

Having teen groups just to talk about all kinds of subjects and to meet others. Sometimes just having others to talk to really helps.

Having a designated ally (friend or staff member) as a source of support to talk through emotions or experiences—being able to bring them to uncomfortable meetings.

Yoga, meditation, Tai Chi classes as a PE course or after school and open to all students

It would be great if teachers were trained in breathing techniques and de-stress activities and meditation and they used them or encouraged us to use them in class.

Therapy dog

Having a school where students and teachers really care about each other and there is a lot of trust because my anxiety causes me to have trust issues.

Source: © 2020 The Centergy Project.

Figure 4.1: Flip chart showing students' full-spectrum suggestions for stress and anxiety.

"10 Things to Know About Me," while other suggestions required a schoolwide approach, like offering support groups. Still other suggestions involved infrastructure, like having a place for students to go when their social anxiety peaks, and some suggestions might require a change of practice or policy, like allowing students access to a therapy dog.

Many schools are increasingly interested in addressing social-emotional growth as a means to improve academics. In an *Education Week* forum on integrated supports, Robert Balfanz (2019) contends:

> As the study of education moves from a practice-based field to one that is more evidence-informed, it is becoming increasingly clear that developing students' social-emotional skills not only has value on its own, but, when based on emerging findings from the learning sciences, also improves academic outcomes.

A full-spectrum approach takes this one step further by providing programming outside the classroom to address underlying barriers that impede development of the whole child.

Community Asset Mapping

At this point, you have identified and prioritized student needs as well as sought student input regarding full-spectrum programming. Now you are ready to align these needs and ideas with the assets accessible in your community.

When asset mapping, your goal is to emerge with a list of potential volunteers, donors, and partners to invite into your wraparound efforts. Leaders commonly think they have a grasp of organizations and resources in their community, especially if they've been at their school for a while. Leigh, who was principal of the high school she graduated from and well connected in the community, was delighted to learn of services and programs she didn't know were available. For example, she remembers being pleased to find out that a local Methodist church had a GED class and grief-support services available for families who were not members of the church.

Enlist counselors, social workers, and other student support staff in the creation of a Community Asset Map to ensure a more comprehensive sampling of resources and service providers. This map, an example of which is pictured in figure 4.2 (page 110), translates the wraparound services graphic from figure 1.5 (page 28) into six categories of services: (1) health and wellness, (2) basic needs, (3) community services, (4) academic opportunity, (5) college and career transition, and (6) safety and justice. As a broad illustration, this example map may go beyond the breadth of a map you would build for your school, so don't let the number of items overwhelm you.

To develop your own Community Asset Map, use the template in figure 4.3 (page 111). You can employ this tree map as a working document to help you flesh out specific community resources you identify. Note that when developing your own Community Asset Map, list specific organizations and groups from your community, as opposed to the more general categories listed in figure 4.2. As you fill out this template, you may discover redundancy in your district's asks of your community with multiple organizations focused on too few programs. You might also find that your district has targeted only a few organizations for

The Centergy Project: A Student Wraparound Initiative
Whole School, Whole Community, Whole Child

Health and Wellness

Public health
Community services board
Health-care partners
Wellness
- Nutrition
- Fitness
- Exercise
Clinical services
- General: Social, emotional, and mental health services
- Addiction
- Stress release and anxiety management
- Self-harm and suicide prevention
- Sexual abuse and domestic violence
- Grief
- Family counseling
- Faith-based
- Eating disorders
- Conflict resolution: Anger management and mediation

Basic Needs

Food
Clothing
Toiletries
School supplies
Housing services
Homelessness services
Laundry services
Access to technology
Transportation services

Community Services

Department of Human Services
Sexual abuse and domestic violence support, recovery, and shelter
Job assistance
Faith-based assistance
Immigration assistance
Teen pregnancy and parenting
Mentoring
Navigators and life coaching
Adult education
- GED
- English
- School 101
- Parenting
- Finance
- Computer skills

Academic Opportunity

Tutoring
Educational advocacy
Test prep
Extended-day programming (after school or before school)
Early learning
Credit recovery
Career pathways
Alternative suspension programming
Rigorous coursework and systems of support
Access to technology

College and Career Transition

YouScience
Chamber of commerce
Institutions of higher learning
- Universities
- Colleges (including technical colleges)
Dual enrollment
College financial-assistance planning
Application and scholarship assistance
Apprenticeships
Military recruitment services
Soft-skills and job-skills training

Safety and Justice

Legal aid
Probation and parole services
Juvenile justice or juvenile court programming and services
Law-enforcement education, support, and services
Personal safety training
Services related to incarceration
Restorative discipline programming

Source: © 2020 The Centergy Project.

Figure 4.2: Community Asset Map.

Community Asset Map

Health and Wellness	Basic Needs	Community Services	Academic Opportunity	College and Career Transition	Safety and Justice

Source: © 2020 The Centergy Project.

Figure 4.3: Community Asset Map template.

*Visit **go.SolutionTree.com/leadership** for a free reproducible version of this figure.*

several different needs. For example, is your district tapping the same church for grief support, transportation, emergency needs, and school supplies? The Community Asset Map will help you narrow and prioritize your requests of organizations so they don't feel overtaxed. You may also discover gaps where you are missing needed services.

This map, combined with the Centergy Cycle framework, lets you determine how to implement services at a pace fitting your situation. There is no one right way. Let student voice, the capacity of your school, and community connections inform your timeline and priorities. The level of connection between your school and the community has a big impact on the speed at which you can roll out services. Building trust between school and community leaders takes time; once trust is established, you'll be able to move quicker.

To guide you through this asset-mapping process, the following sections address identifying community services, involving community organizations in asset mapping, and choosing an initial approach to building an asset map.

Identifying Community Resources

Let's look at ways you can mine your school and community connections to discover what services are available in your district. You're on the lookout for potential partners who are culturally competent and able to provide year-round services, ideally in the school building or within walking distance (Center for Popular Democracy et al., 2016). There are a variety of knowledgeable people you should contact when doing this work, including reaching out to the following.

- Student- and family-support staff
- Faculty
- School and district staff
- Community

We explore each of these groups in the following sections. As you go through the process of identifying resources, be sure to vigilantly inquire about people's firsthand experience and knowledge of a potential resource. You'll want to discover whom *not* to approach as well as whom to approach. Be wary of organizations that are less interested in the joint mission and more interested in gaining credibility or billable hours for their agency. The organizations you'll ultimately partner with must have the "capacity to move the needle on the results the community school seeks" (IEL & CCS, 2017, p. 10). Use your Community Asset Map as a guide to fill areas needing support with the names and contact information of organizations best suited to deliver that support.

Student- and Family-Support Staff

School counselors and affiliated social workers typically have the most connections with outside organizations providing social services, which makes them an ideal place to start. Provide them with copies of your Community Asset Map, and brainstorm which community organizations might support your wraparound center's efforts, focusing first on organizations with whom they have firsthand knowledge, experience, or known points of contact.

Faculty

Devote a faculty meeting to asset mapping. Introduce the concept of wraparound services (if faculty are not familiar), and establish the purpose of asset mapping as we've outlined in this chapter. Share the priorities of focus along with any relevant student voice documentation, such as narratives from focus groups and data from the Student Voice Needs Survey. Post flip charts with headings for various services from your asset map—mentoring, legal aid, housing assistance, grief counseling, and so on—and ask faculty to do a carousel walk to add names of organizations they have personal experience with. Have them include their own names so you can follow up with them after the meeting.

School and District Staff

Tap into your school and district staff's established relationships with community organizations. Not only will this teach you more about the assets in your community, but you'll also have a head start on developing relationships with the organizations. Informally survey school and district staff, asking which organizations they volunteer for and if they serve in a leadership capacity (like on a board of directors).

Community

Reach out to your community to discover resources and potential partners by connecting with the organizations listed next. The ultimate goal is to have the ear of the agency head who has the authority to make a go or no-go decision. Who from your school district is best to make the initial contact depends largely on your district's unique social network, ranging from the superintendent to the principal to the person tapped to lead the wraparound initiative.

- Government agencies (police and health departments)
- Hospitals
- Nonprofits
- Local foundations
- Community services boards
- Chambers of commerce
- Food banks
- Local colleges

Involving Community Organizations in Community Asset Mapping

When building asset maps, some schools join with local organizations such as United Way, chambers of commerce, community services boards, and local foundations to conduct a communitywide assessment of both the needs and the available services in their community. While this approach takes more time, the benefits include building the community's collective capacity to deliver services, publishing comprehensive data, networking and increasing collaboration with social service agencies, and maximizing social capital.

We found that joining together with our local partners was imperative in order to create the right conditions for collective impact. Through our community-wide assessment, we were able to identify common 'pain points' to use as a starting place for our work. For instance, we were able to identify mental health support as a tremendous need after finding our provider-to-patient ratio was not at the same level as that of other communities. [Visit www .unitedwayhallcounty.org/gameplan to learn more.] Of course, we felt the effects of this in our schools, but this was a tremendous issue for our health system as well due to strains on the local hospital's emergency department. Through the initial mapping and subsequent work to address this problem, we now have more entities than we ever imagined "sitting at the table" as we collaboratively work to address this important issue in our community.

—Sarah Bell, deputy superintendent, Gainesville City Schools, Georgia

Choosing an Approach

On completion of a Community Asset Map, we find schools usually choose which partners to approach, as part of the next phase (chapter 5, page 119), in one of two ways.

1. Flesh out one branch of the tree map.
2. Focus on a few elements across branches of the tree map.

The following sections focus on these two approaches.

Flesh Out One Branch

Choosing a single area of focus may make sense for your school if one or more of the following criteria are true.

- Your students' needs are concentrated along a particular branch, and you have corresponding community resources.

- You're looking for a low-risk entry into wraparound services and you'd like to streamline your approach.

- You'd like to align this work with existing initiatives. For instance, if your district is building a College and Career Academy, you might want to expand tiers of student support to include aptitude testing or increase college assistance and career-mentoring services.

For example, if your school is already focused on expanding career readiness, it makes sense to build on that momentum and add wraparound services related to college and career transition, such as a high-quality program for aptitude testing. Such programs might include YouScience (www.youscience.com), SAT or ACT prep courses, military recruitment programs, job fairs, career exploration featuring *be-there* experiences such as apprenticeships and internships, job shadowing for course credit, and after-school or weekend seminars utilizing community members to assist with résumé writing or mock interviews.

For high-poverty schools, addressing basic needs is often a logical entry point into the world of wraparound services. For starters, opening care closets—student food pantries, clothes closets, or school supply closets—is a relatively low-risk activity. You're also likely to find pockets of care closets already in your building—the media specialist with a drawer of snacks and school supplies, the teacher with a bin of sweaters and coats, or the school counselor with a stash of toiletries.

Basic needs are also an easy ask. Most communities have churches and civic organizations eager to help young people with tangible items that fill practical daily needs. By reaching out to those organizations, you provide an opportunity for direct, relevant, and related service projects that support your mission while building a sense of community.

Also, expand your thinking about basic needs beyond food, clothing, and school supplies. According to the Pew Research Center (Anderson & Perrin, 2018), nearly one in five U.S. students can't complete their homework because of a lack of access to online connectivity, electronic devices, and device software they need. The number is even higher in low-income communities (Anderson & Perrin, 2018). This lack of equity around technology creates a barrier to success in college-prep coursework such as Advanced Placement or International Baccalaureate (IB). Consider 2020. As schools relied on online instruction during COVID-19 quarantining, the digital divide became a daily reality for these homebound students without access to technology to complete their schoolwork, with 29 percent of parents reporting it's "at least somewhat likely their children will have to do their schoolwork on a cellphone" (Vogels, Perrin, Rainie, & Anderson, 2020).

As always, telling a personal narrative can mobilize a community initiative. Leigh remembers how students' stories related to the digital divide became the backdrop of a grassroots initiative aimed at providing laptops for underresourced, high-potential students enrolled in rigorous coursework. Because of an established partnership with the local Kiwanis club, which provided laptops through a program called One Byte at a Time, many students gained access to needed technology. (You'll learn more about this in chapter 8, page 187.) If your school has students who lack a computer or internet access, seek donors to supply computers or home internet.

Similarly, if you have students and families who would benefit from having washers and dryers installed on campus, you might approach a local appliance store or scratch-and-dent appliance outlet with quantitative and qualitative school data related to poverty and the need for laundry services. You don't need an MOU to provide a washer and dryer for students and their families to use. We have found such establishments will commonly donate a set of appliances to a school. In this scenario, it is important to destigmatize using the on-site laundry services. For instance, in one school we know, on a morning when many students were caught in a heavy rainstorm while waiting on buses, students were invited to the laundry and clothes closet to choose dry clothes to borrow and wear for the day while available staff, volunteers, and students washed and dried their wet clothes.

Another way to ensure basic needs services aren't stigmatized and are inclusive is to intentionally promote a clothes closet as a resource for all students. Banneker High School in Metro Atlanta named its clothes closet Future Fits. Students go there for tips on both fashion and dressing for success, including access to fully coordinated outfits.

voices
FROM THE FIELD

We don't limit our basic needs services to students and families; we include the community as well. When one of our parents came to us for job assistance, we helped outfit her from head to toe—and she landed a job! Our laundry facility is staffed with volunteers from 9:00 a.m. to 2:30 p.m. daily for students living in extended-stay hotels and serves about thirty families a day. Our food pantry, the Ice Box, distributes about six thousand to eight thousand pounds of groceries to our community every week. We have a fantastic team to pull this off—from ROTC students, faith-based organizations, and faculty to sororities and fraternities and local businesses.

—Igola Richardson, director of the Student and Family Engagement (SAFE) Center, Banneker High School, Atlanta, Georgia

At another school, students have published fashion features in the school newspaper with clothing from the clothes closet. Available outfits are regularly accessorized and displayed in the hallway for all students to see. During prom and homecoming, girls bring in dresses to donate or to swap a previously worn dress for another one. In this same school, students receiving discipline consequences for dress-code infractions can offset those consequences by choosing an appropriate alternative outfit from the clothes closet and wearing it for the remainder of the day; these same students can work in the clothes closet for one hour before or after school to offset the detention they received for the infraction. The school has also made it possible for students to earn community service hours by working in the clothes closet. Finally, students at the school can also borrow clothes for emergency situations, like not bringing socks on gym day, forgetting a jacket and tie for a sports banquet, or needing a certain color shirt for a spirit day.

By taking a single-branch approach, your school will develop similar partnerships, services, and expertise concentrated in an area. Once your services in a specific area are established, you can revisit your student voice data to determine if there is a need to grow the initiative by finding other branches of the asset map to explore for additional services.

Focus On a Few Elements Across Branches

Choosing to focus on more than one branch introduces more complexity into the initiative because diverse needs require diverse expertise. As we explore in chapter 7 (page 163), it is best to undertake this approach when your school has built buy-in in the community and created infrastructure by doing the following.

- Hiring a director to oversee wraparound operations

- Rearranging the organizational structure to consolidate student support functions and staff into the wraparound center

- Allocating space to deliver services and host embedded partnerships to meet a variety of needs

Compare your student voice data with your completed Community Asset Map to find areas of need that correspond with potential partners for your first round of implementation.

For example, a school might choose college and career transition, basic needs, and health and wellness as the areas of focus based on student voice as well as supporting data and community resources. In such a scenario, the district would begin digging into related data, gathering additional voice concerning these three branches, and networking with organizations whose services and staff are aligned with mentoring, college transition, and provision of personal items and school supplies. In addition, it would reach out to agencies who provide services and expertise in the areas of physical, emotional, and mental health. Those choices would inform which organizations to approach about potential partnership and what particular services are needed most to provide needed support for students and families. More information and examples related to a broader establishment of multi-branched partnerships, the securing of funding, and the creation of infrastructure to serve and support a variety of needs are covered in the next three chapters.

Conclusion

In his book *Them: Why We Hate Each Other—and How to Heal*, Ben Sasse (2018) laments the disappearance of the "shoulder on the road"—the social capital families need "to navigate the bumps and disruptions that life inevitably brings" (p. 34). With wraparound services, schools become the hub of a network of services designed to create equitable access to both opportunities and full-spectrum services. For example, Gainesville City Schools in Georgia named their wraparound center *The Hub* and worked with students to create a graphic (figure 4.4) showcasing the breadth of services offered to their students, families, and the greater community.

Source: © 2019 Gainesville City School System.

Figure 4.4: Graphic for The Hub, Gainesville City Schools' wraparound services center.

By asset mapping your community, school leaders can serve in the role of connector and navigator—quite literally creating pathways of social capital for students and families. As you identify resources and service providers who are willing to actively partner with you and others to address equity in a meaningful manner, step 4 of the Centergy Cycle, establish partnerships, provides essential guidance on turning these community resources into formal, sustainable partnerships.

Chapter 5

ESTABLISH PARTNERSHIPS

The Success Center is a unique way to provide services to students in need who otherwise may be unable to access them. I know [from students] the Success Center has provided countless opportunities for students to have a voice. Schools are a cornerstone of the community, and this collaborative approach is innovative but also makes sense. It took a passionate and active belief that students need a holistic approach as it relates to them being successful. This partnership gives me a great deal of hope.

—Grachelle Sherburne, wraparound services partner and licensed professional clinician

Up to this point, you've gathered student voice and identified resources to support wraparound services that align with your students' and families' needs. This chapter leads you through processes to formalize partnerships to create a network of partners engaging in "a set of collaborative practices: shared ownership for results, strategic community partnerships, resource coordination, data-driven planning, and inclusive leadership" (IEL & CCS, 2017, p. 9). To facilitate this, we focus this chapter on three key topics for establishing partnerships.

1. Choosing credible partners

2. Conducting a community strategic-planning meeting

3. Building strong partnerships

Each of these topics is fundamental to finding and maintaining strong partnerships to support your school's wraparound services center. In *The Power of We: Succeeding Through Partnerships*, Jonathan M. Tisch and Karl Weber (2004) explain that partners will take:

> An approach to leadership that is not divisive, but unifying; not competitive, but collaborative; not based on a zero-sum philosophy of scarcity, but on

abundance—the economic, intellectual, and spiritual abundance that human beings can produce when their talents and energies are unleashed. (p. 1)

To facilitate this vision, hold a community strategic-planning meeting with the credible partners you select to focus on launching wraparound services in schools. This begins the journey by bringing all potential partners together to collaborate about goals, essential questions, purpose, outcomes, and so on.

A wraparound center creates the opportunity for your school to bring in partners to deliver on-site services based on your students' and community's need. Table 5.1 gives an overview of the processes used to formalize partnership agreements.

Table 5.1: Start-Up Processes—Step 4

	Process	Purpose
Step 4: Establish Partnerships	Choose credible partners	Analyze opportunity and risk. Hold partnership planning meetings. Establish parameters of an MOU.
	Conduct a community strategic-planning meeting	Introduce partners to one another. Provide an overview of initiative. Develop a mission statement. Build collective energy.
	Strengthen and sustain partnerships	Reciprocate the partnership. Introduce partners to your school. Establish regular communication.

Choose Credible Partners

Especially when you get started, the potential partners you identify should be credible organizations with known track records. But how do you make such determinations? According to Stephen Covey (2018), three variables inform your analysis to extend trust:

1. What is the opportunity (the situation or task at hand)?
2. What is the risk involved?
   - What are the possible outcomes?
   - What is the likelihood of the outcomes?
   - What is the importance and visibility of the outcomes?
3. What is the credibility (character/competence) of the people involved? (p. 294)

You're looking for partner organizations with solid reputations and leaders willing to embrace a collaborative and innovative approach of shared accountability. In particular, you are seeking expertise and resources to bring into your school. Find those organizations with the capacity to work with you as a thought partner—organizations capable of creatively responding to a common vision, staffing, funding, and, most important, the student voice you've gathered. While many organizations may express interest in joining the effort, pursue the right partners; do not welcome any and every potential partner (IEL & CCS, 2017). In general, avoid newly formed organizations, those without verifiable results and references, or those who seem to have ulterior motives.

Evaluating the credibility of a potential partner for wraparound services hinges on trust in the partner's character and competence (Covey, 2018). The reverse is also true as organizations evaluate whether to partner with your school. In chapter 4 (page 103), your school's staff identified organizations to approach as potential partners. If someone from your school or district has an established relationship with the organization, have that person make the initial introduction. If not, arrange for your school's principal to reach out to the organization. As the face of your school, the principal is in the best position to get through obstacles to reach the organization's leader. In addition, a Pew Research Center (2019) poll shows K–12 public school principals are the most trusted professionals by U.S. adults with regard to caring about others, providing fair and accurate information, and handling resources responsibly. Use this built-in asset of the principal's role to approach partners you'd like to join your wraparound initiative.

It takes time to establish the high degree of mutual, relational trust necessary for success. When first establishing relationships for potential partnerships, school and organization leaders should learn about each other's immediate and long-term goals and the community challenges they have in common. For example, while meeting with agency heads who are potential partners, school leaders should be prepared to share data related to identified student achievement and graduation barriers. In terms of developing students, supporting families, and strengthening the community, your qualitative and quantitative student voice and survey data, as well as demographic, achievement, discipline, and attendance data, may prove valuable to unlocking the potential of innovative collaboration and programming.

If your school leadership and a potential partner reach a consensus that their missions align, each can then further explore the potential of partnering as described in the rest of this chapter.

Partnerships will launch at different speeds depending on relationships, complexity, leadership, and funding. As schools stretch themselves to embrace the whole child approach with wraparound and embedded on-site service providers, they are making an intentional decision to approach equity in an actionable manner. By doing so, schools make several transitions in mindset, methodology, and the manner in which they support students and families. As you embark on this process, hold in your mind the idea that wraparound work is a journey from:

- Random acts of good intention to intentional strategic partnerships
- Community silos to associations of care
- External referrals to embedded synergistic services
- A consequence focus to a service focus
- Fear of liability to smart trust

When selecting community partners to provide services in your school's wraparound center, it's imperative they are motivated by more than just the paycheck. Especially when partners fill the gap of the physical and behavioral health services so many communities lack, the mission of the organization or company must be community service focused, and the organization's leaders must be willing to devote their time and energy to building the partnership beyond what they are billing. For example, the mental health organization our school district contracts with not only provides high-quality and diverse mental health services, but the clinical and regional directors of the organization with whom I work directly devote hours of unpaid time consulting with me and the many school staff members in our thirty-one schools, attending meetings and school events, and presenting at parent and community information sessions. Their devotion to our wraparound program far exceeds the contract provisions.

—Rachel Czerepak, socioemotional services coordinator,
Columbia County School District, Georgia

As these items make clear, the collaborative practices demanded of a wraparound initiative require that the school's and potential partners' leaders have a particular mindset; specifically, they must be open-minded, trustworthy listeners with the ability to collaboratively problem solve. It's likely that both the partner and the school will need to change their organizational structure and adapt processes as the partnership evolves, meaning risk taking and flexibility are assets.

A Word About Mental Health, Trauma, and ACEs

In his article titled "Giving Teens a Place at the Table," Eric Hardie (2019) asserts:

The problem of students suffering from anxiety or depression, self-injurious behavior, and even suicide has become all too commonplace, and while schools try to help, their mental health resources are often strained.

Compounding the problem is that the possible solutions to teens' mental health often come from the wrong place. Well-intentioned adults make their best guesses about what might help, but they often forget to directly include the students themselves in developing solutions. Adult perceptions are clouded by the way we hope students experience our schools, missing, at times, the hard truths of our teens' day-to-day experiences, both inside and outside of school. (p. 18)

Record observations based on your initial conversations with potential partners using the Partnership Planning Guide. The version of this guide pictured in figure 5.1 provides details on how to use each section within the guide. This guide will help you clarify the degree of alignment and compatibility between your school and a potential partner.

Scope of the Partnership

Define the partnership.

Initial conversations between schools and partner agencies should occur among leaders with the authority to make decisions related to staffing, programming, funding, and policy—typically the equivalent of the CEO. In determining the partnership's level of engagement, leaders should clarify and gain a broad, mutual understanding of the partnership's scope—its goals and opportunities as well as the potential risks and problems. Once those high-level issues are addressed, other individuals may be tasked with logistics and implementation. Consider this a starting point, expecting adjustments as the partnership develops.

Focus or Mission of the Partnership

Find a shared mission.

First seek to understand the agency, asking questions such as the following.

- "What is your mission?"
- "Whom do you serve?"
- "What is your scope?"
- "Is there a way our school or district can help you better achieve your mission with our students and families?"

Partnerships are based on the premise that everyone shares ownership of the educational enterprise (IEL & CCS, 2017). When approaching a potential partner, look for specific overlap between the partner's mission and your school's mission. For example, a school might engage with a local agency providing conflict resolution counseling because anger management popped up on the Student Voice Needs Survey and is also a significant source of discipline referrals. Finding the shared mission guides the rest of the conversation.

Goals and Measurables

Define goals and measurables.

You'll want to ground your goals and measurables in qualitative and quantitative information you've gathered, including student voice information from conversation circles, focus groups, and individual focused conversations. Pay close attention to the focus groups' and individual focused conversations' documentation as a source of innovative approaches to services and interventions. You'll also get a sense of the mindset and desires of your students by taking the time to listen and read their input.

Be mindful to invite your partner to share data relevant to its mission as a basis of determining mutual goals and measurables for the partnership—what matters to each of you. Examine all mutually relevant information as necessary, such as demographic, achievement, discipline, and attendance data from your school, or community data obtained through public health, law enforcement, or other agencies.

Staffing Needs

Determine staffing needs.

Review your Student Voice Needs Survey results to project potential levels of need and caseloads. Look for all student voice responses related to a partner's expertise. For example, the need for conflict resolution counseling could appear as conflict resolution, anger management, or healthy relationship building. Some partnerships may utilize volunteers to meet the needs of students and families; others will require the use of paid staff. If the agency already serves your students and their families, as may be the case with the local Department of Human Services, the housing authority, or juvenile probation, on-site support may not require the funding of new personnel but may result in the co-location of an individual the agency already employs. To partner with an agency not already serving a caseload of students or families, the school district and the agency may need to cowrite a grant for funding services on-site. Alternatively, billable services may offset the cost of an employee involved in this partnership, such as might be the case with an on-site clinician or public-health expert.

Figure 5.1: Partnership Planning Guide.

continued ▶

Space Needs

Identify on-site space needs.

The space requirements of the partnership will largely depend on the services provided. Some services require special space needs, such as dedicated private space allocated for therapy. Likewise, probation officers conducting drug screens need private access to a bathroom. For partners embedded in the school, you'll need to designate a permanent place for the staff. Some schools use instructional classroom space for services delivered outside school hours. Optimally, you would cluster service providers into one area within the school. Take an objective look at office space, bookrooms, computer labs, teacher planning areas, staff lunch areas, and classrooms. As schools expand or renovate, we've known them to repurpose media center spaces, weight rooms, career and technical education classrooms, field houses, or small classrooms formerly used for pullout purposes.

Schedule

Determine a schedule.

When planning the schedule of services, think at three levels: (1) the typical weekly school schedule, (2) the potential of after-school and weekend hours, and (3) the seasonal rhythms of a school calendar, such as school breaks and testing times. Be sure to consider transportation—school buses and public transportation—when planning services outside the school day. Determine with your partner how to manage those times when the school is closed (such as breaks). Some services (such as clothes closets) are easier to temporarily suspend than others (such as therapy).

Agency Needs

Determine needs the agency must have met to fulfill its commitments.

These needs are highly variable depending on the agency and the mission. Examples include the need for a collaborative referral process, access to student and parent information, an office space, access to a printer, access to a copier, and the need for cooperation on seeking grant funding.

School Needs

Determine school needs relative to agency capacity.

School needs often depend on what the agency requires. For example, your school might desire a partnership embedding service providers on campus or need a voice in the selection of the embedded staffperson. The school district might need customized programming based on the Student Voice Needs Survey and the input of students or parents during focus groups.

Note: Agency and school needs may be as simple as discussing the need for background checks, or they may be more complicated, such as determining and crafting specific guidelines for data sharing.

Supply Needs

Determine supply needs.

Think through what the partner will need to do the job—for example, access to a copier, office supplies, a lockable file cabinet, a desk, a computer, or a dedicated phone line.

Level of Partnership

Determine the level of partnership and whether an MOU is necessary. (Why or why not?)

When you have a high level of trust between your school and the partner, an MOU might feel like overkill (at best) or a distrustful communication (at worst). Also, the level of partnership might not seem like it warrants a full-scale MOU. And it may not. For example, a local civic club may be willing to provide laptops for students and host mock interviews. In this case, the program may thrive with a simple document laying out the framework of the program rather than a more formal MOU.

On the other hand, one compelling reason to develop and execute an MOU with each agency revolves around *sustainability*. An MOU clarifies the partnership agreement in the inevitable event of leadership changes at either the school or the partner agency. Having a formal document that spells out the terms of the partnership, rather than relying on informal or personal understandings, improves the likelihood of a smooth transition.

The Nonprofit Risk Management Center (n.d.) asserts, "The process of developing an MOU is an instructive and potentially invaluable experience in partnering." When developing MOUs, you'll likely learn about partners' responsiveness, their attention to detail, and perhaps how they handle disagreements—all valuable insights before finalizing an agreement (Nonprofit Risk Management Center, n.d.).

Of course, formalizing a partnership introduces more bureaucracy into the arrangement, which can sometimes slow things down, especially when involving attorneys, other people, and departments outside your wraparound center. District policies may also drive much of this process. If possible, keep your MOUs to agreements signed by the leader of your wraparound center, the district superintendent, and the head of the partner agency. In *all* cases, work with your district's legal counsel before executing an MOU.

Funding

At this point, you'll want to be open-minded about funding. Potential sources are district funding including state and federal funding; local donors; in-kind donations; and collaborative funding options involving third-party funding sources such as grants, foundations, and state agencies. The district should be prepared to provide funding for academic and college- and career-related services—SAT and ACT prep, tutoring, transportation to and from school, school supplies, and college and career counseling.

With regard to wraparound school personnel, the district should consider the reorganization of individuals working in nonintegrated student support roles such as credit recovery staff, tutors, school social workers, graduation coaches, parent and community strategists, partnership coordinators, academic screeners, academic counselors, college and career counselors, paraprofessionals, and in-school suspension supervisors.

In general, most schools lack coordination and synergy among these staff members. Rather than hiring additional staff to work in the area of wraparound services, the district might need to coordinate as well as reorganize, repurpose, and refocus existing staff. The only position that the district must hire for and fund is an individual to coordinate wraparound services and the direction of the school-based center.

Primary Point of Contact

As you are establishing the partnership agreement, the primary point of contact for the partner will be the head of the agency. As the implementation proceeds, the leader may designate someone to handle the day-to-day aspects of the partnership's services. On behalf of the school district, the wraparound director, the superintendent, or a member of the cabinet who serves as his or her designee should be involved as the commensurate counterpart to the head of the agency.

Initial Action Steps

Your first step is to gather student voice, but your next steps will depend on a variety of factors, such as the complexity of the partnership, space requirements, or the number of students accessing services. Set a realistic pace for your implementation, and choose your action steps accordingly. The higher the level of trust between the district and partner, the faster you'll be able to implement new wraparound services. If the leaders of the district and partner organizations are not acquainted, expect things to move a little slower as the organizations build relationships and explore common programming.

Intake and Screening Processes

As much as possible, you'll want to streamline your intake processes to avoid duplicate data collection. You don't want students or families filling out multiple forms asking virtually the same questions. While the *how* of pooling the intake processes comes later, here is the place to identify and learn about the partner's established protocols to begin looking for ways you can streamline and assimilate them with various partners'. You'll also want to understand legal and organizational rules of confidentiality when establishing intake and screening processes.

continued ▶

Rules of Confidentiality

Protecting student and family confidentiality undergirds all the work of wraparound services because keeping confidences demonstrates the most basic form of respect. Your work will quickly unravel if students or their families think you are casually sharing their business with others. For that reason, it's best to keep your records separate from the general student information portal, where many people have access to student records. Rely on law and local policies to inform practices to ensure confidentiality as well as proper documentation regarding information release and sharing.

Federal Laws

This is the place to educate your partner about the Family Educational Rights and Privacy Act of 1974 (FERPA), a federal law protecting the privacy of student education records. Basically, the act requires written permission to share any student's education records beyond "directory information" (name, address, phone number, and so on) while allowing for parents and students to opt out of sharing directory information. Exceptions include defined parties, such as financial aid institutes, schools to which students are transferring, and law enforcement (U.S. Department of Education, 2018). Use your district's policies to guide the conversation between the district and partner, keeping in mind to seek parental permission before sharing student information.

Additionally, some partners, such as health-care providers, will be delivering services requiring compliance with the Health Insurance Portability and Accountability Act (HIPAA). The act addresses both privacy and security of defined protected health information (U.S. Department of Health and Human Services, 2013). Ask your partners for their policies, waivers, and permission forms, and then consult your district policies to iron out practices and ensure compliance with HIPAA.

Local Protocols

Use your district guidelines when establishing whether you need parental permission to offer specific services and what language to use for permissions forms. In general, requiring parental permission largely depends on the degree of one-on-one contact with a student. For example, you probably wouldn't need parental permission for a student to participate in a conflict resolution session, but, would need it for a student to participate in individual therapy related to mental health.

Here is some sample parental permission language:

> Your child has requested to participate in one or more of the following activities within our school's wraparound center. Our center was created based on students' suggested topics of interest and requested services. Our mission is to provide wraparound services for our students in an effort to safeguard their wellness and increase their ability to learn and graduate on time with their class.
>
> (List services.)
>
> I understand that by signing, I consent to my child's participation in services at the wraparound center. I also understand that at any time, I can revoke my consent by written, dated communication.
>
> If you have any concerns or questions regarding services provided, you may contact the Center directly.

Barriers

Anticipate potential situations that could present obstacles to connecting students and families with services. Some barriers may be logistical, like after-hours access or lack of transportation. Others might be more sensitive or rooted in societal stigma, like allowing students to meet with young adults in recovery for universal screenings or mentoring sessions related to decreasing or ceasing substance use. Additionally, be prepared to identify the point of contact and discuss the preferred process for solving problems related to instances of inefficiency or ineffectiveness on school or partner staff's behalf.

Data to Collect

Each partner will measure success differently based on its mission and expertise. For example, a food bank might measure success by pounds of food distributed as well as the number of students and families participating. A conflict resolution therapist might want to measure the rate of recidivism for students receiving anger-management counseling. A mentoring program might want to compare the mentored students' graduation rate with the overall graduation rate of the school. Among other things, schools will want to track the number of students and families participating in services and programming; decreased days of suspension; improvement in the attendance, discipline, or credits earned by a specific caseload of students; improvement in graduation rates; and qualitative information gathered from students and families regarding program effectiveness.

*Visit **go.SolutionTree.com/leadership** for a free reproducible version of this figure.*

A Word About Mental Health, Trauma, and ACEs

According to Hendershott (2016):

> Wounded students face many issues that are not only hard to deal with, but also hard to hear. When we are entrusted with insight into a wounded student's life, we need to protect that child further by honoring their confidence. Whether this information comes through information offered by parents/caregivers or the child themselves, reassurance should be given that you can be trusted to keep this information as a tool for better understanding how to best serve this student. The only reason for a breach in this confidentiality would be if there was a concern regarding a child's or other person's safety. At that time, proper protocol should be followed for involving professional help. (p. 57)

Of particular note from the Partnership Planning Guide is the Level of Partnership section, which addresses whether the partnership requires a formal MOU. When schools and partners craft a formal MOU, they typically use these agreements to spell out the following.

- Services descriptions
- Personnel selection and management
- Space, equipment, and other needs
- Insurance requirements
- Licensure requirements
- Means of handling expenses (including insurance when applicable)
- Parental permission guidelines
- Compliance with local or federal regulations

As we indicated in figure 5.1 (page 123), these agreements are not always necessary, depending on the nature of the partnership. However, if you or your partner determines such an agreement would be beneficial, you may use figure 5.2 (page 128) to serve as a discussion guide.

Memorandum of Understanding Discussion Guide

1. Record the full legal name of each party (organization).

School district: _____ Agency: _____

2. Describe the parties involved in the MOU, including any current or historical ties to the project.

School district:

Agency:

3. Describe the intent and role of each party as related to wraparound services.

School district:

Agency:

4. Describe each party's responsibilities. Include the co-location of people, space and equipment requirements, and specialized expertise and services.

School district:

Agency:

5. Define the terms of the agreement and any notice expected prior to termination or renewal.

6. Record any data-sharing needs or requirements.

7. To develop appropriate practice guidelines, exchange codes of conduct and ethics regarding interaction with students either individually or in groups. Record any items requiring action.

8. Discuss and record funding streams, payments expected, and each party's role and expectations in obtaining funding and sharing costs.

9. Discuss and record any risk-sharing or insurance needs, including minimum liability limits and coverage.

10. Identify proper signatories with the authority to bind each organization.

11. Establish no sharing of employees. Each party retains the responsibility of supervision, training, and certification of its employees. Initial below.

_____ Initial _____ Initial

Date: _____

Figure 5.2: Memorandum of Understanding (MOU) Discussion Guide.

Visit **go.SolutionTree.com/leadership** *for a free reproducible version of this figure.*

Conduct a Community Strategic-Planning Meeting

Once you have your initial committed partners, set up a time with all your partners for a community strategic-planning meeting. At this point, most of your contact has likely been with the heads of the partner organizations. This is a good time to ask each partner to bring one to three others who will help implement the partnership going forward. Use the Community Strategic-Planning Meeting Guide (figure 5.3, page 130) and your draft of the Community Asset Map (figure 4.3, page 111) to ensure you invite the proper people and have the materials you need. We suggest scheduling this as a full-day meeting or as a series of shorter meetings. In either case, expect to devote approximately six to eight hours to this process.

With people possibly unfamiliar with the concept of wraparound services, you will need to spend some time on foundational information. Don't worry if it's repetitive for some; everyone can benefit from a collective conversation using common language to ground the work. Let's take a closer look at the elements of your community strategic-planning meeting and eight steps you can take to structure the meeting so that it achieves all four purposes outlined in figure 5.3.

1. Introduce partners to one another.
2. Establish a shared vision of graduates.
3. Provide an overview of the whole child approach, wraparound services, and student voice.
4. Share student voice data.
5. Invite partners to share their mission and services.
6. Develop a wraparound mission statement.
7. Have partners complete an asset map.
8. Conclude the meeting.

Purpose	Introduce your partners to one another. Provide an overview of the whole child approach, wraparound services, and student voice. Develop a wraparound mission statement. Build collective energy.		
Participants	School Representatives (District leaders, principals, wraparound director [if hired], and so on)		

Name	Title or Role

Partners (Provide enough space for those invited. It is preferable to keep this number less than forty-five.)

Name	Organization	Title

Materials	Provide the following for engagement activities that will take place during the meeting.

- A blank poster-size copy of the Community Asset Map
- Blank flip chart pages to post on the walls with the following questions
  - What will we be celebrating in a year?
  - What are key questions to keep our work grounded?
  - Who is missing from this meeting?
- Markers
- Tape (if needed to hang the flip charts)

Distribute the following to each table. Participants will use the items to record their feedback on the preceding engagement flip charts.

- Sticky notes
- Blank paper (for notetaking)
- Writing utensils
- A copy of documents related to developing a wraparound mission statement for each person; double-space all documents to facilitate written feedback.
- Copies of supporting documents, such as research articles, graphics, presentation handouts pages, Student Voice Needs Survey results, and so on; all documents should have page numbers and be printed on different colors of paper for quick access and ease of facilitation.
- Commitment cards

Location	Large meeting room to accommodate table seating and small-group work.

Figure 5.3: Community Strategic-Planning Meeting Guide.

*Visit **go.SolutionTree.com/leadership** for a free reproducible version of this figure.*

In addition to completing these steps (which we detail in the following sections), during breaks or transition times, capture the group's enthusiasm by inviting participants to use sticky notes to answer the following engagement questions and post their answers on the charts you have posted in the room.

- "What will we be celebrating in a year?"
- "What are key questions to keep our work grounded?"
- "Who is missing from this meeting?"

Before the meeting concludes and people depart for the day, remind all participants to make sure they have posted a response to each question.

Introduce Partners to One Another

Suggested time: Twenty to thirty minutes (depending on the number of participants)

Start the meeting by asking everyone to introduce themselves, including their names and titles. After a brief welcome and introduction of the purpose for the meeting, continue with this icebreaking think-pair-share activity or with time dedicated to small-group sharing, asking participants to respond to the following questions. These questions will help engage the participants on a personal level.

- "Why are you here today?"
- "What do you care about?"
- "What gives you hope?"
- "What helps you come back from something difficult?"

Depending on how much time you have left for this segment, you may choose to facilitate a brief large-group follow-up discussion on these questions. You might also direct the attention of participants to similar student voice charts you have on display requesting those in attendance take some time during an upcoming carousel walk to review the answers students gave to these questions.

Establish a Shared Vision of Graduates

Suggested time: Ten minutes

After introductions are complete, begin the meeting with an activity designed to establish a vision of what attributes participants want their local graduates to possess. The purpose of this is to demonstrate the need for communities to embrace a collaborative approach to whole child success. To facilitate this activity, introduce the prompt "I want our graduates to be . . ." and supply a starter answer of your own, like *trustworthy* or *curious*. Avoid providing an academic starter answer, such as *achievers*, since your goal for your audience is to think broadly and beyond the classroom. Likewise, ask participants not to use the word *successful* as it is too opaque, and the goal is to identify those attributes that are the components of a successful life.

Give people about three to four minutes to individually respond with a list of words on one sticky note. The goal is for each participant to brainstorm seven to ten one-word descriptors. After this period of individual brainstorming, ask the participants to circle their top three answers and compare their answers in duos or triads. When these small-group conversations are complete, facilitate a large-group response, asking volunteers or individual participants (depending on group size and time) to say aloud the three attributes they determined to be of most value.

Inevitably, you will establish a list of characteristics having very little to do with finite achievement, SAT scores, grade point average, or scholarship dollars earned. Instead, this prompt evokes descriptions of productive, healthy citizens, ones who are *resilient*, *connected*, *employed*, and *optimistic*. Then, ask the group, "Whose responsibility is it to develop these kinds of graduates?" Expect to hear answers involving families, churches, schools, and the community. Indeed, the answers you hear are likely to further validate the notion schools can't go it alone and educating the whole child is the whole community's responsibility.

At the end of this activity, collect everyone's responses. After the meeting, use online tools like https://wordart.com to turn them into word art, as in figure 5.4. You can use this output in publications, posters, or other promotional materials. Also note this kind of activity is equally useful for venues such as faculty meetings and PTA meetings.

Figure 5.4: Community ideals for graduates.

Provide an Overview of the Whole Child Approach, Wraparound Services, and Student Voice

Suggested time: Two hours

With the introductions and initial activity complete, you'll need to tailor your overview of the need for services based on the audience. If you've met individually with everyone in the meeting, you'll be able to keep your comments fairly high level. However, if you have people new to the initiative (such as people your partner is introducing for the first time), plan to provide a packet, brief presentation, or overview that includes the following.

- Definitions of the whole child approach and wraparound services

- Reasons your district has chosen to provide wraparound services

- A summary of your student voice processes

- Primary barriers your students have identified

- Methods you intend to use to prioritize initial wraparound services

- Any supporting documentation relevant to your community (newspaper articles, presentation handouts pages, and so on)

Share Student Voice Data

Suggested time: Sixty to ninety minutes

By this point, you should have student voice data in the form of flip charts from conversation circles and focus groups, and you should have copies of your Student Voice Needs Survey results, which provide quantitative data about students' needs. Post the flip charts around the room, and invite participants to do a carousel walk. Prompt organic conversations by asking the following questions before they begin the carousel activity. (You might also display these questions on a presentation slide.)

- "What affirms your thinking?"

- "What surprises you?"

- "What do you perceive as positive?"

- "What is concerning to you?"

- "Is there something missing?"

- "How does this information influence your approach to children and teens in our community?"

- "What is a requested service that would be relatively straightforward to implement?"

- "What groupings of needs, if any, have emerged that could be addressed together in a clustered approach?"

Another approach is to give participants a sheet of small stickers (stars, dots, and so on) and allow them to self-select flip chart comments that resonate with them as affirming their thinking or influencing their perspectives or the work of their agency. They can place stickers next to the comments they find the most thought-provoking.

Encourage participants to dig deep and ask questions about your student voice data. In our experience, the transparency from students revealed in student voice data often surprises participants. This inevitably leads to concern at the volume and severity of the challenges students face. Take the opportunity to explain the survey data are a snapshot of interest rather than a diagnostic tool. For example, as we explained in Dealing With the Big Four (page 68), if a high number of students show interest in services related to one of the big four barriers, like suicide prevention, it is not the same thing as a student reporting suicide ideation. Spending time to review the data will likely create a sense of urgency for your wraparound efforts.

Invite Partners to Share Their Mission and Services

Suggested time: Thirty to forty-five minutes

Because you will no doubt reach out to multiple partners, you need to develop a holistic approach to wraparound services that breaks down silos. Partners need to understand how their work integrates with the other partners' services. Ask your partners (a designated person from each organization) to come prepared to share a brief overview of their mission, services, and connection with your wraparound initiative (about three to five minutes). Consider doing this before you have a hard stop (like before lunch) to create a time pressure so people are brief.

Develop a Wraparound Mission Statement

Suggested time: Forty-five to ninety minutes

A mission statement answers the question, Why do we exist? Education experts Richard DuFour, Rebecca Dufour, Robert Eaker, Thomas W. Many, and Mike Mattos (2016) argue that a strong mission establishes a clarity of purpose that "can help establish priorities and becomes an important factor in guiding decisions" (p. 39). A well-crafted mission statement will ground the wraparound work as well as focus your communication with internal and external stakeholders. The process of developing a mission also establishes a shared understanding of the wraparound center's purpose and its aspirations for the future (Allison & Kaye, 2005).

TopNonprofits (n.d.) suggests you aim for three criteria when creating a mission statement.

1. **Clarity:** A reading level between eighth and tenth grade

2. **Brevity:** Keep to five to fourteen words and try for no more than twenty

3. **Usefulness:** Informs, focuses, and guides

Very likely, your school has a mission statement already. However, the mission of your wraparound center requires an emphasis on social-emotional learning that many school mission statements lack. We find modeling a wraparound center's mission after other non-profit organizations can help distill the focus such that it better aligns with the preceding criteria. Consider the following examples.

- **Smithsonian National Museum of Natural History (n.d.):** To promote understanding of the natural world and our place in it

- **The Nature Conservancy (n.d.):** To conserve the lands and waters on which all life depends

- **Monterey Bay Aquarium (n.d.):** To inspire conservation of the ocean
- **Children's Museum of Atlanta (2018):** To spark every child's imagination, sense of discovery and learning through the power of play

The community strategic-planning meeting affords you the opportunity to have purposeful conversations about the mission of your wraparound initiative. There are many ways to approach this task depending on any number of variables such as the urgency of completion, the availability of people to help, and your other priorities. Here are just a few options to consider.

- Gather a small group of trusted colleagues to draft a statement to present in the meeting. At the meeting, solicit feedback from your partners and update the statement accordingly.

- Appoint a facilitator to embark on a larger, community-based approach by developing a brand for your wraparound center using processes as spelled out in *Building a StoryBrand* (Miller, 2017) or *Strategic Planning for Nonprofit Organizations* (Allison & Kaye, 2005).

- Create a simple, open-ended wraparound mission questionnaire, like the one shown in figure 5.5, for participants to complete in the meeting. Ask for volunteers who will form an ad hoc committee and turn the answers into a formal statement to bring back to the group.

WRAPAROUND MISSION QUESTIONNAIRE

Name: _____

Organization: _____

Date: _____

1. Why does the wraparound center exist?

2. What services does the wraparound center provide?

3. Who benefits from the services of the wraparound center?

4. What problems are solved by the wraparound center?

Figure 5.5: Sample wraparound mission questionnaire.

*Visit **go.SolutionTree.com/leadership** for a free reproducible version of this figure.*

Each method has pros and cons. Depending on the method you choose, you may only have enough time to begin the process in this meeting. In any case, if your partners are relatively unknown to each other, conversations around mission can help jump-start the interpersonal relationships you'll need for effective collaboration. If your partners come with established positive relationships, you might choose a more streamlined process to quickly move to more nuts-and-bolts aspects of establishing the partnerships.

Have Partners Complete an Asset Map

Suggested time: Ten minutes before the meeting ends

Utilizing a blank poster-size version of the Community Asset Map, invite partners to place their organization's name or a business card on the map. Request that partners resist the urge to post their organizations on multiple branches of the map and instead identify only one branch. This requires them to prioritize a primary area of service and support so your school is not overreliant on a few organizations to meet many needs, which can sometimes lead to partner fatigue.

Conclude the Meeting

Suggested time: Fifteen minutes

To end the meeting on a high note, ask each partner organization to collaboratively complete a commitment card, like the one in figure 5.6. Ask participants to share their commitments to build collective energy based on the possibilities of your shared mission to make a difference in your community. Collect these cards at the end of the meeting and compile them into a single document.

WRAPAROUND COMMITMENT CARD

Organization: _____

Preferred point of contact: _____

Phone number: _____

Please collaboratively answer the following questions.

- What are you excited about?

- What resources and support can you provide?

- How can the wraparound initiative help your organization be more effective?

- What can your agency commit to the wraparound initiative?

Figure 5.6: Sample commitment card.

After the meeting, follow up with a thank-you to all participants, including a summary of all decisions and any supporting material you think the participants need (graduation graphic, photos of flip charts, and so on). Additionally, include contact information to facilitate partners' connecting with each other.

Build Strong Partnerships

During partnership planning, the district and the partnering agency met to explore their shared mission, determine the level of partnership, and define goals and measurables as well as roles and responsibilities. In co-designing the programming and services to be delivered, the school district publicly aligns itself with the partner agency and leverages the expertise of the partner to better serve its students and families. Like any relationship, partnerships require some effort to keep them vibrant and healthy. In this section, we provide three ideas to ensure your partnerships thrive: (1) introduce partners to your school and community, (2) establish regular communication, and (3) reciprocate and celebrate the partnership.

Introduce Partners to Your School and Community

It is important to publicly announce your partnerships, and you might consider one of the following as a means for doing so: a signing ceremony; banners displayed in your center, in your schools, and at the partner's offices; a press release; recognition at a board of education meeting; a parent-teacher-student association (PTSA) meeting or sporting event; and publication in the school and district newsletters. Once you establish a partnership, integrate the partners into your school and community with activities such as the following.

- Invite partners to faculty meetings, possibly for professional learning on their area of expertise. For example, if you have a substance abuse clinician, allow time for the clinician to present on the science of addiction.

- Publicize your partners' work, staff members, and services in newsletters and on social media.

- Introduce your partners at a PTA or parent-teacher organization (PTO) meeting. Include your partner agencies in your Open House and start-of-school events.

- Cohost with your partners a provider, health, or job fair that is open to your entire community.

- Cohost with your partners a symposium focused on a communitywide issue, such as substance use, homelessness, or mental health challenges.

By continually looking for ways to include your partners, they will become a part of the fabric of your school's culture, becoming more like a part of the family than a guest.

Establish Regular Communication

Like any relationship, frequent communication keeps a partnership evolving. With embedded service providers, you'll have daily interaction with the partner staff in your school. Regardless, you'll want to establish regular check-ins between the heads of your wraparound center and the partner agency. Initially, set these monthly. As the partnership grows and strengthens, you can reduce the frequency of check-ins to quarterly, biannually, or as needed. In addition, host periodic meetings with *all* partners to evaluate progress, reconnect with the mission, celebrate the union and any successes, and orient any new partner representatives.

Reciprocate and Celebrate the Partnership

True partnership is a two-way street. You build trust and connection when your school and partners mutually support one another, not when your school positions itself as a recipient of partners' largesse. You'll forge authentic partnerships only when you are genuinely prepared to treat your partners' concerns as equal to your own (Tisch & Weber, 2004). To ensure this happens, actively seek ways for your school to contribute to your partners' missions. If your partners are looking for people to be members of their boards of directors, offer school staff (not just the superintendent) to serve. Show up to their galas and fundraisers. Grant them free access to your school facilities for their events. Publicly celebrate any recognition or milestone your partnership agencies achieve. Publish an annual report and include information, photos, and services-related data on all your partners. The bottom line—don't just ask your partners for support without providing support and recognition in return.

Conclusion

During the era of NCLB (2002), Jonathan M. Tisch and Karl Weber (2004) argued, "The right solutions [to education] will come about when the educational system is reformed in an atmosphere of partnership, not treated as a political football" (p. 183). The Partnership for the Future of Learning's (n.d.) *Community Schools Playbook* stresses the impact collaboration has on a community's ability to make substantial changes. Through forging high-trust relationships with a full range of community partners, you'll streamline access to services while intentionally making your school a welcoming space for your students, families, and communities. While these partnerships bring many benefits, it is critical to consider funding and its role in making this initiative possible and sustainable.

Chapter 6

SECURE FUNDING

This chapter was coauthored with Margaux H. Brown.

Please accept my sincere gratitude for your assistance during a very stressful time. I'm a single mother. My daughter has just started college, and my son is a senior in high school. Things changed for us financially when she went off to college. I found myself struggling to assist her and maintain household expenses. I emailed [the Center], stating our food supply was low and my bills were behind. The staff replied and set up a time to meet me. We received food for the week, and we were connected with assistance regarding our immediate bills, college expenses, more affordable housing, and assistance with services. The face-to-face meeting was so important. I love knowing the Center is a place of support for the entire family.

—High school parent

One of the first questions school leaders ask when learning about a wraparound center is "How much is this going to cost?"

There's good news. If you embrace the framework we present, much of the funding for your wraparound work could come from external sources, not your school budget. Embrace your school district's role as a pillar and architect in this work. This is grassroots community building, and the school district must step forward to assist in the lift. If the school district foots the bill for most of your services, you'll miss opportunities to partner with and engage your community—a vital component to sustainability (see chapter 9, page 207).

While fundraising is easier in some communities than others, *all* communities can leverage people-powered assets for the good of students and families. Be mindful to approach this opportunity with a future-focused, asset-minded, and optimistic perspective; this work is hopeful, and momentum builds with each stakeholder who leans in and then steps forward. Without question, securing state and federal dollars and intentionally braiding them with local funding, in-kind donations, and grants is critical to the hoist and the long-term impact and sustainability of wraparound work. This chapter spells out a myriad of funding streams potentially available to you from public and private sources. Please note that many of these funding streams are based on our knowledge of U.S.-based resources; however, if you live outside the United States, this chapter still offers knowledge and ideas that can point you in the right direction for funding options specific to your community, province, and nation.

When it comes to funding, find the right balance between budgeting school funds for wraparound services and asking others for financial and in-kind support. A school district needs its own skin in the game when it comes to financially supporting wraparound services, particularly services targeted to academic opportunity and college and career transition. For instance, a school district should cover costs related to tutoring, bus transportation, and school staffing as well as facilities and operations. However, individuals and community organizations can help close equity gaps by mentoring students, providing goods, donating services, and supporting the costs of needs and services for students and families. Beyond revenue and cost savings, you may find in-kind contributions an effective way to cultivate supporters and build capacity (Engelhardt-Cronk, n.d.).

In the following sections, and as depicted in table 6.1, we examine all these avenues that make up step 5 of the Centergy Cycle: state and federal school funding, fundraising and other external funding streams, and braided funding of all sources together.

Table 6.1: Start-Up Processes—Step 5

	Process	Purpose
Step 5: Secure Funding	State and federal school funding	Understand the ESSA (2015) and how it developed.
		Review federal title funding programs.
		Explore intervention funding.
	Fundraising and other external fundraising streams	Clarify the role of the wraparound director.
		Learn about 501(c)(3) organizations and funding streams.
		Establish systems for bookkeeping and donation tracking.
	Braided funding	Plan for melding both federal and state funding with community-driven funding, including cash donations, in-kind donations, and grants.

State and Federal School Funding

Understanding U.S. funding at the state and federal levels requires some understanding of how U.S. education funding programs have evolved since 1965. As paradigms shift and the perpetual pendulum swings, the ESSA (2015) reauthorized a civil rights law, the Elementary and Secondary Education Act (ESEA) of 1965. Initially signed into law by President Lyndon Johnson, ESEA passed at a time of promise and optimism in the federal government's ability to improve the lives of all Americans (Brown, Lenares-Solomon, &

Deaner, 2019). Passed within a year of the Voting Rights Act of 1965, the Civil Rights Act of 1964, and the Economic Opportunity Act of 1964, ESEA aimed to alleviate poverty through education.

ESEA established Title I as part of an outline of federal resources for economically disadvantaged youth (Gamson, McDermott, & Reed, 2015). However, federal involvement in education was controversial during that time, so the federal government's role in ESEA regarding education was laissez-faire (Gamson et al., 2015). ESEA's reauthorization in 1994, titled the Improving America's Schools Act (IASA) of 1994, ushered in federal accountability for standards-based reforms—a first for the federal government, which had not previously had a hand in curriculum. To receive funding, states had to demonstrate accountability for schools and districts in setting standards, assessing learning in mathematics and English, and devising improvement plans. The spirit of the act was to move beyond addressing students in poverty to incentivizing educational reform (Gamson et al., 2015).

Post-9/11, the law was reauthorized and renamed No Child Left Behind (2002) with the goal to continue to improve K–12 education through increased federal involvement (DeBray & Blankenship, 2016). NCLB continued to build on the accountability in IASA by including a subgroup accountability model for adequate yearly progress and mandating all students reach proficiency in mathematics and English by 2014. Schools had to show progress in all subgroups of students, and failure to do so resulted in a series of reforms (Gamson et al., 2015). Though the goal was to ensure all students' progress toward the 2014 targets, the imposed reforms for increasing adequate yearly progress standards crippled schools and districts with more students of color, students learning English, and students with disabilities. Reforms were too narrowly defined, and in practice, more reforms meant more time spent on testing for the sake of accountability (Gamson et al., 2015).

The ESSA (2015) is the most recent reauthorization of ESEA. The ESSA maintains the spirit of accountability for states to set high standards for educating all students. However, states and districts enjoy more flexibility to set goals for standards, decide how to measure growth (including growth in nonacademic factors), and determine consequences for insufficient performance. ESSA has expanded many teacher-only provisions (such as for professional development) to include school staff in general, from leaders to paraprofessionals to school counselors. It has also expanded student subgroups to reflect changing demographics of school-aged youth and include students with parents in the military, students in foster care, and homeless students (ASCD, 2015). ESSA emphasizes the coordination of services among school and community entities, such as colleges and universities, nonprofit organizations, and businesses. It includes phrases like *in partnership with*, *coordinated*, and *rich collaboration* that honor the act's original purpose to reduce disparities through education, but ESSA tailors this purpose to a contemporary milieu. The legislation and corresponding state report cards require more transparency, not only in graduation rates but also in postsecondary enrollment. ESSA also emphasizes using data to inform decision making (ASCD, 2015).

The following sections examine how state and federal funding of the nature described here can serve to support or enhance wraparound services at your school. In these sections, you will consider ESSA's flexibility regarding wraparound services and the various categories of title funding, intervention funding, and charter funding.

ESSA Flexibility, the Whole Child Approach, and Wraparound Services

The purpose of ESSA is "to provide all children significant opportunity to receive a fair, equitable, and high-quality education, and to close educational achievement gaps" (National Association of Secondary School Principals [NASSP], n.d.a). In the article "Educating Students in Poverty: Building Equity and Capacity With a Holistic Framework and Community School Model," Rea and Zinskie (2017) show ESSA's alignment with a whole child approach. If your district requires research supporting ESSA funding for evidence-based practice, this article is a good resource. Rea and Zinskie (2017) also explain how ESSA grants school districts flexibility to serve students with a well-rounded education. They further assert school districts have the flexibility and opportunity to promote caring, safe school climates that support students' learning, well-being, and social and emotional development. They state:

> ESSA emphasizes not only family engagement but also community engagement for school improvement and student success (Adelman & Taylor, 2016). ESSA goes beyond NCLB to allow federal funding for community engagement approaches such as the Integrated Student Supports (ISS). According to Moore et al. (2014), ISS is an evidence-based approach to community engagement that provides wraparound community services to support the success and healthy development of low-income students and their families (e.g., dental, medical, mental health services, etc.). (Rea & Zinskie, 2017, p. 10)

Some eligible family and community engagement activities schools can incorporate include integrating health practices, implementing mental health awareness training programs for school staff, and expanding access to school-based mental health community partnerships. Health education and physical education are also included in ESSA's emphasis on a well-rounded education.

Another important requirement of ESSA is the use of a needs assessment during initial planning. As mentioned in chapters 3 and 5 (page 63 and page 119), you have many types of data to consider as part of your needs assessment—universal screenings, attendance data, discipline data, social worker referrals, and community health and law-enforcement data. Additionally, the Student Voice Needs Survey (both the anonymous and individual), plus the off-track interviews with individual students, serves as a collective keystone for keeping your programming relevant and the story your data tell fresh while also satisfying ESSA needs-assessment requirements.

Title Funding

Let's take a look at the six federal-funding title categories that are most relevant to this initiative and their potential impact on wraparound services and a whole child approach: Titles I, II, III, IV, V, and IX. (Each of these categories exists within ESSA [2015].) See NASSP (n.d.a) for more valuable information on title funding from the ESSA Fact Sheets.

Title I

Title I, "Improving Basic Programs Operated by State and Local Education Agencies," is funding intended to close achievement gaps. While ESSA differs from NCLB in that it eliminates the School Improvement Grant program and specific school-improvement

When we started planning our wraparound initiative, we had limited district funds. We began brainstorming internal and external resources and then started filling in holes with federal programs and community resources. The flexibility provided in ESSA and its focus on whole child development made it easier to align the needs of the wraparound program with the intent of the title programs. As a safeguard, we stayed in close contact with our federal program managers to write budget descriptors and design programming that would be approved by our state education agency (SEA). With a constant eye toward collaboration, most of the federal programs now play a role in the sustainability of our wraparound program in addition to community and school district resources.

—Brian Campbell, director of student learning for high schools,
Columbia County School District, Georgia

strategies, it specifies state education agencies must set aside 7 percent of their Title I funds to support school-improvement initiatives at schools performing in the bottom 5 percent. In accordance with increased flexibility, ESSA makes allowances for schools that do not meet the threshold of having 40 percent low-income students.

The accountability system lies with the state instead of federal purview, and school quality measures can include school climate, school safety, student engagement, and other measures beyond academic achievement indicators. Wraparound services addressing these broadened indicators of school success can receive Title I funds. Schools can also use these funds to hire wraparound directors who conduct needs assessments, coordinate resources, garner community partnerships, facilitate family and community engagement, and oversee the integration of student supports.

A Word About Mental Health, Trauma, and ACEs

Barr and Gibson (2020) write:

> Though no demographic category is immune to ACEs, students living in poverty are more likely to experience high levels of trauma and ACEs than more economically advantaged peers (Brendtro, Brokenleg, & Van Bockern, 2019; Child Trends, 2019; Hughes & Tucker, 2018). In fact, living in poverty is related to, or found alongside of, many traumas listed in the ACEs survey (National Council of Juvenile and Family Court Judges, 2006), like homelessness and incarceration of a parent, as well as adverse experiences not listed in the original study (Felitti et al., 1998), such as living on a reservation, being an immigrant or refugee, or walking to school through streets rife with drugs, gangs, and violence (Hughes & Tucker, 2018). Youth living in poverty are six times more likely to experience significant levels of adversity than high-income peers, with 25 percent of children living in poverty reporting three or more ACEs by adolescence (Center for Promise, 2017; Child Trends, 2019). (p. 38)

Title II

Title II, "Preparing, Training, and Recruiting High-Quality Teachers, Principals, or Other School Leaders," is designed to allocate funds for staffing and professional development. ESSA (2015) includes two major changes to Title II: (1) the funding formula now weighs poverty over population, and (2) states are allowed to blend Title II, Part A funds with other ESSA funds (such as Title III and Title IV funds).

Title II changes relevant to creating and supporting wraparound services include an expanded use of funds for professional development for more than teachers and principals. Title II includes the following provisions for in-service training of school personnel:

(i) The techniques and supports needed to help educators understand when and how to refer students affected by trauma, and children with, or at risk of, mental illness;

(ii) The use of referral mechanisms that effectively link such children to appropriate treatment and intervention services in the school and in the community, where appropriate;

(iii) Forming partnerships between school-based mental health programs and public or private mental health organizations; and

(iv) Addressing issues related to school conditions for student learning, such as safety, peer interaction, drug and alcohol abuse, and chronic absenteeism (U.S. Department of Education, n.d.)

A Word About Mental Health, Trauma, and ACEs

In the article "Trauma-Informed Teaching Strategies," Jessica Minahan (2019) writes:

> Traumatized students are especially prone to difficulty in self-regulation, negative thinking, being on high alert, difficulty trusting adults, and inappropriate social interactions (Lacoe, 2013; Terrasi & de Galarce, 2017). They often haven't learned to express emotions healthily and instead show their distress through aggression, avoidance, shutting down, or other off-putting behaviors. These actions can feel antagonistic to teachers who don't understand the root cause of the student's behavior, which can lead to misunderstandings, ineffective interventions, and missed learning time. (pp. 30–31)

Minahan (2019) suggests the following eight trauma-informed teaching strategies for fostering a feeling of safety.

1. Expect unexpected responses.
2. Employ thoughtful interactions.
3. Be specific about relationship building.
4. Promote predictability and consistency.
5. Teach strategies to "change the channel."
6. Give supportive feedback to reduce negative thinking.
7. Create islands of competence.
8. Limit exclusionary practices.

Title III

Title III, "Language Instruction for English Learners and Immigrant Students," is designed to ensure that English learners, including immigrant youth, attain English proficiency and school personnel develop their capacity to serve English learners. This is meaningful for wraparound services because schools can use Title III funds for translation services, additional English tutoring, or professional development for educators to serve students learning English. Title III also promotes parent, family, and community participation in language instruction programs for English learners.

Since 2017, Title III funds have been increasing (NASSP, n.d.c); advocate for these funds to benefit your students and families.

Title IV

Title IV, "21st Century Schools," is meant to support the whole child and has increased significantly in scope and amount since ESSA passed. It includes the Student Support and Academic Enrichment program, which provides state education agencies, local education agencies, and schools the flexibility to tailor investments to the needs of their unique student populations (Georgia Department of Education, 2019b). A key clarification in Title IV is its emphasis on parent involvement, making its intent more active and less passive. It places the onus of initiating family engagement on the school instead of on the parents.

Formerly restricted to safety and drug-free schools, Title IV emphasizes three buckets related to whole child wellness: (1) a well-rounded education for all students (classified as *well-rounded*), (2) a focus on improving school conditions (*safe and healthy*), and (3) support for digital literacy and technology (*educational technology*). In November 2019, the Georgia Department of Education (2019b) provided guidelines to help its local education agencies adapt their practices by listing the individual criteria and requirements within Title IV's three buckets. This guidance can well serve any district in the United States. The *well-rounded* bucket includes the following criteria:

- Access to all
- Core and/or Beyond the Core Curriculums (Fine Arts, Foreign Languages, Health, Physical Education)
- College and Career Counseling
- Social Emotional Learning
- Advanced Placement opportunities (AP Exams for low-income students)
- Supplementary endorsements (STEM, ESOL, Gifted) (Georgia Department of Education, 2019b, p. 3)

The *safe and healthy* bucket includes the following criteria:

- Parent engagement
- School-based mental health services
- Reduction of exclusionary discipline
- Promoting positive climate and culture
- Nutritional and/or healthy lifestyle; active lifestyle habits

- Awareness and prevention education for risk behaviors
- Trauma-informed practices
- Mentoring
- Dropout programming/Re-entry
- Skills to improve safely recognizing coercion, violence, or abuse
- Establishing community partnerships (Georgia Department of Education, 2019b, p. 3)

And the *educational technology* bucket includes the following criteria:

- 85% must be utilized for the support of professional development (Non-Reg Guidance)
  - STEM/STEAM PD/PL
  - Computer Science PD/PL
  - PD/PL that uses technology to impact student achievement via the development of personalized/blended learning programs
- Discover/adapt/share educational resources
- Computerized assessments
- Inform/collaborate instructional strategies with web-based data
- Digital learning technologies
- Assistive technology
- Infrastructure (equipment, software, applications, platforms, digital instructional resources, one-time IT purchases)—15% cap on spending (ESEA Sec. 4109(b)) (Georgia Department of Education, 2019b, pp. 3–4)

The Georgia Department of Education (2019b) adds the following about conducting a needs assessment as it relates to the use of Title IV funding:

> Due to the unique flexibility of Title IV, Part A, [local education agencies] and schools should delve more deeply into the root causes of deficiencies to identify needs and develop initiatives/interventions designed to provide all students with access to a well-rounded education, improve school conditions for student learning, and improve the use of technology in order to improve the academic achievement and digital literacy of all students to determine specific needs. (p. 4)

As the preceding guidance highlights, Title IV is highly flexible and can constitute the majority of school funding for wraparound services. Examples of services schools can provide using Title IV funding include social-emotional learning, comprehensive mental health awareness training, school-based counseling, prevention programming (including for violence and bullying), nutrition and health services, and integrated systems of student and family supports.

Title V

Title V, "Flexibility and Accountability—Rural Education and Achievement Program," provides support and flexibility to meet the unique needs of both small rural and rural low-income school districts. These districts frequently lack personnel and resources to effectively contend for federally competitive grants, and they receive formula funds in amounts too small to meet their intended purposes (NASSP, n.d.a). Therefore, Title V funding may be an option for rural districts interested in obtaining supplemental financing so they can provide increased access to wraparound services.

Title IX

Title IX is part of the Education Amendments of 1972; it provides protection and prohibits discrimination on the basis of sex in any federally funded educational program. Varying political pressures between presidential administrations has made it so a federal definition of what *sex* means is still lacking, which leaves schools in a murky position. Regardless of definition, Title IX prohibits discrimination based on sex, including harassment, bullying, and sexual assault, and schools must protect students at school, on buses, and at school-related events. Writing for the National Federation of State High School Associations, Lee Green (2018) asserts:

> Schools must have procedures in place consistent with Title IX for accepting reports of harassment or bullying of LGBTQ students, for investigating such complaints as required under Title IX, and for resolving such disputes using the same policies and procedures used in all complaints of harassment and bullying of students.

This means that districts are required to have district-level coordinators who oversee discipline policies and activities around sex-based harassment. Title IX also charges schools with implementing strategies that safeguard students from such behavior, whether perpetrated by school personnel or by peers, and effectively addressing misconduct when it occurs on campus or in connection with any educational or extracurricular program (Green, 2018). Depending on student voice in your school, you may closely collaborate with your district's Title IX coordinator to help support victimized students with wraparound programming and services and to help school leaders address climate issues that perpetuate harassment.

Synthesis of Title Funding

The Federation for Community Schools, an Illinois-based nonprofit supporting community schools, recommends using ESSA to leverage funds to promote comprehensive, efficient, effective, and collaborative programming for students and families. As mentioned, ESSA's intent is to ensure schools have funds to provide a wide range of services for students and families. Creatively and intentionally blending financing across title funding affords schools greater opportunity and flexibility for the positive development of students.

Table 6.2 (page 148) utilizes information from the Federation for Community Schools (2017) in combination with NASSP (n.d.a) fact sheets to clarify how schools might classify funding needs according to titles. As a cautionary note, please remember *all* funding decisions are subject to each state's interpretation and approval from federal programs staff.

Table 6.2: Funding Needs and Title Classifications

Resource Coordination and Access to Supports	Title Classification
School site coordinator	Use a combination of Title I, Title III, and Title IV funding to hire a school-site coordinator tasked with integrating services for families and engaging parents in school-improvement plans.
Resource coordinator	Use Title IV funding to hire a resource or partnership coordinator to align supports as well as identify and build partnerships through shared leadership structures.
Partnerships to promote student mental health	Allocate Title IV, Part A funds to create partnerships between schools and public or private mental health organizations.
Wraparound services	Use Title I and Title IV funding to support wraparound services.
Positive Youth Development	**Title Classification**
21st century community learning centers	Use Title I and Title IV, Part B funding to create out-of-school opportunities for extended learning time aimed at promoting achievement and positive youth development.
Family and Community Engagement*	**Title Classification**
Needs assessments	Use Title I, Part A funds to allocate expenses related to the yearly needs assessment that Title I, Part A requires Title I schools to conduct. Use Title IV funds to further engage the community in asset mapping and thereby identify potential partnerships for whole child or safe-and-healthy schools programming.
Parent leadership teams	Use Title I, Part A or Title II funds to create diverse and representative parent leadership teams that will work with school staff in the area of school improvement. These teams increase parent capacity within a shared-governance framework.
Bilingual family liaisons	Allocate Title III funds to hire bilingual family liaisons to assist with English learner parent-engagement activities and coordinate supports. Schools can also use this funding stream to develop bilingual family literacy trainings and English as a second language classes for parents.
Professional learning and family engagement	Blend Title I and Title II funds to provide professional learning for school staff that focuses on engaging parents and community members in support of increased student learning and school improvement.
School Climate and Culture	**Title Classification**
Positive school climate	Use Title IV funds to promote whole child development and healthy learning environments through mentoring and counseling for students. Mental health services, bullying prevention initiatives, schoolwide universal screenings, restorative programming, and evidence-based drug and alcohol prevention activities are allowable opportunities for schools to promote health and wellness among students. Use Title II funding for professional development in any of the aforementioned areas.
Cultural competence	Blend Title II and Title III funds to create professional development experiences related to cultural competence, equity, and family engagement.
Trauma-informed professional development	Use Title II funding to offer school personnel professional development in supporting or appropriately referring students affected by trauma, influenced by adverse childhood experiences, or at risk of mental illness.

*Title I, Part A requires districts to allocate 1 percent of Title I funds to parent engagement. The purpose of the Title I, Part A funds is to increase parent capacity.

Source: Federation for Community Schools, 2017; NASSP, n.d.a.

Intervention Funding

The ESSA (2015) requires every state have a plan to identify schools for support or improvement based on two designations: Comprehensive Support and Improvement and Targeted Support and Intervention Schools. According to the NASSP (n.d.b):

> As an intervention, [state education agencies] use a 7% set-aside from Title I to assist identified schools for improvement and support. In [comprehensive support and improvement] designated schools, states determine the number of years for intervention, districts determine intervention, and states determine exit criteria. Schools meeting the following criteria can receive state support:
> - Schools in the bottom 5 percent according to the state's performance metric
> - High schools graduating fewer than 67 percent of students
> - Schools consistently underperforming for any subgroup after a state-defined number of years
>
> Additionally, states must identify schools for Targeted Support and Improvement: Schools that are low performing for one or more subgroups [performing as low as the bottom 5 percent]. In this case, districts determine timing and type of intervention, unless the school is then defined as a school for comprehensive support and improvement.

In figure 6.1 (page 150), Georgia's Department of Education (GaDOE) clearly illustrates its intention to support schools focusing on the whole child while also following a continuous strategic-planning cycle aligned with ESSA.

On November 13, 2019, Georgia's deputy superintendent of school improvement Stephanie Johnson (2019), recognized across the United States as an innovative leader committed to whole child supports, spoke to the state superintendents of all fifty states to expand on the GaDOE's use of funding to support whole child innovation in schools:

> In Fall 2017, our GaDOE School Improvement Department began a wraparound initiative case study to place an intentional focus on providing a centralized support model to address non-academic barriers that impact student outcomes. We provided more than $1 million to help schools create wraparound centers for their students on school campuses. The initial funding was part of our comprehensive and proactive strategy to target schools federally identified as low performing for support by GaDOE's School Improvement division with Title 1, Section 1003 funds. However, we are now witnessing the expansion of wraparound centers in schools with no identification.
>
> The wraparound centers operate before, during and after the traditional school day, connecting students and families with resources in order to support and improve student achievement. Through the centers, students have access to community resources like food pantries and clothes closets; mental health counseling; tutoring and academic support; workshops on college applications,

Figure 6.1: GaDOE's whole child wheel for continuous school improvement.

résumés, interview skills, and money management; help connecting with local job opportunities; and more.

The initial funds totaling $1,040,000 provided by GaDOE and approved by the State Board of Education fund a regional Wraparound Coordinator in each of Georgia's 16 Regional Education Service Agencies (RESAs). This was a first-of-its-kind position established to help schools identified for comprehensive and targeted support under Georgia's ESSA plan create and coordinate their wraparound centers. Each wraparound coordinator was charged to lead a pilot in their RESA targeting two to three of the schools in that RESA receiving support from GaDOE School Improvement annually. The goal is to expand the pilot to impact more schools in future years.

Our GaDOE School Improvement wraparound initiative was a response to the growing need to address non-academic barriers to student learning and to a body of research that shows students are better able to learn and achieve when those barriers are removed.

Charter Schools

If your state embraces the provision of charter funding, these dollars may be a resource for your whole child or wraparound initiative. In some states, for example, charter funds are available for innovations designed to meet local needs, and the state grants each school district flexibility in how to use the funds. John Floresta (personal communication, December 5, 2019), chief strategy and accountability officer in Georgia's Cobb County School District, states:

> Policymaker rhetoric to "modernize education" is rarely matched with the dollars to make political speeches a reality. However, state and federal charter policies, which provide start-up funding for innovative approaches, are promising as they can be effectively used in the same way the private sector uses an angel investor. Educational practitioners should be ready for the long-term "business model" questions demanding answers related to sustainability. Lastly, beware of becoming reliant on charter funding for wraparound services as it is vulnerable to the whims of policymakers and to changes in district leadership.

If your state has similarly earmarked charter flexibility and funding for whole child or innovation, your district should explore using charter funding to launch wraparound services.

Fundraising and Other External Funding Streams

When seeking funding outside of federal, state, and local education funding, let your student voice and community data drive your asks. As much as possible, think of the school as funding academics while external sources can support other wraparound work—including academic supports that families typically fund (such as personal technology or fees associated with field trips or college visits). For instance, if students mention they need assistance in paying athletic fees when they fill out your Student Voice Needs Survey, you could approach your alumni association to donate the athletic fees for student athletes in need.

Sometimes, you'll need to take a piecemeal approach to meeting needs. For example, opening a clothes closet can involve various avenues of funding, such as the following.

- The school system designates space for the closet and runs water supply lines for clothes washers and dryers.

- A local home organization store designs the organizational layout and supplies needed.

- United Way awards a mini-grant for the material costs of shelving and racks and pledges a sustainable supply of gently used teen clothing.

- Junior League donates feminine products.

- A local appliance store donates scratch-and-dent washers and dryers.

- Individuals donate cash to purchase toiletries and new underwear.

- Students and community members donate gently used teen clothing, hangers, and laundry supplies.

Notice how meeting the need for a clothes closet involves the school plus individuals and organizations in the community through cash, in-kind donations, and grant funding. Of note, faith-based and other service or mission-related organizations are often eager to partner on initiatives related to basic needs. In our experience, many seem to appreciate being able to focus their efforts on one school or one feeder pattern of schools and to respond to specific needs.

In the following sections, we will focus on topics that are each critical to raising funds for your school's wraparound center.

- The role of the wraparound director
- 501(c)(3)s
- Funding streams
- Bookkeeping and donation tracking

The Role of the Wraparound Director

The part the wraparound director plays in securing initial funding depends on when he or she is hired. Optimally, a school will hire a director early in the process for establishing wraparound services, but understandably, the hire may be funding- or calendar-dependent due to the natural contract cycle. While this section includes content regarding the director's role in funding, you will find more detail on the characteristics, duties, and hiring of the director in chapter 7 (page 163).

As the primary face of the wraparound center, the director naturally promotes the center's work by continually endorsing a WSCC approach to education. This includes organizing activities such as the following.

- Hosting periodic tours for community members and potential donors
- Holding a family open house at least twice a year
- Speaking to local civic clubs as well as faith-based and community services organizations
- Sending press releases regarding partnerships, grants awarded, and donations to local media
- Publishing an annual report for distribution to partners, donors, and the community

These types of public relations activities promote your wraparound work as part of your community's story and build momentum for community involvement. The director must have a brief, adaptable elevator speech he or she can give on a moment's notice to partners and members of the community. The speech should underscore not only the gathering of student voice most relevant to the audience but the need for schools to work with their communities to produce graduates ready for life.

The director also oversees the wraparound center's budgeting and finances—including fundraising. For the purpose of funding, the director must nurture relationships with partners, donors, and potential donors. Sometimes, this means choosing less efficient means for meeting student and family needs. For example, Leigh remembers reaching out to the local bar association to cover a single mother's testing fees so she could take the 911 dispatcher test. Facilitating this ask took more time than simply reaching for the checkbook, but it paid off nonetheless by deepening the web of connections among the school, the bar association, and the mother.

The director must intentionally build social capital with key stakeholders to develop credibility. Nurturing partner relationships to build this capital often involves showing up for partners' events, such as galas, or making presentations for boards of directors—meaning the director will need to be available for extended hours, beyond the school day. When you show up for events without asking anything in return, you demonstrate respect for your partners' impact beyond your school's self-interest.

501(c)(3)s

A 501(c)(3) is a nonprofit corporation that is formed for charitable, educational, religious, or scientific purposes (Foundation Group, n.d.). Your community may have a 501(c)(3) foundation that serves as a fundraising avenue for your school district. These nonprofits are separate from the school district and operate under their own rules of incorporation. If possible, work with your local school or community foundation to receive donations. By doing so, you'll be able to take advantage of the foundation's donation and accounting processes. In addition, your school district will not be burdened with additional bookkeeping responsibilities inherent in accepting donations.

Some centers and schools have started their own 501(c)(3)s to support their wraparound initiatives. Depending on your local district's stance and the amount of funding you believe will be incoming, this is also an option worth considering as a way to keep designated funds for services separate from school or district accounts.

Funding Streams

In addition to educational funding opportunities, you may have access to a variety of potential income streams to support your wraparound work, including cash donations, in-kind donations (goods and services), and grants. An important lesson we learned when asking for funding or donations is to be specific with your ask. Carefully think through the initiative you're undertaking. If you want to give every family participating in a food pantry a slow cooker (a wonderful gift for those living in spaces that lack full kitchens), ask a local church for the *exact* number of cookers you need. If you want to create a way to provide girls with bags of feminine products, ask a women's group, specifying the number of bags you need and what you need in each bag. If you want to provide twenty-five laptops a year for high-potential, low-opportunity students who are participating in honors classes, explain to members of the potential funding organization the ramifications of the digital divide, specify the number of laptops you need, detail how qualifying students will be chosen, and then articulate the cost of sponsoring one student with a laptop.

The following sections each explore key funding resources (cash donations, in-kind donations, and grants) in more detail.

Cash Donations

Some donations come in as cash, either for general use or designated for a specific purpose. When a donor gives an undesignated contribution, take the time to find out what is important to the donor—such as first-generation college attendance, food stability, and assistance for teen parents—and then try to utilize the donation in alignment with those priorities. In all cases, keep an accounting of all funding received and how the wraparound center uses that funding so you can provide an update to funders upon request and also for the purpose of documenting when you've sent a written acknowledgment to the donor. See Bookkeeping and Donation Tracking (page 158).

Designated donations can come in small amounts, such as fees for college applications or money for toiletries. Other designated donations can be more significant, such as endowing a room in your wraparound center by donating the costs for all furnishings and supplies. In the case of large donations, such as the endowment of a room, work with the donor to determine the appropriate public acknowledgment, such as commemorative naming or a wall plaque. It is also possible some donors will prefer to remain strictly anonymous.

In all cases, create cash donation processes that are easy for donors to use. For example, provide a Donate button on your website; use an online need-meeting platform, such as Purposity (www.purposity.com) or One Need (www.oneneed.org); or offer access to a payment-processing app, such as Payanywhere (www.payanywhere.com) or Square (https://squareup.com). Finally, promote any online or cash-giving opportunities on your social media platforms.

In-Kind Donations

When setting up your wraparound center, a variety of needs are candidates for in-kind donations. Remember, you are creating a common space designed for the purpose of housing goods and delivering services the students and families of your community need. In-kind donations are contributions of goods, counsel and expertise, or services—instead of cash—directed toward developing your infrastructure, intended for general use or consumption, or designated for a special purpose. The following sections explore each of these contributions.

Goods

The supplies and furnishings you need depend largely on your services and the spaces you will furnish, such as office space for external partners, private spaces for counseling, and a coffee corner. For ongoing operations, solicit in-kind donations for care closets of clothing, food, toiletries, and school supplies. It is appropriate to reach out to faith-based organizations, civic clubs, private citizens, local merchants, and others to donate items and furnishings or endow donations. For example, in Columbia County School District in southeastern Georgia, the wraparound coordinator asked a local furniture store if it would provide a sofa for one high school–based center in a district that included five high schools, but she also prepared herself to address what else the wraparound center might need as furnishings. She knew this local business had deep ties to the school district and a vested interest in the community. The store ended up furnishing all five high school centers with sofas, rugs, chairs, art, and lamps.

Every community is only as successful as the future it builds. Over a two-year period, citizens and leaders in Gainesville–Hall County identified the mental health challenges facing the community, which included all ages, races and ethnicities, and socioeconomic designations. In disaggregating the information, three key data points were sobering:

1. More than six hundred suicides were attempted by sixth- through twelfth-grade students (city and county schools combined).

2. Only one mental health provider is available per 1,350 citizens (top performers are 350:1).

3. Half (50 percent) of all chronic mental illnesses are diagnosed by age fourteen (eighth grade).

The need to align initiatives and implement them collectively was a theme all stakeholders shared. With Northeast Georgia Health System leading the way to reform our community, the school system leveraged partnerships to maximize a collective vision, The Hub. The Hub at Gainesville High School is only possible due to the partnership of the Medical Center Foundation and the willingness of existing partners to think outside the box for serving our youth. The Medical Center Foundation selected The Hub as their project for 2019. Fund-raising efforts over a few months allowed Gainesville City School System to benefit from $340,000, effectively establishing The Hub. Immediately, major renovation of Gainesville High School commenced while the remaining pieces of the puzzle were pulling together.

The excitement was contagious, and it gave the district the opportunity to review the structure of existing partnerships. Our partnerships with area service providers (Center Point, Avita Community Partners, and Georgia Vocational Rehabilitation Agency, among others) were once separated from day-to-day school operations but are now integrated on campus. Work groups with United Way of Hall County, One Hall committees, and Hall County School System elevated the awareness within the community, and over three hundred community members attended the ribbon-cutting to open the Center. Now, through one voice, we build a better future.

—Jeremy H. Williams, superintendent, Gainesville City Schools, Georgia

If needed, consider asking your community (individuals, corporations, or civic organizations) to provide technology (such as internet, laptops, or Wi-Fi access) for students lacking the resources to succeed in rigorous classes. Or collaborate with your community on seeking state and federal grants so that you can close this digital divide. Regardless of the means of supplying and furnishing your spaces, consult the student voice in your school to guide the feel of your wraparound center.

Services

In-kind services manifest themselves in two major ways: (1) professional experts volunteer for the benefit of students and their families, and (2) partner service providers deliver services on-site at your school. Both present opportunities to grow the number of individuals and organizations actively involved in your wraparound center, thereby expanding its network of support.

Some services requested through your student voice processes provide you the opportunity to connect students and their families with experts in your community, such as lawyers, bankers, health-care professionals, or immigration specialists. Those connections may come via seminars such as first-time-home-buyer classes or English language classes, in addition to individual assistance. This individual assistance often comes in the form of pro bono professional services, like legal aid or dental care.

Co-locating partner staff also counts as an in-kind service. Co-located staff members retain employment from the partner organization while creating an on-site satellite office of the partner. Examples of in-kind services include on-site staffing from the Department of Human Services, the Department of Public Health, the Department of Juvenile Justice, the housing authority, a local mentoring organization, or the Communities in Schools organization. Universities and other postsecondary institutions are also a source of in-kind services and can provide social and human services, professional learning, and counseling interns to serve as auxiliary staffing in your center.

Grants

Public and private grants are available for projects that launch and provide public services. If your school district has a grant writer, consider yourself lucky, and work with that individual to seek out grants to fund various aspects of your work. If your district does not have a grant writer, do not let the prospect of writing grants overwhelm you. We've found many partner agencies and organizations have their own grant writers, and they know the funding streams in their area of expertise or service better than you do. Regardless of who writes the grant proposal, seeking collaborative grants with your partners offers two main advantages.

1. Many grants give preference to collaboration. According to Barbara Floersch, executive director of the Grantsmanship Center in Los Angeles, "A deeply collaborative program plan demonstrates dedication to making a difference by leveraging available expertise and resources" (as cited in NonProfit Times, 2015).

2. Many nonprofits and agencies bring grant proposal expertise to the table—meaning you will be a source of data rather than a primary author. If you have facilitated conversation circles, a Student Voice Needs Survey, and focus groups, you possess powerful student commentary, innovative ideas, and hard-to-get qualitative and quantitative data. Many organizations are eager to have this information (in a nonidentifying format) so they can include it in grants and use it to inform staffing, programming, and so on.

As the organizations' partner, your school offers data, programming suggestions, office space, and coordination and shared supervision. This is a common-sense, contagious, and hopeful approach, meaning it has wide appeal. With partners, you may be able to coapply for collaborative or competitive grants from organizations such as the following.

- Local or community human service organizations

- Local and national corporations (wireless providers, home-improvement stores, grocery stores, and so on)

- Civic clubs (Kiwanis, Rotary, Optimist, Junior League, and so on)

- Charter school foundations

- Public and private health organizations

- Hospital foundations

- Organizations (Community Catalyst, the Center for Social Innovation, the National Alliance on Mental Illness, the Hilton Foundation, Target, Home Depot, the Gates Foundation, and so on)

- State agencies (the Department of Behavioral Health and Developmental Disabilities, the Department of Corrections, the Department of Human Services, the Department of Community Health, and so on)

- Private advocacy foundations

- Public service foundations and agencies

- Faith-based organizations

- School and alumni foundations

- Local country clubs and benefits (Inquire whether they have an application or mini-grant process to apply for the proceeds of their community events, such as galas, golf tournaments, and auctions.)

Equally, districts should explore the wealth of mini-grants available for specific programming and staff needs. Mini-grants are typically smaller in every facet—a shorter application, a shorter window of time, smaller financial amounts available, and fewer reporting requirements. In our experience, the eagerness of potential partners amazes school districts.

Grants can be a significant funding stream if you have the time, resources, and partnerships to track them down. They come in many forms—public and private, corporate and individually funded, broad and narrow—and each has its own criteria, application timeline, and reporting requirements. Pay attention to the reporting requirements of grants, and steer away from those with excessive time requirements. Some small grants may require so much time with regard to reporting and compliance that they would have almost no return on investment. On the flip side, some sizable grants from organizations aligned to your work may require minimum applications and oversight but have a big payout.

As mentioned, student voice tells a compelling story to unlock funding. For example, Leigh worked with a local nonprofit agency to create an on-site teen advocate position that would provide full-spectrum services related to sexual abuse and domestic violence. Neither the school system nor the agency had financing available to fund the position. At the agency's recommendation, they coauthored a grant proposal to the Georgia Department of Corrections. In the proposal, they restated the Department of Corrections' data about the number and percentage of inmates who were survivors of sexual abuse and domestic violence; they recorded the number of students requesting services related to sexuality and abuse; and they included documentation of innovative programming and partnership ideas that students had suggested. In essence, they used student voice to make a compelling case for a collaborative approach to full-spectrum services. The Department of Corrections agreed to fund four one-year contracts for an on-site licensed teen advocate. These contracts were renewable at the end of each year dependent on student participation and feedback.

voices FROM THE FIELD

"

In Columbia County, Georgia, we have been fortunate to partner with the AmeriCorps Volunteers in Service to America (VISTA) program. AmeriCorps has provided a full-time staff member, known as a VISTA, at each of our five high schools. This co-located colleague is tasked with finding and supporting the launch of new community resources within our wraparound program. Each VISTA costs our district $4,000. We allocate Title IV to pay the $4,000 fee for each high school. Through this partnership, we have hired five full-time employees at a cost of $20,000 to our district.

—Brian Campbell, director of student learning for high schools, Columbia County School District, Georgia

"

Bookkeeping and Donation Tracking

It is important to establish a relationship with your school or district bookkeeper so you can align your processes with the requirements of your local educational agency. For sure, programs such as QuickBooks can be an easy-to-use resource. Be sure to also acknowledge every donation with a receipt and a follow-up thank-you letter. Writing a letter will let the donor know of your appreciation, and it will strengthen the relationship between your program and your donor. In this section, we highlight two forms you can use for this purpose.

1. **In-kind donation form:** Create an in-kind donation form, like the one depicted in figure 6.2, and ask donors to complete it to ease the process of recording, reporting, and acknowledging donations of goods. In-kind forms should include the following information (Engelhardt-Cronk, n.d.).

   - The date the gift was received

   - The donor's contact information

   - A description of the gift, noting whether the gift was used and, if so, its age and its condition

   - The donor's estimated value of the gift's fair-market value and how the value was determined

2. **Gift-acknowledgment form:** Acknowledge all cash donations shortly after receiving them through a written thank-you letter, like the example in figure 6.3.

It is also advisable to recognize significant contributors or partners at board of education meetings. Not only does this allow you to acknowledge the donors and partners, but it also serves to keep the initiative at the forefront of the minds of board members as well as community members and other potential donors.

```
Wraparound Center: _____

Name: _____  Date: _____

Address: _____

Email: _____  Phone: _____

Donation description and estimated fair market value: _____
```

Contributions of goods are deductible for income tax purposes to the extent allowed by the law. The Wraparound Center does not assign a financial value to your gift(s). That is the privilege and responsibility of the donor.

Thank you for your donation!

```
Received by: _____
```

Figure 6.2: Sample in-kind donation form.

*Visit **go.SolutionTree.com/leadership** for a free reproducible version of this figure.*

```
Dear _____,

On behalf of _____ [school system], I thank you for your generous
financial donation to the Wraparound Center. We acknowledge your gift of $_____
(include check number if applicable) on ____/____/____. This donation will be [or
has been] used for _____.
```

As you know, the Wraparound Center is a resource center for all students who are working to maximize their potential. We concentrate on providing support aimed at increasing academic achievement while also assisting our students in the areas of college and career preparedness, overall wellness, and counseling and recovery, as well as providing additional wraparound services needed by their families. Because of concerned, engaged, and future-focused community members like you, we can provide our students with many of the items and services they need to be successful in school and beyond.

Sincerely,

Director, the Wraparound Center

Figure 6.3: Sample gift-acknowledgment form.

*Visit **go.SolutionTree.com/leadership** for a free reproducible version of this figure.*

Braided Funding

Local school leaders must do their homework regarding education funding and grants, but they must also work with partners and external leaders to create plans that involve bringing it all together by braiding sources of internal and external funding. Learning how to use funds in a braided manner maximizes the potential and sustainability of your wraparound initiative. Figure 6.4 shows a full-spectrum implementation funding model for mental health services.

voices
FROM THE FIELD

Effective leaders in high-performing organizations communicate, collaborate, innovate, and include both influencers and stakeholders when making decisions that impact services and funding—especially funding.

—Stephanie Johnson, Georgia deputy superintendent of school improvement

Figure 6.5 (page 162) illustrates a model for federal, state, and local funding used in combination with grants and contributions. Because actual percentages will vary based on your district's circumstances, your own braided numbers may be significantly different from what you see here. Still, we find this graphic a useful illustration for understanding the big picture as it relates to funding your wraparound center.

Conclusion

Having diversified funding streams is a wise way to approach the start-up and sustainability of a wraparound center. Educators who worked in schools during the era of NCLB (2002) must intentionally shift their mindset regarding funding flexibility and strategic planning. In the years of NCLB, educators often looked first to what funding descriptors said was allowable, restricting their thoughts to only academic achievement in the areas of language arts, mathematics, science, and social studies. *Then*, school leaders determined their strategies and programming. Under ESSA (2015), educational leaders conduct needs assessments and may use a broader lens to support the whole child, first asking themselves what their students need and then turning their focus to how to fund those needs. Additionally, educational leaders need to collaborate with state and district funding leaders to increase their understanding of new funding flexibility, and they need to explore opportunities provided through the avenue of consolidated funding if their states and local districts allow it. It is appropriate that educational leaders ask the question, "Is what I am asking people or organizations to provide prohibited, or do funding guidelines simply not designate it as permissible? Who can we ask for further guidance?"

Now that you have some background and options based on establishing needs and setting priorities (revealed through student voice processes) and how to fund them, you are ready to create a structure for connecting students and families with services.

Prevention

Programming	Funding Source
Question, persuade, and refer (QPR) training for suicide prevention	Title IV
Yoga, meditation, and tai chi as a PE elective	In-kind goods, expertise, or services District instructional budget or charter budget Cash donation
Schoolwide participation in mental health screenings for depression, eating disorders, and substance use	Special-purpose public health and educational funding related to health barriers Title IV

Education and Awareness

Programming	Funding Source
Parent education events on mental health topics that include practitioner panels and moderated question-and-answer sessions	In-kind goods, expertise, or services Title III for translation services
Professional development for school personnel on active listening, mental health first aid, trauma-informed practices, and de-escalation strategies	Title II
Updated curriculum in health classes utilizing individuals from public health and health care, law-enforcement professionals, first responders, and clinicians as speakers	In-kind goods, expertise, or services Title II for staff planning or professional development

Support and Intervention

Programming	Funding Source
A safe place or room for de-escalation or relaxation	In-kind goods, expertise, or services Cash donation
Sources of Strength training and programming for peer-led support groups	Provider agency Provider grant
Cognitive-behavioral therapy (CBT) support groups led by a clinician (for example, anger, self-esteem)	Health-care mini-grant In-kind goods, expertise, or services Title IV
One-on-one therapy	Billable through insurance Title IV as a supplement
Therapy dog	Endowment Cash donation
Alternative to suspension on-site for tutoring and connection with services	Title I Title IV

Sustainability and Recovery Support

Programming	Funding Source
One-on-one therapy	Billable to insurance through provider Title IV as a supplement
Support groups led by a clinician (for example, support groups on grief or substance use)	Health-care provider mini-grant In-kind goods, expertise, or services Title IV as a supplement
Family counseling	Billable to insurance through provider Title IV as a supplement
Schoolwide response and planning for the aftermath of a crisis or suicide	School safety funding or grant

Figure 6.4: Coordination and allocation of funding for the purpose of providing full-spectrum services in the area of mental health.

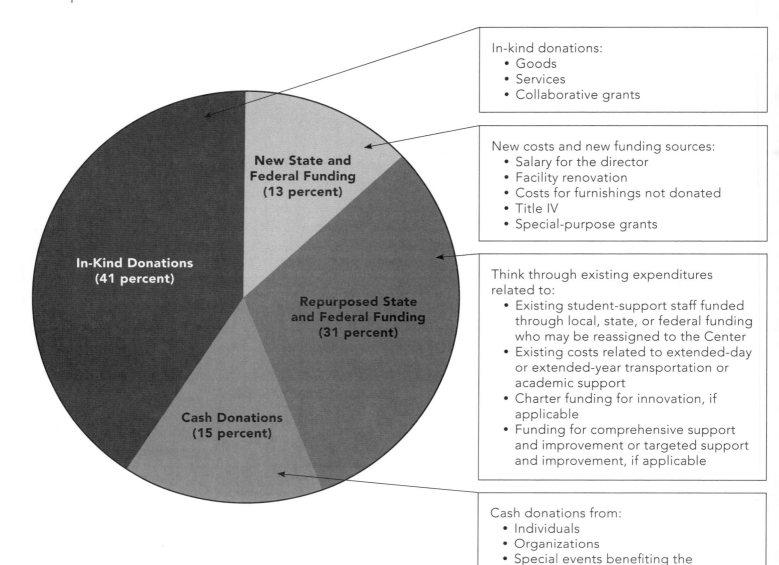

In-kind donations:
• Goods
• Services
• Collaborative grants

New costs and new funding sources:
• Salary for the director
• Facility renovation
• Costs for furnishings not donated
• Title IV
• Special-purpose grants

Think through existing expenditures related to:
• Existing student-support staff funded through local, state, or federal funding who may be reassigned to the Center
• Existing costs related to extended-day or extended-year transportation or academic support
• Charter funding for innovation, if applicable
• Funding for comprehensive support and improvement or targeted support and improvement, if applicable

Cash donations from:
• Individuals
• Organizations
• Special events benefiting the wraparound initiative

Source: © 2020 The Centergy Project.

Figure 6.5: An example of a consolidated funding model.

Chapter 7

CREATE YOUR STRUCTURE

Academically, [our center] is a place where teachers tutor each day after school to help students comprehend difficult content or prepare for tests. Emotionally, my kids feel they have an open door to counselors who are willing and able to help them. Physically, kids receive food, clothing, and just about anything a family might need. Compassion is the name of the game in the Center, and our kids know it! It has fostered more open and honest relationships with my students. It is a special place!

—Marie Sherbondy, high school teacher

Consolidating student-support efforts under the umbrella of wraparound has the dual benefit of avoiding having staff working in silos while also integrating interventions. In silos—with their fragmented reporting structures and prescriptive funding sources—individuals ostensibly working toward a common goal of providing comprehensive student support may be paid through various prescriptive funding sources, often with very little coordination of goal setting, service rendering, and data collecting. This well-intended yet ineffective configuration results in diffused rather than focused efforts. With wraparound, student-support staff are on the same team, which naturally results in synergies as they develop processes for streamlining and improving their intervention efforts.

Lack of synergy and coordination across worthwhile student support initiatives—such as credit recovery, extracurricular responsibilities, restorative practices, trauma-informed processes, PBIS, and social-emotional learning—can leave the most empathetic and conscientious teachers carrying unwieldy, heavy loads, struggling to meet the multifaceted needs of students and their families. According to a report on teacher turnover from Desiree Carver-Thomas and Linda Darling-Hammond (2017), educators are leaving the profession at an unprecedented rate of 8 percent per year, and two-thirds of teachers leaving the profession are leaving for reasons other than retirement. Reports are growing of teachers, counselors, and principals experiencing compassion fatigue, secondary traumatic stress, and moderate depression due to exposure to their students' poverty, grief, family concerns, and other problems (Walker, 2019).

According to Richard Ingersoll of the Center for the Study of Teaching and Policy, a key feature of teacher retention is "being empowered to enact positive change for young people and their schools" (as cited in Center, 2018). With an approach focused on offering wraparound services, your school gives your staff an accessible avenue to find help for their students without shouldering the burden themselves. We've seen some schools start to look at including their faculty in their wraparound efforts. For example, Banneker High School in metropolitan Atlanta opened a teacher space called The Well. Designated as a teacher self-care zone, teachers are welcome throughout the week to visit for moments of respite and renewal. Every Friday, Igola Richardson, the wraparound director, arranges programs such as live music, catered lunches, self-care lunch-and-learns, or chair massages—all from local businesses, organizations, and individuals wanting to show their appreciation to teachers.

At this point—with priorities established and partnership planning underway—you're ready to start the nuts-and-bolts planning that will set the stage for delivering services. Table 7.1 lists the start-up process associated with step 6 in the Centergy Cycle.

Table 7.1: Start-Up Processes—Step 6

	Process	Purpose
Step 6: Create Your Wraparound Structure	The *what*: Developing programming based on student voice	Review student voice data. Review partnerships. Continue gathering student voice.
	The *how*: Developing an organizational structure	Hire a director. Determine staffing. Create a student board of directors.
	The *where*: Designing spaces for connecting students and families with services	Select a space for wraparound services. Involve students in designing your spaces.
	The *who*: Reaching the whole school, identified groups, and individual students	Plan services for the entire student body.

As you can see from table 7.1, in this chapter, we examine four areas related to creating a structure for your wraparound services.

1. **The *what*:** Developing programming based on student voice

2. **The *how*:** Developing an organizational structure

3. **The *where*:** Designing spaces for connecting students and families with services

4. **The *who*:** Reaching the whole school, identified groups, and individual students

The *What*: Developing Programming Based on Student Voice

As you begin addressing prioritized student barriers, rely on student voice data, particularly the Student Voice Needs Survey, focus groups, and individual focused conversations. We find students are much more likely to participate in programming tailored to their needs and interests rather than canned (predetermined) programs. For example, suppose a school identifies a need for personal safety training through a Student Voice Needs Survey. Subsequently, focus groups give the following feedback with regard to desired content.

- How to avoid sexual assault on a college campus
- Self-defense
- How to interact with law enforcement

Share this detailed feedback with partners so they can tailor their service offerings or contributions to meet these specific suggestions. Based on the student feedback in this example, the district should probably consider partnership with a local agency focused on preventing sexual assault and the local police department.

To make final determinations about what programming your wraparound center requires, you should review student voice data, review the partnerships you have established, and continue gathering more student voice. Table 7.2 puts these Centergy Cycle step 1 and 2 processes together.

Table 7.2: An Overview of Student Voice Processes

	Process	Purpose
Step 1: Identify Needs	Conversation circles	Gather broad information about academic achievement, social-emotional wellness, and family engagement.
	Off-track interviews	Conduct personal conversations with off-track students to learn about barriers and develop action plans when appropriate.
	Graduation stories	Gather reflective feedback from graduates on their school experiences.
Step 2: Establish Priorities	Student Voice Needs Survey	Anonymous (large group and aggregate): Quantify student needs to establish priorities and project potential caseloads. Individual (personal and identifiable): Connect individual students with services.
	Focus groups and individual focused conversations	Delve into specific barriers to understand student perspectives and elicit programming suggestions.

Review Student Voice Data

Steps 1 and 2 of the student voice processes tell your school's story through qualitative and quantitative data necessary to understand student and family needs, develop programming, and project potential caseloads. Begin by sharing Student Voice Needs Survey data related to your partner's area of expertise. Additionally, whenever possible, augment your survey's quantitative data with relevant anonymized narratives from off-track interviews or graduation stories. Focus group discussion charts and notes from individual focused conversations related to school response (refer to the starred questions in the Personal Reflection Notes document, page 87) will also provide detailed student perspectives related to programming, activities, and staffing. Figure 7.1 documents students' ideas during a focus group discussion about full-spectrum services related to healthy relationships, sexuality, and sexual activity.

Altogether, your collected student voice tells a data story that will guide discussions with partners to unpack student-identified barriers and develop customized programming and an array of services. Let's walk through an example from Leigh's experience. The step 1 student voice processes identified a cluster of factors concerning or potentially related to sexuality, sexual abuse, and domestic violence as barriers to learning and graduation. The Student Voice Needs Survey yielded the following areas of interest, based on a total of 1,274 completed surveys. The parenthetical numbers document the number of students who responded they would benefit from services on the specified topic.

- Anger management (352)
- Social-media management (203)
- Bullying and harassment (158)
- Sexual activity (137)
- Sexual identity and LGBTQPIA (124)
- Teen parenting (124)
- Sexual abuse (108)
- Pornography exposure and habits (101)
- Domestic violence and violence at home (74)
- Building healthy relationships (54)

In some cases, such as the preceding data cluster, the data indicate a need for full-spectrum programming (inclusive of prevention, education, support, and sustainability strategies). Such programming requires a deep dive that is multifaceted and -tiered, providing educational opportunities that are appropriate for the whole of the student body and others that are individualized to students in greater need. By relying on student voice throughout the planning and implementation of programming, you are laying the groundwork for a stigma-free culture where students feel comfortable discussing their needs and participating in a variety of experiences and services.

PREVENTION

* Information on healthy relationships like 10 Signs of a healthy dating relationship, 10 Signs of an unhealthy dating relationship

* Personal safety training related to social media, sexting, abduction, assault/aggression, rape prevention, domestic violence, and human trafficking

* Training on how to avoid sexual assault at college

* Understanding Consent

SUPPORT

* Skill development on conflict resolution, relationship drama, and ending toxic relationships

* Help in responding to pornography exposure and habits

* Beginning/Supporting a Gay Straight Alliance Group

* Managing anger and learning to trust after being a victim

* 1:1 Counseling and Support groups

* Help coping with and stopping sexual bullying and harrassment

* Dealing with sexual violence and domestic violence at home

EDUCATION

* Identifying/Defining personal property rights like "How do I say no after I have said yes?"

* Understanding teen laws related to sexual activity

* School awareness campaign about teen dating violence

* Knowing what is meant by key terms related to sexuality, sexual identity, sexual abuse/assault, etc.

* Improvement to the Health Curriculum with "real" and relevant information related to sexual activity, women's health, healthy/unhealthy choices related to sexuality and birth control

* Preparing for fatherhood in the future (for boys who have been exposed to domestic violence and/or those growing up without a father in their homes, and also teen fathers)

RECOVERY and/or SUSTAINABILITY

* Help in recovering from sexual assault and abuse through 1:1 counseling and support groups

* Teen parenting classes for pregnant students and new moms

* Peer led advocacy groups focused on assertiveness, self-esteem, positive body image, and empowerment

* Promoting a school of culture and respect

Source: © 2020 The Centergy Project.

Figure 7.1: Focus group chart related to full-spectrum services for healthy relationships, sexuality, and sexual activity.

Review Partnerships

As you analyze student voice data, in some instances, you may find that programs and services your partners offer are perfectly suited to your students' requests. Continuing the previous example, if your students request programming on healthy relationships, it only makes sense to review existing programs for alignment with these requests. In this case, an existing partnership with the Georgia Network to End Sexual Assault's (n.d.) Step Up. Step In. program could help teach students and those who influence them about healthy interactions, healthy friendships, and healthy relationships. However, in the absence of an obvious partner, school leaders may review their Community Asset Map (page 110) to identify community organizations with related expertise, such as the following.

- **A related community agency or nonprofit:** Such organizations are focused on prevention, education, support, and recovery related to sexual assault and domestic violence and could provide curriculum and full-spectrum programming.

- **The local board of health:** The board can provide sex education and instruction and programming on healthy life choices in health classes. Or it can provide this instruction and programming as an after-school option to offset suspension in cases of behavioral infractions of a sexual nature.

- **Clinical counseling services:** Many counseling services provide expertise and services related to anger management, conflict resolution, healthy relationships, and recovery from abuse.

- **A teen pregnancy and parenting program:** This programming provides education and mentoring for teen mothers.

- **The police department:** Police can provide personal safety seminars to students and families on topics such as social media, sexting, abduction, assault and aggression, rape, domestic violence, and human trafficking.

At this point, it's crucial to understand that reviewing your school's data story and partnerships does not mean the work of gathering student voice stops or even pauses.

Continue Gathering Student Voice

Gathering student voice should not be a one-and-done activity conducted only in the early stages of wraparound development. Consistently connecting with your students to gather their voices fuels trust—the oxygen of wraparound services—and keeps your work relevant to your students' lives. Intentionally develop opportunities to thoughtfully listen to students, such as by doing the following.

- Create processes to receive reflective feedback about the wraparound center.

- Institute student teams to update the Student Voice Needs Survey and review data.

- Conduct conversation circles about schoolwide topics (for example, how to reduce trash on campus; how to improve the school's response to a tragedy, such as the death of a student; and how to increase student or family participation in events, such as health fairs, job fairs, or provider fairs).

- Conduct ongoing focus groups on identified student needs, known barriers, or community concerns. Family changes, grief, anger, immigration struggles, and sexual identity, to name a few, are realities for students and families, and these personal challenges impact learning and future success.

By keeping student voice a vital part of the feedback loop, your wraparound center's programming will continually serve the evolving needs of your students and their families. At the same time, you'll develop closer relationships with your partners while helping them become more relevant to their constituencies.

The *How*: Developing an Organizational Structure

The *what* of wraparound services begins with developing programming aligned to those barriers that students assert most impact their learning and graduation. The *how* involves school leaders strategically restructuring existing staff and partnering with outside agencies to make their school a full-service school—creating a one-stop shop of support for all students and their families.

As the school creates the organizational structure of wraparound services, it must also internally map assets related to the district's student-support-services personnel. For example, does the district already have contracted or employed individuals working as intervention specialists (PBIS specialist, family or community liaison, graduation coach, social worker, mental health clinician, mentoring coordinator, Communities in Schools site coordinator, academic screener, school psychologist, counselor, and so on)? School districts eager to increase staffing in the areas of counseling, student support, and administration may be best served by first considering reorganizing, repurposing, and refocusing existing staff. A key part of this process includes hiring a director to fully implement and systemize the continual gathering of student voice while also creating and supervising the wraparound center's day-to-day operations.

Hiring a Director

Districts *must* designate one person singularly responsible for the management and oversight of the wraparound initiative. The wraparound initiative aims to pivot a district from random acts of good intention to intentional, strategic partnerships. Hiring a wraparound director avoids diffusing responsibility among multiple staff members, which dilutes the synergies gained from a consolidated approach. We find that the most effective structure to increase wraparound services' impact is to designate the wraparound director as a district-level staffer with a K–12 reach within a cluster of schools that have a high school feeder pattern. Optimally, the wraparound director has the authority to respond on the district's behalf to students, their siblings, and their family as a whole. For example, when a student self-refers for access to the food pantry or requests grief services due to a loss, siblings and other family members in the district likely need similar support, and the wraparound director can help them get it.

The wraparound director also oversees creating and coordinating the system of care for a cluster of schools. In addition to managing student- and family-support staff members, the wraparound director facilitates referrals, workflows, programming, connections with partners, funding, and service provisions. The salary is typically equivalent to that of an assistant principal on an extended-year contract, a principal, or a district-level director, depending on the number of staff, partnerships, and schools involved in the initiative.

The following sections detail aspects of hiring a wraparound director that schools should address, including the necessary characteristics and capacities of a director, the job description, and the director's place within the organizational structure.

Characteristics and Capacities

The leader of your wraparound initiative needs to have both the characteristics and the capacities to innovatively leverage resources to solve problems. The ideal wraparound director engenders trust through authentic, open-minded, and respectful communication with all stakeholders—students, faculty, school and district leaders, and community members. Balancing realism and asset-mindedness allows the director to be what author and investor John Doerr (2018) describes as "a blue-sky thinker" who keeps his or her "feet on the ground" (p. 4). In addition, because the wraparound initiative requires managing change and taking risks, the wraparound director needs flexibility, a high tolerance for stress and ambiguity, and a willingness to challenge the status quo. This person must also be tenaciously optimistic so that he or she can persist even when attempts to help a student or family fail. Given this need for executive-level decision making, it's best to find someone with leadership experience, either as a school administrator or in a social service or therapeutic capacity.

Wraparound directors must be cognizant of the new work and collaborative change they are leading. During the launch of this initiative, competing agendas, philosophies, and personalities may rise to the surface. The wraparound director must have knowledge of the social systems already in place, be sensitive to who the proposed changes will affect, and be able to maintain a focus on the wildly important goal of connecting students and families with the support and services they need. In *Leading for Learning*, Phillip C. Schlechty (2009) spells out three capacities schools need to successfully support and sustain such *systemic changes* and *disruptive innovations*:

- The capacity to establish and maintain a focus on the future
- The capacity to maintain direction once a clear focus has been established
- The capacity to act strategically by reallocating existing resources, seizing opportunities, and creating a new future (p. 224)

A large part of seizing opportunities requires the wraparound director to seek new streams of funding for programs and services, such as those we established in chapter 6 (page 139). Your wraparound director must not be shy about asking for financial support. He or she must let the story of your student voice data capture the hearts, open the minds, and inspire the generosity of your community. And he or she must always treat your students' stories with respect when informing your community—*never* exploiting them for financial (or any other) gain.

The director must come in knowing how to ethically live in the gray. In the gray is where problem solving, networking, and interpreting student voice resides. I think the director's mindset to welcome the uncertainty means that he or she will problem solve through the unknown, just like our students have to in times of uncertainty.

—Tonya Sanders, director of The Hub, Gainesville City Schools, Georgia

Job Description

Naturally, every wraparound director's job description is tailored to the district's standards and protocols. Figure 7.2 shows a sample job description you may use as a starting point for developing your own.

Wraparound Director Job Description

Reports to: Assistant superintendent of student services

Requirements

- Graduate degree in education, social work, sociology, or public policy
- Working knowledge of state public education rules and regulations
- At least three years of successful experience working with students at risk
- Experience collaborating with community partners

School administration or organizational leadership experience preferred

Purpose Statement

The job of the wraparound director is to work collaboratively with district and school administrators to provide supports for students, families, and the community so that student success before and after graduation increases.

Skills, Knowledge, and Abilities

Skills are required to perform multiple nontechnical and technical tasks, with a potential need to upgrade skills to meet changing job conditions. Specific skill-based competencies required to satisfactorily perform the functions of the job include preparing and maintaining accurate records; operating standard office equipment; utilizing pertinent software applications; communicating effectively and in a timely manner; and working as a liaison between district-office staff members and schools as well as community members and service providers.

Knowledge is required to communicate information to others and analyze situations to communicate effectively. Specific knowledge-based competencies required to satisfactorily perform the functions of the job include knowledge of English grammar, punctuation, spelling, and vocabulary; office equipment and software; and a variety of school procedures and office practices.

Ability is required to gather, collate, and classify data; work with varied types of data, utilizing specific, defined, and varied processes related to collection, innovation, problem solving, and strategic planning; and use basic job-related equipment. Flexibility is required to work with others in a wide variety of circumstances. Problem solving is required to identify issues and create action plans. Specific ability-based competencies required to satisfactorily perform the functions of the job include maintaining confidentiality; adapting to changing priorities; working with frequent interruptions; communicating and working with diverse groups and individuals; initiating activities and projects as needed; and displaying tact and courtesy.

Figure 7.2: Sample job description for a wraparound director.

continued ▶

Responsibility

Responsibilities include developing processes under limited supervision; following standardized practices and methods; guiding and coordinating others; and operating within a defined budget. Utilization of resources from other departments may be required to perform the job's functions. Fundraising related to use of in-kind donations; grants and collaborative partner funding; appeals to foundations and organizations; and use of state, federal, and charter funding will also be required.

Work Environment

The usual and customary methods of performing the job's functions require moderate physical demands, such as some lifting, carrying, pushing, and pulling; some stooping, kneeling, crouching, and crawling; and significant fine finger dexterity.

Generally, the job requires 40 percent sitting, 35 percent walking, and 25 percent standing. This job is performed in a generally clean and healthy environment.

Essential Functions

- Assist in the identification, design, and implementation of support services related to academics (inclusive of college and career), life skills, and social-emotional development, and assist partners with the coordination of support services for students and families.

- Manage students assigned to counseling and clinical services for restorative practices and programming related to behavioral infractions.

- Create, support, and adhere to processes for identifying students who are behaviorally at risk, and align services to student needs.

- Continuously assess student needs through conversation circles, off-track interviews, graduation stories, focus groups, individual focused conversations, Student Voice Needs Surveys, and other data to identify additional community resources.

- Coordinate with service providers and nonprofits in the community as well as state agencies.

- Develop procedures for students and families to receive food, clothing, toiletries, and other supplies related to basic needs.

- Collaborate with student-support-services personnel, such as social workers, school counselors, and others, as well as human-services partners and others to provide supports for students and families.

- Collaborate with counselors and the career and technical education department to conduct workshops that assist with college applications, résumés, interview skills, and so on.

- Collaborate with the career and technical education department to facilitate career-exploration events, seek employment opportunities for students, and maintain job postings.

- Seek new partnerships with community resources based on district needs.

- Increase public awareness of services offered at schools.

- Work collaboratively with the district, community leaders, and donors to build sustainable funding sources.

- Work with district personnel and community partners to increase awareness of known barriers to learning (such as mental health, substance use, family changes, transience, immigration, poverty, and trauma); provide programming and training for staff and community members on the impact of those barriers; and provide evidence-based strategies related to prevention, education, support, and sustainability.

- Leverage support from professional organizations that provide behavioral and social-emotional health counseling.

- Draft and implement MOUs with outside service providers in coordination with the superintendent and the district's attorney.

- Perform other duties as required, including on nights, on weekends, and before and after school.

Organizational Structure

The wraparound director provides program oversight and day-to-day supervision of all staff and services in the wraparound center. MOUs should clearly state the wraparound director is the primary point of contact and on-site supervisor for programming and services that third parties deliver within the school district. However, providers co-located within the school district should maintain their employment status with their parent organization, meaning their protocols, billing processes, licensure, salary and benefits, correspondence, and continuing education remain with their employer. For example, if a school opens a student health clinic staffed with nurses or a doctor from the Department of Public Health or another health-care provider, the health-care organization continues to oversee the work of its personnel assigned to the school-based clinic.

With this dual staff management, it is essential there be a high level of relational trust among the wraparound director, the agency head, and the on-site service provider. In Leigh's case, she created MOUs ensuring she would have input in the selection and evaluation of any service providers working within her wraparound center. This helped further clarify the organizational structure between internal and external wraparound staff. Figure 7.3 (page 174) shows a sample organizational chart, including both existing district and partner staff. Note that the school district's reporting structure for the wraparound director (who the director reports to) is dependent on the organizational structure and scope of the Center as well as whether the position is considered a school- or district-level position.

Creating a Student Board of Directors

Having a student board of directors is a way to keep student voice alive. Select a diverse group of students—consider age, race, socioeconomic status, and school experience—who can advocate for themselves and others. Deputize them to serve as advisors to school leadership and ambassadors to both the student body and the community. As advisors, these students serve a valuable role in the creation of the space that will become the Center (colors, vibe, furniture and artwork selection, room layout), design and refinement of programming, scheduling of activities, rollout of schoolwide surveys, and promotion and marketing of events and services, as well as peer support. Don't make this student board of directors merely window dressing; authentically lean on these students' experience to continue to seek the truth and speak the truth on behalf of students.

The *Where*: Designing Spaces for Connecting Students and Families With Services

Where to house a wraparound center will vary according to the resources within a school, district, or community. We have seen schools use the following, but do not restrict your thinking to these spaces.

- Repurposed media centers
- Repurposed classrooms, storage closets, and offices
- Mobile classroom units
- Off-site hubs with satellite facilities

Wraparound Director	
Existing District Personnel	**Community Partners**
Based on district staffing, one or more of the following district personnel should be considered for assignment to the director of wraparound services.	Based on community availability, one or more community partners, such as the following, should be considered for co-location within the district to provide equitable access to goods and services.

Existing District Personnel

Based on district staffing, one or more of the following district personnel should be considered for assignment to the director of wraparound services.

- 504 coordinator
- Academic screener
- College and career counselor
- Computer lab supervisor (virtual learning, online, credit recovery, or writing lab supervisor)
- Core content intervention teachers
- Graduation coach
- Homeless liaison
- In-school suspension or out-of-school suspension facilitator
- Mentoring coordinator
- MTSS coordinator
- Paraprofessional
- Parent and community liaison
- PBIS coordinator
- School counselor
- School psychologist
- Social worker
- Student support team facilitator

Community Partners

Based on community availability, one or more community partners, such as the following, should be considered for co-location within the district to provide equitable access to goods and services.

- Boys and Girls Club
- Case manager for the Department of Human Services
- Case manager for housing
- Communities in Schools
- Department of Public Health
- Faith-based organization
- Human services, social services, or counseling interns from the local college or university
- Juvenile justice or probation
- Military recruitment officers
- Police department
- Behavioral health services provider
- Community services board
- Family services coordinator
- Sexual abuse and domestic violence specialist
- Recovery community organization
- United Way
- YMCA or YWCA

Figure 7.3: Sample organizational chart of a wraparound center's personnel.

Design your wraparound space to reflect the services provided, and seek generous input from students about the layout, furnishings, and supplies of the individual rooms. Having student input about the *where*'s setting and atmosphere often results in warm touches, like turning spirit T-shirts into pillows, decorating the walls with student photos, and including social-emotional learning and therapeutic tools. Your wraparound center may be relatively small, with space for only a wraparound director and a couple of partners; or it may be more extensive, with multiple rooms designed for a variety of purposes. Figure 7.4 shows a floor plan of repurposed rooms for Gainesville City Schools' wraparound center,

The Hub. These rooms were previously a media center, supply closets, offices, a computer lab, and classrooms.

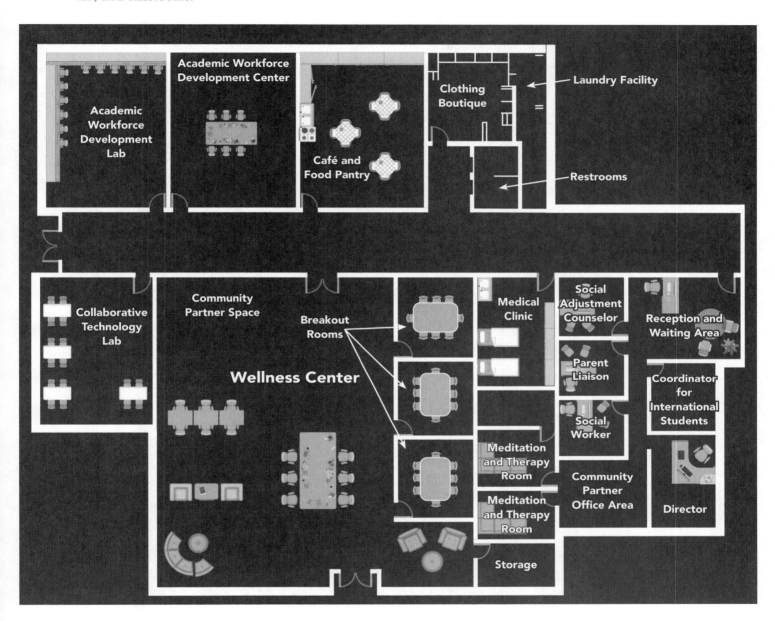

Figure 7.4: Layout of a wraparound center housed in repurposed rooms.

Figures 7.5 (page 176), 7.6 (page 176), and 7.7 (page 177) show sketches of a meditation and therapy room (designed as comfortable meeting spaces for de-escalation, mediation, individual counseling, and more), an academic workforce-development area (used as flexible space for college visits, career exploration, military recruitment, and soft-skills training), and a food pantry (used for students and families who experience food instability).

Source: © 2020 The Centergy Project.

Figure 7.5: Meditation and therapy room.

Source: © 2020 The Centergy Project.

Figure 7.6: Academic workforce-development area.

Figure 7.7: Café and food pantry.

In addition to viewing these images, you can take a virtual tour of a wraparound center by going to the Centergy Project website (www.thecentergyproject.com) and selecting View a Model from the homepage's drop-down list. Then, use the menu on the top left to change room settings. While viewing the rooms, you can select the *i* button at the bottom of the screen to see additional information on the purpose, staffing, and funding for each space.

The *Who*: Reaching the Whole School, Identified Groups, and Individual Students

Effective outreach strategies are critical to ensuring your wraparound center reaches a broad spectrum of students, and they will vary based on the audience. When planning for the *who*, the wraparound director must think of the entities and groups comprising the entirety of the student body so all students are welcomed. This includes wraparound services for the whole school, identified student groups who may require specialized services, and individual students in need.

Whole School

By thinking whole school, the wraparound director will naturally offer programs that appeal to the entire student body. This includes prevention and awareness curriculum relating to healthy relationships, substance use, and self-care or tutoring, and it includes programs on academic and work skills such as interviewing, social-media management, time management, test prep, or college and job application assistance. For example, one school we are familiar with offered after-school classes titled "Five Meals You Need to Learn to Cook Before Living on Your Own," and another school's center offered a whole day of student-suggested Adulting 101 sessions, such as basic sewing, how to change a tire, the essentials of résumé writing, and healthy strategies for dealing with stress. They had a large menu of options, and students could sign up for the sessions they wanted to attend. In addition to whole school programming, make your wraparound spaces available for activities like study groups, student council meetings, and the like.

In short, regularly promoting and hosting events with mass appeal ensures that visiting your wraparound center is an entirely normal thing for any student to do—resulting in destigmatizing seeking your wraparound center's services.

A Word About Mental Health, Trauma, and ACEs

In the article "For School Leaders, a Time of Vigilance and Caring," John Rogers (2019) asserts:

> Schools must draw from a fuller set of strategies than merely intensifying security and surveillance. What's more likely to reduce the incidence of violence at schools is turning to a public health model that emphasizes systems and supports to promote safety and that gets to the source of the problems behind threats or violent acts (Interdisciplinary Group on Preventing School and Community Violence, 2013). This approach calls for principals to focus attention on establishing a school climate in which students feel a sense of connection with, and responsibility toward, one another. It also entails investing in counselors, psychologists, and social workers who can identify students in need of counseling and provide mental health services. As a long-term strategy, this approach would also address conditions outside schools that endanger students during school hours.

Identified Groups

While your aim is to build a culture where students exercise self-care and self-improvement by seeking out services and support, don't wait for students to come to you. Instead, build a prioritized caseload of student groups based on specialized criteria—usually students who are faltering academically, students with high potential who are facing barriers related to basic needs and low support at home, students who are frequently absent, and students who are exhibiting behaviors related to emotional and behavioral health.

Additionally, reach out to students struggling with a specific need, such as grief or anxiety. Ask teachers, counselors, and administrators to refer students for participation in programming, such as topic-specific focus groups, support groups, mediation services, and lunch-and-learn opportunities. While you continue to open your doors and welcome students who are self-referring, utilize the connections and influence of participating students to grow the number of students participating in groups and services. Much like the initiatives of PBIS and RTI or MTSS, wraparound services range from generalized to individualized and must be malleable to the level of support or intervention needed.

A Word About Mental Health, Trauma, and ACEs

In the article "What's Love Got to Do With It?" elementary school principal and trauma survivor Rita Platt (2019) asserts schools must make a plan for supporting students. As part of this plan, they must respond to students' unmet needs by incorporating the following effective strategies, which will help students struggling with trauma.

- Support students in meltdown.
- Build relationships.
- Offer tools to help students self-regulate.
- Teach students to scale the problem and the response.
- View students as more than their trauma.

Individual Students

Collaborate with school staff to create and continually update a list of priority students identified for a variety of reasons as needing wraparound support such as basic needs (food, clothing, school supplies), clinical therapeutic services, recovery support, de-escalation, and crisis response. Use positive language and messaging to target these students for outreach and connection with services, such as emphasizing the use of restorative practices that address a student's unique needs.

The launch of a wraparound center is also a wonderful opportunity to revisit professional learning priorities and discipline policies as they relate to strengthening relationships as well as establish restorative and alternative disciplinary practices that prioritize services and support over consequences and punishment. Consider that traditional discipline practices rely on blame, guilt, and punishment, rather than repairing harm, restoring relationships, and addressing root causes through restorative action. According to Betheny Lyke and Spencer Byrd (2018), restorative practices are worth the effort because they help students understand their behavior, accept responsibility, and make amends. Their work through the Illinois Center for School Improvement to improve discipline practices in Mounds, Illinois, resulted in a two-thirds decline in out-of-school suspensions (Lyke & Byrd, 2018). Barr and Gibson (2020) further encourage schools to become safe havens where students can connect and build relationships, not places that further traumatize and reject them. Recognizing zero-tolerance policies make schools no safer and push out students (sometimes forever), many schools are embracing the proven reform of restorative practices and positive behavior practices (Dingerson, 2015).

A Word About Mental Health, Trauma, and ACEs

Brendtro and colleagues (2019) write:

> Building restorative relationships is not limited to those with formal training in counseling. An adult who is involved in ongoing daily events has many opportunities to show small acts of kindness and respect. While trained therapists make important contributions, everyday supportive relationships are the most potent way to heal trauma. (p. 36)

Clinical psychologist Ricky Greenwald (2005) further affirms this thinking:

> You do not have to be a therapist to create a therapeutic or healing relationship with a child. Parents, counselors, teachers, coaches, direct care workers, case managers, and others are all in a position to help a child heal. The quality of your relationship is the vehicle for healing. (p. 37)

Our experience with teens backs up the research. We have yet to hear any students say that shame and isolation helped them come back from something difficult. Instead, we've found students eager for the second chances that come with restorative practices. The responses we've received from students, illustrated in figure 7.8, make this abundantly clear.

Of the responses pictured in figure 7.8, consider the following in particular.

- "Being treated with respect even though I screwed up or did something wrong"
- "Not being judged continually by the adults in the building for my worst 'bad day'"
- "Learning from my mistakes"

These comments show students' willingness to admit their mistakes and a desire to recover and learn from them. Restorative practices provide students grace and support as they work to change their behavior and learn new skills.

Your focus group artifacts will prove valuable to including restorative practices in your wraparound approach. The Personal Reflection Notes (page 87) and the focus group discussion flip charts described in chapter 3 (page 63) include questions that reveal root causes and suggest restorative school responses. Share this data story with your faculty and administrative team to develop restorative practices—in the classroom and for the whole school. If your wraparound center includes a space to offset suspension with on-site tutoring and connection with services, add appropriate staffing, such as tutors and paraprofessionals.

When you struggle in how to use restorative practices to best address student issues that are complicated and sensitive, use your student voice processes to gain insight into what students need and how you can approach concerns in an effective, student-centered manner. For example, figure 7.1 (page 167) showed student-generated requests concerning full-spectrum support and sexuality-related services. In high schools, sexual misconduct can be a precipitating reason for discipline and suspension; however, punishment alone for the offender rarely adequately addresses the downstream impact of the offense to the

What helps you come back from something difficult?

Asking for and receiving forgiveness

Forgiving myself and forgiving others

Being given some space, options, and control

Using my experience or mistakes to help someone else

Having some privacy and time to come to terms with what happened and then begin to figure out how to move forward so I am not dwelling in the past.

Think about the big picture

Finding a source of motivation and hope

Having someone to talk to, someone who will listen

Being given another chance by someone who believes in me

Being treated with respect even though I screwed up or did something wrong

Having some quiet and alone time to think through my next steps

Talking with someone who understands because they have been through something similar

Not being judged continually by the adults in the building for my worst "bad thing"

Having teachers who really know _me_ not just how I act

Unpacking "it" then packing "it" back up

Doing something physical to work it out (the stress, figure out the problem, get my mind off it, etc.)

Someone who knows where you are coming from

Someone you trust

Admitting what I have done to someone else, getting it off my chest

Apologizing and accepting my responsibility

Having a mentor

Learning from my mistakes

Knowing I will know how to avoid making this mistake in the future

Accepting the consequences that come my way and then moving on

Having teachers or others respond with caring and compassion even though I've messed up

Finding a positive place or being with non-judgy people who help me move on

Being able to talk to someone who listens

Focusing on a positive and important goal

Figure 7.8: Student responses to a question on overcoming difficulty.

accused or the victim. Some of these infractions, such as sexual harassment and sexting, also have a negative impact on school climate. In these instances, discipline policies typically mete out consequences of shame and isolation, and schools miss opportunities to thoughtfully respond with respect, education, healing, changes in mindset, and restoration when appropriate.

In some communities, the Department of Public Health funds and facilitates training called the Personal Responsibility Education Program (PREP; Family Youth and Services Bureau, n.d.) using the evidence-based Reducing the Risk curriculum (Success Center for Sexual & Reproductive Health, n.d.), which provides abstinence and contraception education to prevent pregnancy and sexually transmitted infections. Taught by registered nurses (one male, one female), the PREP course also incorporates adulthood-readiness topics such as healthy relationships, sexual education, and other student-requested content.

During Leigh's tenure as a center director, some students involved in sexual infractions could offset suspension by completing the PREP course over the course of eight weeks in weekly two-hour sessions. Students, administrators, and parents at her school reported this approach was beneficial to students, their peers, and the overall school culture. Other examples might include how a student found to be in possession of alcohol or drugs might offset suspension by having scheduled mentoring sessions with a person in long-term recovery (see the appendix, page 227, for much more about addressing substance abuse through wraparound services) or how a student reported for insubordination or willful refusal might be able to offset time out of class by attending and participating in an anger-management support group. Each of these examples demonstrates how student voice, wraparound services, and restorative practices can work together to transform a school's approach to discipline and better serve students at the same time.

voices FROM THE FIELD

Before the Center, discipline was handled punitively—mainly with in-school suspensions and out-of-school suspensions. These consequences fail to address the actual behaviors or put any strategies in place to keep the behaviors from happening again. Our center has allowed the administrative team at our school the ability to truly impact students' lives by giving us the resources to determine the root cause for behavioral issues; provide information and support related to the infraction; provide direct academic support to students during a time they would have separated from the school; and provide students with social-emotional counseling, mediation services, and the opportunity for restoration during a time they would have previously been sitting at home. By strategically using the Center, we have dramatically reduced, or offset, our total days of suspension, while at the same time helping students address many of the barriers that lead to the negative behaviors. Addressing barriers and infractions in this manner has reduced our days of suspension, lowered the rate of repeat offenses, and positively impacted our school culture.

—Jason Meade, high school administrator

Conclusion

Structuring your facilities for wraparound work means consolidating and realigning your internal resources and actively partnering with service providers to deliver a variety of student-informed, coordinated student services. By collaborating with staff, partners, and students, you'll be prepared to work synergistically with regard to planning, reporting processes, services, staffing, funding, and physical spaces.

Student voice is the lifeblood of keeping your work relevant to the lives of your students and their families. Consult students whenever possible—from designing spaces to developing and revising programming. You'll be most effective and remove stigma when you design programming that appeals to all while intentionally seeking those most in need of services. Look for ways to incorporate restorative practices to improve school culture and reduce harmful behaviors.

Once you have your wraparound center's structure sketched out, you will be ready to focus on what matters most: connecting students and families with services.

Part IV

LAUNCHING AND SUSTAINING WRAPAROUND SERVICES

Chapter 8

CONNECT STUDENTS AND FAMILIES WITH SERVICES

I am the parent of a ninth grader, and we are new to this area. It has been lonely and scary starting over. I've been struggling with obtaining work, and my daughter is still getting adjusted to our life changes, a new school environment, and new friends. She started seeing a therapist at the Center who has given her support and helped her motivation to do good in her classes. The therapist also offered her assistance after learning more about what we are going through. She suggested I come to the Center to seek some help. Since then, I have felt so welcomed and at ease. We have been able to get food and help with some of our bills, and they are trying to help me find a job. Everyone I've come across has been friendly, compassionate, and caring. I am still in financial crisis, but I am not facing my problems alone. Knowing that my daughter's school has resources to help us fight our way through all of this means the world to me.

—High school parent

When you developed your wraparound mission statement (see chapter 5, page 119), you declared your *why*—your wraparound center's reason for being. This chapter is largely about execution—getting the work done. Larry Page, cofounder of Google, puts it this way: "Good ideas with great execution are how you make magic" (as cited in Doerr, 2018, p. xi). Measuring the magic—meaning the impact or results—of wraparound services presents a challenge in the quantitative world of strategic planning, SMART goals (strategic and specific, measurable, attainable, results-oriented, and time-bound; Conzemius & O'Neill, 2014), and annual measurable outcomes. The world of wraparound work requires the strategic, analytical educator to deeply consider what measurements matter the most. How does one measure the impact of equitable access, social capital, and trusting relationships? As sociologist William Bruce Cameron (1963) famously said:

> It would be nice if all the data which sociologists require could be enumerated because then we could run them through IBM machines and draw charts as the economists do. However, not everything that can be counted counts, and not everything that counts can be counted. (p. 13)

In general, these measurement efforts should be grounded in a continuous cycle of query and response to three questions.

1. **What do we need?** Augment student voice with community data to form the foundation of identifying needs.

2. **What are we doing?** Collect and report data about services delivered to your students and families.

3. **How is it going?** Intentionally seek qualitative feedback, usage data, and academic impact measures to evaluate effectiveness and guide improvement efforts.

With measurement systems in place that address these questions, you'll be prepared to use various warm, personal referral processes to connect students and their families with services designed to meet their needs. This chapter will frame your thinking on the topics of measuring what matters, establishing procedures and processes that ensure and enhance connections with services (including referral processes), and developing an Individual Student Voice Needs Survey to connect students and families with services. Table 8.1 breaks down the process and purpose behind step 7 in the Centergy Cycle.

Table 8.1: Launching and Sustaining Wraparound Services—Step 7

	Process	Purpose
Step 7: Connect Students and Families With Services	Measure what matters.	Answer the following questions. • What do we need? • What are we doing? • How is it going?
	Establish processes and procedures that ensure and enhance connection with services.	Conduct a school-year kickoff. Establish walk-in and referral systems.
	Develop an Individual Student Voice Needs Survey..	Determine individual student needs.

Measure What Matters

In *The 4 Disciplines of Execution*, Chris McChesney, Sean Covey, and Jim Huling (2012) urge leaders to focus on one or maybe two *wildly important goals* and say no to other good ideas. They contend that, without a clear overriding goal, secondary activities are likely to distract your team. Although its publisher markets this resource as a business book, we find the content applies to schools and will help leaders and educators develop productive habits.

In wraparound services, your wildly important goal is straightforward: connect students and families with services. If you stopped there, you'd technically achieve your goal by serving only one student and family. When determining your targets, your wraparound team needs to balance what is achievable against a stretch goal—an aspirational goal requiring commitment and focus (Doerr, 2018, p. 135). If you make your targets too easy, your team will lose steam and coast. Make your targets too hard, and you may endanger team efforts with "narrowed focus, unethical behavior, increased risk taking, decreased cooperation, and decreased motivation" (Doerr, 2018, p. 9).

Including measurements for your wildly important goal, in the form of stretch goals, adds clarity and focuses your team's efforts on high-leverage actions to impact the wildly important goal. Keep in mind two critical measurements when creating stretch goals for your wraparound center: (1) the number of services or partnerships your wraparound center provides and (2) the number of unique students and families it serves.

Here's an example of a measurable wildly important goal: *During the 2020–2021 school year, we will connect 30 percent of our students and 15 percent of our families with wraparound services.* In this case, your team will be able to monitor progress toward the goal during the school year, and it will know at the end of the school year whether it met the goal. With *connections with services* as your wildly important goal, your subsequent strategic plans will follow suit and focus on keeping score of service-oriented objectives such as the following, which are based on the services your school will be offering.

- Use of care closets (food, clothing, toiletries, and school supplies)
- Days of offset suspension through restorative practices
- Student and parent attendance to events
- Families with more than one child participating in services
- Caseload numbers

By rounding out these quantitative measurements with qualitative feedback, you'll augment your data story with the voices of your students and families—important outcome information that counts but can't be counted (Cameron, 1963).

While keeping score is critical to maintain focus and momentum, beware of creating a measurement monster. Don't chase numbers that get in the way of your wildly important goal—connecting students and families with services. Only collect truly useful data regarding student and family needs, delivery of services, and quality of services provided. To avoid creating processes that get in the way of meeting student and family needs in a timely manner, strive to achieve a balance between the collection and completeness of data and the ease of access to services. The following sections address this balance by asking the three questions we introduced at the start of this chapter: (1) "What do we need?" (2) "What are we doing?" and (3) "How is it going?"

What Do We Need?

Throughout your engagement with the Centergy Cycle, you've been collecting insight to inform the connection of your students and families with services. From gathering student voice to establishing partnerships, you traveled a journey of query regarding needs and opportunities. Here's a summary of the data about student voice you should have by this point to inform your answer to what you need.

- Charts from conversation circles
- Notes from off-track interviews
- Narratives and trends from graduation stories
- Requests of services from Student Voice Needs Surveys
- Information and artifacts from focus groups

In addition, your efforts to identify resources and establish partnerships (chapter 4, page 103, and chapter 5, page 119) facilitated your review of school and community data related to academic achievement, discipline, attendance, demographics, and poverty as well as public health and local law-enforcement priorities. Chapter 9 (page 207) spells out ideas for creating a rhythm for keeping these processes alive.

What Are We Doing?

This question tasks you with collecting data about the services you've delivered to students and families. Just as your gathered student-voice data do, these data tell a story. Figure 8.1 shows an example from The Centergy Project of how a wraparound center can report its impact through a graphic data story using both aggregate and disaggregate data as well as various numbers related to students, families, partners, and funding. You can share this graphic with a broad spectrum of stakeholders inside and outside the school through newsletters, flyers, posters, and annual reports.

As this figure illustrates, the data you collect should reflect the partnerships you have in place and the services you're offering. Ask your partners what measures are important to them. For example, a food bank stocking your food pantry will likely want to know the number of families served and the pounds of groceries distributed.

Table 8.2 (page 192) lists some possible measurements that can help you answer the "What are we doing?" question for the wraparound service categories. When collecting and reporting aggregate numbers of unique students and families or caseload numbers, use the descriptors in this table as a starting place and adapt to the services your wraparound center offers. In accordance with privacy laws, you should never report individual student or family names when documenting measurement data.

Ask your wraparound team—school employees and partners—to collect and regularly report the services they are delivering. For example, a graduation coach might report the number of students participating in off-track interviews, a college and career counselor might report the number of college acceptances or scholarship dollars students receive, and a substance use counselor might report the number of students participating in universal screening, brief intervention, and referral to treatment (SBIRT). Aim to keep your

The Wraparound Center: By the Numbers

856

Students visited the supply closet stocked with items courtesy of Our Town Church Network

MORE THAN 125

students and their families received professional counseling

315 Students completed ACT/SAT Prep courses

25+ Partnerships with state & local agencies, non-profits, colleges, and universities

An Average of **7,000lbs** of food distributed monthly through the organization Food for Thought

178

Thanksgiving meals delivered to families from Families First

225 Community members attended tours of the center

193

Students matched with community mentors through Mentoring Matters

$1.3mil

estimated value of services delivered to students and their families this year

youscience®

1,200 Students completed YouScience aptitude assessment

The Wraparound Center helped **205** Students recover 976 instructional days

An average of **20**

Students per day visited the clothes closet supplied by Simple Gifts

Source: © 2020 The Centergy Project.

Figure 8.1: Sample data story graphic of services delivered.

Table 8.2: Potential Wraparound Measurements

Basic Needs

- Number of families accessing a food pantry or pounds of food the pantry has distributed
- Number of visits to a clothes closet and laundry facilities
- Types and general quantities of supplies distributed (such as toiletries, slow cookers, housing supplies, and car seats)
- Number of families receiving housing assistance or assistance related to rent and transportation
- Number of families assisted in crisis due to emergency situations (such as appliances, furniture, clothing, and shelter)
- Number of families receiving holiday assistance

Community Services

- Number of providers and types of services offered
- Number of students and families receiving clinical and therapeutic services
- Number of students in a mentoring program with community-based leaders
- Number of teen mothers participating in a mentoring program
- Number of students participating in support groups (such as groups related to anger, LGBTQPIA identity, incarcerated loved ones, anxiety, and substance use)
- Number of parents attending English language classes
- Number of parents attending a provider fair, job fair, or health and wellness fair

Academic Opportunity

- Number of students participating in tutoring or utilizing a technology lab
- Number of out-of-school suspension days displaced through restorative practices
- Types and general quantities of school supplies distributed (such as book bags, notebooks, and trifold boards)
- Number of students supplied with technology (such as Wi-Fi, laptops, and graphing calculators)
- Number of days for provision of homebound or extended-year services for students academically at risk due to health issues, discipline problems, or lost credits
- Number of students participating in online courses for enrichment or credit recovery

College and Career Transition

- Number of students completing a YouScience assessment and attending a feedback conference to debrief results
- Number of students attending college presentations or seminars
- Number of parents attending financial seminars related to college savings and costs
- Number of students participating in SAT or ACT prep classes
- Number of students participating in apprenticeship or internship programs or career-shadowing opportunities
- Number of students receiving assistance with college (such as applications, scholarship opportunities, and college visits)

Safety and Justice

- Number of students managed in juvenile court caseload through on-site probation services (caseload specifics)
- Number of students and parents participating in police-taught self-defense classes
- Number of drug test kits distributed to parents
- Number of contacts or supervised visits by Department of Human Services staff with students and families (caseload specifics)
- Number of parents and community members attending seminars offered by law enforcement and first responders (such as seminars on gun safety, crisis response, CPR, risk avoidance, and personal safety)
- Number of students completing a driver's education or defensive driving course

Health and Wellness

- Number of health provider partnerships and clinical services offered
- Number (or hours) of students participating in yoga classes and mindfulness training
- Number of student and family participants in nutrition and cooking classes
- Number of students receiving annual physicals for athletics
- Number of students and families participating in on-site health screenings
- Number of students and parents participating in health education opportunities
- Number of students and families participating in substance-use and recovery-support services
- Number of student visits to and services provided by a student health clinic
- Number of students participating in SBIRT for substance use (see the appendix, page 227)

data-collection processes simple to avoid time-consuming reporting processes getting in the way of delivering services.

How Is It Going?

Answering this question requires you to seek qualitative data that can tell you how your efforts have impacted the lives of students and their families. To get qualitative feedback from your student body, partners, and parents, periodically provide a questionnaire or feedback form similar to the one in figure 8.2 (page 194). This document asks students about their experiences and ideas. The wraparound director or his or her designee then compiles the narratives in a report to use for improvement planning, annual reports, presentations to boards of education, grant applications, and promotional materials. The report should anonymize identifying comments when it makes sense to do so.

In addition to a formal questionnaire, look for informal ways to continually collect feedback. For example, you might end focus groups with a quick discussion of what worked and ideas for improvement (spoken or on sticky notes). You might create a suggestion box (or email address) and ask a different question each month, such as "How can we make pep rallies more engaging?" or "How can we decrease the litter on campus?" Or, you might hang blank focus group charts and invite students to add their thoughts.

Establish Procedures and Processes That Ensure and Enhance Connections With Services

This section is devoted to the importance of having procedures and processes related to daily interactions with students and families. As part of this exploration, we address how schools can connect students and families with wraparound services through marketing and start-of-the-year materials providing an overview of services offered and by establishing a system for accessing services via walk-ins and referrals.

School-Year Kickoff

Before the school year begins, make sure the school's first-day packet and other school-year kickoff documents include a parental permission form regarding wraparound services. Ensure this parental permission form is also included in the registration package for new students who enroll throughout the school year. This schoolwide parental communication on wraparound services has three purposes.

1. Gain parents' permission in the least complicated manner possible.
2. Notify all parents of the services available within the Center or district.
3. Destigmatize concerns related to asking the school for assistance.

Figure 8.3 (page 195) shows an example parental permission form. Notice that it includes opt-in wording, although you may instead choose to handle parental permission with opt-out wording or by gaining parents' permission for specific services—such as mentoring, clinical and therapeutic services, or family support—as needed. While your district may decide students are allowed to access all academic-, college-, and career-related services without additional parental permission or notification, services related to mental and emotional

Students,

We have had an exciting year in our Wraparound Services Center (WSC). We hope you have come to see us and taken advantage of some of the services we are providing. Please help us improve by completing this form to give us some information on what we are doing well and where we might need to do better as we plan for the next school year. Include any ideas or suggestions you have for the Wraparound Services Center.

Have you attended our Wraparound Services Center?

- ☐ Yes
- ☐ No

If you answered *Yes* to the previous question, what services or support did you receive? (Please check all that apply.)

- ☐ Tutoring
- ☐ Mentoring or personal support
- ☐ Graduation planning (alternative scheduling, academic advice, and so on)
- ☐ College and career services (YouScience, military recruitment, SAT or ACT prep, college information, scholarship assistance, and so on)
- ☐ Personal needs (food pantry, clothes closet, housing assistance, and so on)
- ☐ Support groups (yoga, stress management, anger management, self-esteem, and so on)

Please tell us your thoughts on the WSC.

What is going well?

Has the WSC been of assistance to you? If so, how?

Is there something we need to improve? If so, what?

Do you have any ideas you would like to share with us? If so, what are they?

If you could tell another school or another student something about the WSC, what would you tell them?

In what ways, if any, would you be interested in becoming more involved in the WSC? (Please check all that apply.)

- ☐ I would be interested in volunteering my time in the clothes closet.
- ☐ I would be interested in serving on the student board of directors.
- ☐ I would be interested in serving as a WSC tour guide.
- ☐ I would be interested in assisting with service projects related to the WSC.

Contact information is optional but appreciated—especially if you checked any of the boxes above ☺.

Your name: _____

Email address: _____   Phone number: _____

Figure 8.2: Sample student feedback form.

*Visit **go.SolutionTree.com/leadership** for a free reproducible version of this figure.*

Parental Consent for Student Participation in Wraparound Services

We created our Wraparound Center based on student-suggested topics of interest and student-requested services. Our mission is to provide wraparound services for our students to increase their ability to be healthy, to learn, and to graduate on time with their class. All three support areas listed on this form are housed at our school.

Academic Support	Behavioral and Life Skills Support	Counseling and Family Support (Community Partnerships)
Alternative scheduling	Peer mediation and conflict resolution	Group support on the following topics.
Writing lab and access to technology	Anger-management support	• Eating disorders
Training on study skills, time management, and organizational skills	Alternative suspension placement	• Homelessness
Tutoring services during and after school	Yoga classes	• Grief
Mentoring programs	Meditation	• Sexual abuse
Information regarding school clubs and academic honor societies	Behavioral and psychological testing	• Sexual identity, including LGBTQPIA
Community service opportunities	Probation services	• Depression
ACT and SAT fee waiver assistance	Assistance in dealing with bullying and harassment	• Family changes and divorce
Test preparation for the ACCUPLACER, ASVAB, ACT, SAT, and GED	Stress-release and stress-management support	• Sexual activity
College selection and scholarship assistance	Social-media management support	• Mental health
Career shadowing, internships, and jobs	Teacher-student mediation	• Self-esteem
YouScience assessment	Support on building healthy relationships	• Gang resistance
Access to recruiters from all military branches, including National Guard and reserves personnel	Wellness and nutrition assistance	• Violence at home
	Assistance in job skills, including:	• Cutting and self-harm
	• Interview skills	• Substance abuse
	• Résumé writing	• Pornography habits
	• Dressing for success	• Family counseling
	• Professional etiquette	• Teen parenting-skills assistance
		• Suicide prevention
		Counseling for students in families struggling with substance abuse, incarceration, and mental- and physical-health concerns
		Food pantry
		Clothes closet

I understand that by signing, I consent to my student participating in services at the Wraparound Center. I also understand that at any time, I can revoke my consent by written, dated communication.

_____   _____
Student name (printed)   Date

_____   _____
Parent or guardian name (printed)   Parent or guardian signature

_____   _____
Wraparound Center representative signature   Date

Figure 8.3: Sample parental permission form.

health or any services provided by individuals who are not school district employees may require specific permission. We discuss parental permission for one-on-one clinical services at the end of this chapter (page 203).

In addition to providing schoolwide communication to parents and gaining parents' permission for services, conduct your Student Voice Needs Survey in the first few weeks of each school year. As discussed in chapter 3 (page 63), we recommend revisiting your schoolwide Student Voice Needs Survey each year, reviewing the survey content with a small but representative committee of students to make any needed changes. Involving students in the rollout of the survey will help build student trust, buy-in, and transparency. Use this survey to determine and review annual priorities, educate students about opportunities for service, destigmatize conversations about barriers, quantify student interest, and estimate caseloads.

Additionally, we recommend keeping your annual large-group Student Voice Needs Survey anonymous. In our experience, client schools that have conducted non-anonymous surveys schoolwide have found themselves overwhelmed with data requiring immediate response, such as individuals requesting assistance with self-harm, suicide ideation, sexual abuse, or domestic violence. You might also inadvertently create expectations of services being made immediately available unless you word your survey very carefully. Should your school decide to proceed with non-anonymous surveys, consider a phased rollout of the survey with plans in place to quickly respond to urgent requests and those requiring mandatory follow-up and reporting. For example, conduct surveys in ten homerooms every other day, starting with seniors. During the time between survey administrations, allow time for designated staff to immediately review all results and respond as necessary. If you can ensure immediate follow-up, you may even consider adding an item on the survey for students to check if they have an urgent need related to health or safety. Continue through the junior, sophomore, and freshman classes.

Walk-In and Referral System

Make your wraparound center walk-in (what we call a *self-referral*) friendly by keeping procedures simple. Deputize staff members (counselors, family liaisons, or social workers) as navigators who connect students and families with appropriate personnel. Rather than constructing barriers to entry, make sure every door offers a pathway to the right connection so people do not encounter a "wrong door" or come at the "wrong time" when seeking assistance. In the following example, a school's processes (and prerequisites) for providing assistance become barriers to connecting students and families with the wraparound center's services.

> *Parents must attend an evening meeting, where they receive a code to create an account for an online platform to request assistance. Parents and students must each complete an online questionnaire via that platform. Failure to complete the questionnaire by the start of school on the morning of their scheduled appointment results in the appointment being canceled. Wait times for an appointment are frequently several weeks or longer.*

Several problems present in this scenario stand out, particularly the extreme wait times for services that may require immediate attention. Additionally, students whose parents miss the once-a-semester overview evening where programming is explained are at an immediate disadvantage from the start—resulting in overtly inequitable access to services.

Most students and families come to your wraparound center because they have a need. Some needs might be simple, like meeting with a tutor or mentor. For those transactional situations, easy access becomes the top priority of the check-in process. Other situations, such as those involving therapy, basic needs related to poverty, or a student or family in crisis, require a more sensitive, high-touch approach. In any case, you must avoid creating the sorts of roadblocks apparent in the preceding example. Such roadblocks will impede students and families in need and imply the convenience and protocols of the provider are the top priority.

Even when connecting students with clinical services, the feel shouldn't be clinical or sterile. Your designated navigators should guide students through your processes for connecting with services. Choose people capable of establishing a rapport through gentle, respectful communication about student and family challenges and the possibility of engaging in new and healthier behaviors (Naar-King & Suarez, 2011). In all cases, a warm, welcoming environment helps put students and families at ease.

In most instances, referrals will come to your wraparound center from the following avenues.

- Self-referrals (student or family walk-ins)
- Faculty or staff referrals for students and families
- Priority students
- Discipline referrals
- Parent or guardian referrals
- Referrals based on returns from extended absences
- Referrals to co-located external partners

The following sections address each of these and describe how wraparound staff can best facilitate referrals.

Self-Referrals

In addition to hearing about services through the communication efforts of the school, students and families are likely to organically hear service information through word of mouth, from one student or family member to the next. After hearing about the possibility of assistance, expect parents to walk in, often without an appointment, and share their story and their needs. These self-referrals are a clear sign that students and families feel the school wants to help them. As you plan for the day-to-day operations of your center, proactively plan for welcoming these walk-ins, and coach staff in understanding the opportunity these unscheduled encounters represent.

A simple physical or digital sign-in log (whichever is the most appropriate for the situation) lets you keep a running tally of the number of visits, taking care to protect student identity when appropriate. *Never* treat walk-in visitors like a burden or an interruption. One unpleasant experience in your center can create a ripple effect of negative word of mouth that may discourage others from coming.

"

When students come to our center, they check themselves in via a scan of their student ID by choosing the purpose of their visit in a drop-down menu. Our database is updated with this information. In the case of an emergency situation, we first help the student, then document the visit.

As director, I can access all the data, while partners are allowed limited access to the data related to their caseloads.

While it took a bit of work to create, an automated check-in saves us time in the long run by eliminating data entry—giving us more time to work with students and their families.

—Igola Richardson, director of the SAFE Center, Banneker High School, Atlanta, Georgia

"

As previously stated, wraparound staff must be open-minded, flexible, compassionate individuals who are skilled in listening and motivational interviewing. It is particularly important they embrace their role as navigators. Receive visitors with empathy while demonstrating you understand that they may be missing work, they may need assistance with basic needs, they may be coming to share a difficult story, or they may be struggling through a lack of transportation. These individuals and these challenges are your purpose, and these families and students are the incarnations of your wildly important goal.

A Word About Mental Health, Trauma, and ACEs

Barr and Gibson (2020) explain:

> Students impacted by trauma and adverse experiences may exhibit a wide range of behaviors that are detrimental to learning and cause difficulties with developing healthy relationships. These students may struggle with self-regulation, which can lead to impulsivity and aggression. They may overreact to events and misinterpret them as threatening or aggressive, or they may refuse to respond to adults in the school through behaving defiantly, acting out, or becoming passive. Some students suffering from trauma may simply withdraw from their surroundings. When triggered by some perceived threat, be it physical, emotional, environmental, or social (the brain does not differentiate among threats and responds the same way to all), people respond with some form of *fight*, *flight*, or *freeze* (Hammond, 2015). (p. 39)

Faculty or Staff Referrals for Students and Families

Ideally, the faculty and staff at your school will consider themselves part of the wraparound effort; they won't see the effort as something relegated to wraparound staff or separate from the overall school experience. Consider your wraparound staff a resource to connect school or district staff members with professional learning related to social-emotional supports, trauma- and poverty-informed practices, the science of addiction, motivational interviewing, and more. If you've shared your student voice data and artifacts as well as community data with your staff, you're already well on your way to having informed, observant faculty who help students and their families connect with the support and services your center provides.

voices FROM THE FIELD

The following was written in response to this prompt: Think about a time when you were struggling. Who or what gave you hope?

Ms. Nesbitt helped me get the help I needed. She could tell something was wrong, and she didn't just ignore me or just let it go. She asked, and she kept asking. First, she talked to me about the Center, and she encouraged me to go and see it and talk to someone on staff about what was happening. Then, when I came back to class, she asked me about my visit to the Center and asked me how it went. I told her I didn't go. She took me outside in the hallway and encouraged me again to go and get some help for myself, and she gave me a pass to the Center. I didn't go, but Ms. Nesbitt checked, and when I went back to class, she knew I hadn't gone. Ms. Nesbitt talked to me again, but this time, she took me to the Center. Ms. Nesbitt introduced me to the director and stayed with me. Soon, I was able to start meeting with a therapist, and it has really helped me cope with what is going on in my life.

—High school student

School and district staff and faculty need to understand what your wraparound center offers as well as how they can identify needs for those who may not self-refer. Host tours of your wraparound center for staff and faculty (perhaps with their students), explaining the services and activities you offer and how to connect with them. Share student voice examples, like those in figure 8.4 (page 200), to inform staff's student-watching skills. Notice some of the students' comments about what happens when their anxiety peaks, such as *stuttering, talking to myself, foot tapping, looking at my phone,* and *hiding in my clothes.* In isolation, these behaviors would not identify a student as a potential candidate for services; however, to an informed educator who observes the student in a holistic and informed manner, this knowledge might alert the teacher to watch for other behavioral trends or risk factors.

Sometimes, teachers, administrators, counselors, and social workers are the first point of contact for families who receive assistance from the Center. When staff members speak with parents and guardians about a student's concern, they may hear about struggles the family is experiencing. At this point, staff members can make a referral to the wraparound center for follow-up, or they can give a parent or guardian relevant information about services and partners in the wraparound center. By developing all staff and faculty's observation and listening skills, you're more likely to reach students and families who may otherwise fall through the cracks.

When my anxiety peaks at school, others might see... (personal behaviors)

I stutter
aggressive/Mad
fidgeting
panic attacks
I disassociate
Speed walking
breathing fast
talking to myself
Chest pain
Sleeping in class
stupid-or think I'm crazy
nervous laughter
foot tapping
wide eyes
stretching - slapping fingers
Walking out of class
can't focus

Picking at my clothes
Shaking
I walk away
Eyes watering
Itching
leg bounces
not making eye contact
looking at my phone
Isolation
going to the bathroom a lot
↳ I just cry
Avoiding others
crying
Being rude
Stare off in distance
paranoia

Source: © 2020 *The Centergy Project.*

Figure 8.4: Example student voice data on what others would see when students are anxious.

A Word About Mental Health, Trauma, and ACEs

Hendershott (2016) states:

> I believe that the biggest piece missing for most of our wounded youth is the sense of being a valued member of community or belonging. Feeling isolated or having the feeling that no one understands just seems to deepen the sense of hopelessness in the wounded person. (p. 47)

Priority Students

In addition to individual staff referrals, take a proactive approach to prioritize students who are at risk due to both internalized and externalized symptoms. According to child psychology expert Lauren DiMaria:

> Due to the quiet nature of internalizing symptoms, children may not receive treatment as quickly as those with more disruptive or externalizing symptoms. In fact, because they are often disruptive and noticeable to others around them, externalizing symptoms in children have received quite a bit more attention and research than those of internalizing symptoms, but that is starting to change. (DiMaria & Gans, 2020)

School interventions often identify priority students based on those who frequently appear three lists: behavior infractions, academic struggles, or poor attendance. Relying solely on these criteria might overlook internalizers, who DiMaria and Gans (2020) explain are more likely to engage in the following behaviors.

- Withdraw
- Seem nervous or irritable
- Not talk
- Experience unexplained headaches, stomachaches, and other physical symptoms
- Have difficulty concentrating
- Sleep more or less than usual
- Eat more or less than usual

Enlightened staff view these students less as apathetic or troublemakers and more as students with unmet needs. Of note, school nurses are often excellent sources for identifying priority students who may be frequent visitors to the school clinic.

In addition, schools may choose to prioritize those students who are living in foster care or those who are living in an unaccompanied fashion, meaning they are living with fictive kin without the presence of a parent. These students deserve special attention because, according to the Development Services Group and Child Welfare Information Gateway (2015):

> Youth in foster care are often exposed to multiple risk factors, putting them *at risk* for negative outcomes. Intervention and prevention efforts intended to reduce risk factor exposure can be effective, but they may also take longer to show evidence of impact. At the same time, children and youth in foster care

are considered to be already *in risk* given the conditions leading up to their placement in foster care. (p. 1)

As we discussed in chapter 7 (page 163), schools with a wraparound center and co-located service providers can individually, strategically, and compassionately support high-need and off-track students. Encourage faculty and staff to reach out to these students to connect them with services appropriate to their situation.

voices FROM THE FIELD

We develop our prioritized student list from students with discipline, attendance, and academic issues. Each student is assigned a staff member from our student-support team who develops a personal relationship with the student and helps them connect with services in our center.

—Igola Richardson, director of the SAFE Center, Banneker High School, Atlanta, Georgia

Discipline Referrals

One powerful aspect of connecting students with services is it may revise school discipline as it relates to student and staff relationships, disproportionality, and both in-school and out-of-school suspensions. If your school adopts restorative practices as discussed in chapter 7, wraparound services will become one potential path for addressing discipline issues in a manner that helps students repair harm, restore relationships, and address root causes. Some school systems update their discipline policies to include wraparound services as a disciplinary response and as a prerequisite for formal processes such as placement in an alternative setting or tribunals. In extreme instances, services or placement in the wraparound center may not be an option; however, your established partners may still prove to be a resource for the student or family by providing services or support in an off-campus location.

voices FROM THE FIELD

The biggest change in my life that has come from our center is that I am learning to respond to my life and not react to it.

—High school student

The best thing about our center is there is a place I can go in school where I am not judged only by my one worst day.

— High school student

What helps me come back from something difficult is choices and opportunity—having some control over my next steps.

— High school student

A school utilizing services provided through a wraparound center in lieu of out-of-school suspension should strive to achieve three goals: (1) students returning to class with higher grades than they had at the time of the infraction as a result of in-school academic tutoring and assignment completion, (2) a deeper connection with their school and its staff, and (3) an individualized plan of support and intervention that will directly address the infraction's root causes, the ability for the student to voluntarily reconnect with the Center, and the student's growing skills.

voices FROM THE FIELD

When we opened our center, all students who were suspended for fighting were required to attend a professional mediation facilitated by one of our on-site partners. The students were also invited to join the anger-management support group called Wisdom Over Anger. After one to two days out of school, students were offered the opportunity to serve the remainder of their suspension in the Center. There, they completed their daily assignments and made up previously missed work with the help of on-site tutors. We never required any students to come to the Center to offset their suspension, but the option was almost always available. Both students and their parents were eager for an alternative to days out of school. Through restorative practices, the Center was negating an average of eighty-four suspension days a month within the first quarter of opening.

—Leigh Colburn

Parent or Guardian Referrals

In addition to walk-ins (self-referrals), keep it easy for parents and guardians to refer their children for wraparound services. You might develop a simple referral form for parents to fill out, such as the very basic one illustrated in figure 8.5 (page 204). Although you may use such a form (a paper form or online), we advise you to also accept referrals by phone calls and emails. In Leigh's experience, many parent referrals occur in person immediately following a meeting between a parent and an administrator, staff member, or faculty member. When the parent or guardian voices the desire to make a referral, a school staff member walks the parent or guardian to the wraparound center and introduces him or her to a wraparound staff member.

Of course, before parents and guardians can refer their children to your wraparound center, you must establish regular communication and promotion of your center's services so your students' families know about the services you offer. The following ideas will promote your work to your parent and guardian population.

- Include information on how to contact your wraparound center in all communications and on your school website.

- Work with your school administration to include information about your wraparound center in newsletters that go to your parent population.

Name of person making referral: _____

Name of person being referred, along with his or her relationship to the referrer (self, friend, parent, teacher, or other): _____

Need category (or categories):

☐ Academic, college, and career

☐ Behavior and life skills

☐ Community partnerships (outside expertise)

☐ Family needs

List any specific programs under the categories you selected that reflect the nature of your need. For example, family needs could include access to our food pantry, housing assistance, or financial counseling for college expenses. If you are unsure what specific programs might align with your need, please leave this space blank.

Signature of referrer: _____ Date: _____

Figure 8.5: Example referral form for wraparound services.

*Visit **go.SolutionTree.com/leadership** for a free reproducible version of this figure.*

- Attend PTA or PTO meetings to let parents know about the services you offer and ways they can connect with services or volunteer opportunities. Additionally, have your center open for parents to tour and initiate contact during these meetings.

- Host a beginning-of-year open house and a mid-year open house for parents.

- Host events such as career fairs, provider fairs, or health fairs.

- Host an educational event that connects to wraparound services. For example, show the film *Angst* (Skerritt, 2017), which is about teen anxiety, and follow the movie with a question-and-answer session with a panel of local mental health practitioners who can provide support via your wrapround center.

Referrals Based on Returns From Extended Absences

Students returning from an extended absence often need a transition period to ease back into the daily school routine. Whether their absence was related to mental or physical health, the birth of a baby, or discipline issues, students in conversation circles tell us they frequently face social reintegration anxiety simply answering the question, "Where have you been?" or managing the gossip their absence and return generates.

Your wraparound center can help students ease back into school by providing welcomed support as these students return to full-time school. For example, allow students to return to the Center prior to returning to class, if they desire. Offer students the option to have lunch in your center for a few weeks until they are comfortable returning to the cafeteria. Also, position your wraparound center as a facilitator by offering partial days and targeted, individual academic assistance. This assistance can include having the students meet with teachers and tutors in your wraparound center to prioritize work missed and determine how to move forward academically in a manageable and effective way.

Referrals to Co-Located Partners

The parental permission form and referrals we've covered up to this point only allow students to access general school-run services at your wraparound center. When connecting a student with a clinician or other nonschool employee for one-on-one services or support groups, you'll need separate and specific parental permission. Likely, the co-located partner will need more substantial information about the student and, potentially, his or her family. (Think of the kind of information you must provide when visiting a professional practice such as a doctor's or dentist's office.)

To make a difficult process easier for both students and families, work with your partners to streamline this intake process so families don't have to complete redundant paperwork. Also, create a common form asking for the information most provider agencies need, such as directory information, the student's date of birth, parental contact information, a copy of the parent's driver's license, a copy of the insurance card (if the student is insured), and basics of family history (if applicable). You can then copy this common form and attach it to the specialized forms co-located partners require.

Develop an Individual Student Voice Needs Survey

Thus far, we have suggested that you have every student anonymously complete the Student Voice Needs Survey so you can gather aggregate data for determining student needs, projecting caseloads, and planning services and partnerships. However, utilizing a non-anonymous Individual Student Voice Needs Survey serves a vital function in the referral and intake process for identifying the specific needs of a particular student and connecting him or her with services.

You have two options for how you can administer this Individual Student Voice Needs Survey: (1) as a pencil-and-paper survey or (2) as an online survey. You can find an example of the former along with this book's other online reproducibles (visit **go.SolutionTree.com /leadership**). Regardless of your choice, the survey should then lead to one-on-one discussions with students about their needs. To create a warm, personal, and safe environment, use a printed copy of the student's completed survey in the discussion, rather than reviewing the results on a screen. Visual tools are also an excellent way to engage students while reducing eye contact, which can make students uncomfortable (Naar-King & Suarez, 2011).

Use the Individual Student Voice Needs Survey to connect with your students on a personal level—a level of special importance if they come to you for assistance. When approached in a compassionate manner, the completion of an Individual Student Voice

Needs Survey can serve as an informative ticket in the door for a respectful, inquisitive touch base with wraparound center staff. Once the student is in the door, the survey can help a staff member start a one-on-one conversation about the student's perspective about his or her needs. Further, the survey educates the student about the breadth of the services the wraparound center offers while destigmatizing and encouraging self-advocacy around sensitive subjects. These conversations are where your wildly important goal comes to life—connecting students to services.

voices FROM THE FIELD

> Although we do not generally recommend using a survey with a student in active distress, I did so once. I was meeting with a student who was overwhelmed with emotion and could not talk. I introduced the survey as a visual and conversational tool that might help the student put his emotion and needs into words. Using the survey as an educational tool regarding services and a guide for our conversation, we were able to unpack and identify the student's needs.
>
> —Linda Beggs

Conclusion

Connecting students and families with services culminates the work you began with your first conversation circle. Through this journey, you have built trust in your school—not through public relations alone but "almost one person at a time and face to face" (Schlechty, 2009, p. 202). In addition, you are positively influencing three of five primary factors related to socioeconomic mobility that economist Raj Chetty and his colleagues identify (as cited in Putnam, 2015): (1) family stability, (2) school quality, and (3) community cohesion. (The other two factors are residential segregation and income inequality, factors not within a school's or district's control.)

Keeping your work grounded in student voice deepens the web of interpersonal relationships at your school while ensuring your services remain relevant to your students and families. Creating measures meaningful to your school, your partners, and your community allows you to assess your results for what works as well as what needs improvement. The net effect of marrying student voice with meaningful measures is *focus*—meaning day-to-day activities are tied to your wildly important goals (McChesney et al., 2012).

In the next chapter, we examine how you can ensure the wraparound services you've established can sustain long into the future.

Chapter 9

SUSTAIN WRAPAROUND PROGRAMMING

You can't sell a melted popsicle.

—Beverly McAfee, community advocate

The concept of a wraparound center makes sense to students, parents, community members, and donors. We find it easy to get others on board with the concept, but sustainability requires the ability to execute. If your students don't utilize your center; if you don't nurture relationships with students, families, and partners; and if you don't keep your center in the forefront of your community's thinking, it will become last year's (or the last superintendent's) new thing. Donors and partners will find other initiatives to support.

As with any initiative, you'll face plenty of obstacles along the way to distract you from your mission, including bureaucracy, policies, inertia, perceived (and real) lack of resources, competing priorities, and politics. Added to these is a necessary school and district mindset shift toward a whole child approach and wraparound services—a shift partially evidenced by the flexibility and collaboration required to co-locate embedded service providers. The culture change and new behaviors are required of everyone to influence not only the meaningful connection of students and families with services but also the long-range, positive impact of your wraparound efforts.

While your mission statement proclaims your *why*, sustainability requires you to *stay* with your why. This chapter highlights five major practices for maintaining your why and keeping your wraparound center vibrant.

1. Remain grounded in student voice.

2. Assess progress.

3. Navigate leadership changes.

4. Keep the work relevant to the whole school.

5. Manage funding.

As you examine these topics in this chapter, reflect on the full scope of the Centergy Cycle as depicted in table 9.1.

Table 9.1: Steps in the Centergy Cycle

	Process	Purpose
Step 1: Identify Needs	Conversation circles	Gather broad information about academic achievement, social-emotional wellness, and family engagement.
	Off-track interviews	Conduct personal conversations with off-track students to learn about barriers and develop action plans when appropriate.
	Graduation stories	Gather reflective feedback from graduates on their school experiences.
Step 2: Establish Priorities	Student Voice Needs Survey	Anonymous (large group and aggregate): Quantify student needs to establish priorities and project potential caseloads.
		Individual (personal and identifiable): Connect individual students with services.
	Focus groups and individual focused conversations	Delve into specific barriers to understand student perspectives and elicit programming suggestions.
Step 3: Identify Resources	Types of resources	Identify sources of labor, funding, and in-kind donations as volunteers, donors, or partners.
	Full-spectrum programming	Explore four stages of full-spectrum programming: 1. Prevention 2. Education 3. Support (intervention) 4. Sustainability (recovery)
	Community asset mapping	Work with the following groups to identify community resources: • Student-support staff • Faculty • School and district staff • Community Choose an approach
Step 4: Establish Partnerships	Choose credible partners	Analyze opportunity and risk. Hold partnership planning meetings. Establish parameters of a MOU.
	Conduct a community strategic-planning meeting	Introduce partners to one another. Provide an overview of initiative. Develop a mission statement. Build collective energy.
	Strengthen and sustain partnerships	Reciprocate the partnership. Introduce partners to your school. Establish regular communication.

	Process	Purpose
Step 5: Secure Funding	State and federal school funding	Understand the ESSA (2015) and how it developed. Review federal title funding programs. Explore intervention funding.
	Fundraising and other external fundraising streams	Clarify the role of the wraparound director. Learn about 501(c)(3) organizations and funding streams. Establish systems for bookkeeping and donation tracking.
	Braided funding	Plan for melding both federal and state funding with community-driven funding, including cash donations, in-kind donations, and grants.
Step 6: Create Your Wraparound Structure	The *what*: Developing programming based on student voice	Review student voice data. Review partnerships. Continue gathering student voice.
	The *how*: Developing an organizational structure	Hire a director. Determine staffing. Create a student board of directors.
	The *where*: Designing spaces for connecting students and families with services	Select a space for wraparound services. Involve students in designing your spaces.
	The *who*: Reaching the whole school, identified groups, and individual students	Plan services for the entire student body.
Step 7: Connect Students and Families With Services	Measure what matters.	Answer the following questions. • What do we need? • What are we doing? • How is it going?
	Establish processes and procedures that ensure and enhance connection with services.	Conduct a school-year kickoff. Establish walk-in and referral systems.
	Develop an Individual Student Voice Needs Survey.	Determine individual student needs.

A Word About Mental Health, Trauma, and ACEs

According to the Child Mind Institute (2016):

With their concentrations of children and trained caregivers, schools are an ideal place to leverage evidence-based mental health knowledge and make a transformative impact on the mental health landscape of this country.

Young people with access to mental health services in school-based health centers are 10 times more likely to seek care for mental health or substance abuse than those who do not. (p. 13)

Remain Grounded in Student Voice

As we stress throughout this book, gathering student voice should become a pervasive practice, not something done in the early stages of wraparound development and never repeated. Your school's student body is not static. Your school continually receives incoming freshmen and transfer students. Plus, life happens, and students frequently experience the ups and downs that come with adolescence and young adulthood. You can count on your students' needs being dynamic.

Seize the opportunity to keep your work relevant by prioritizing student voice. To do this, revisit the Centergy Cycle step 1 and step 2 voice processes through the lens of sustainability. When you're preparing to launch wraparound services, step 2 builds on step 1. For example, you should design the Student Voice Needs Survey based on data gathered from conversation circles. Once you're delivering services, each student voice process develops with a rhythm of its own.

The following sections offer guidance on how you can continue to gather student voice data for the long term through the processes listed in table 9.1 (page 208) for steps 1 and 2. If you need a refresher on core aspects of each of these topics, it may be useful to revisit chapter 2 (page 35) and chapter 3 (page 63).

Conversation Circles

Your initial conversation circles created the backbone of your Student Voice Needs Survey through inquiry into academic, social-emotional, and family needs. But subsequent conversation circles can serve various purposes, such as the following (as introduced in chapter 2).

- **Inquiry:** Includes identifying student needs and barriers to learning, clarifying perceptions, and exploring ideas or concerns related to instruction, climate, or safety

- **Brainstorming:** Includes generating actionable plans for carrying out items such as grade-level spirit activities, increasing participation in school activities, and planning events

- **Problem solving:** Includes addressing or troubleshooting problems, such as littering on campus or cell phone use during class

- **Improvement:** Includes refining or fine-tuning practices, such as arrival and dismissal processes; pep rallies; and programming, process, and policy development

Continuing these purposeful conversations not only fuels school-improvement efforts but also strengthens relationships while you keep your finger on the pulse of students' lives. Beware of concentrating the facilitation responsibilities of these essential interactions to a few people, because when those people leave (as everyone ultimately does), the practice can easily wither away as "something we used to do." Instead, deputize and train a cadre of staff members—administrators, counselors, social workers, and faculty—who can conduct conversation circles regularly enough for them to become part of the culture. Strive to make the saying, "Let's ask our students," prevalent in your school.

Off-Track Interviews

In many schools, there is no internal or external pressure to engage in individual conversation with struggling students. As such, off-track interviews can slip through the cracks. If your counseling department handles off-track interviews, these conversations with struggling students can quickly take a back seat to scheduling, withdrawals, testing, and college and career counseling. Yet continually holding and refreshing these conversations yields opportunities to help some of your most vulnerable students while learning about barriers other students might face.

Have your wraparound team develop criteria regarding which students to interview, such as those who are more than one year off track for graduation, students with a GPA of less than 2.0, students who counselors and the school nurse identify as internalizers, and students with more than ten unexcused absences. We advise setting a monthly target for the number of off-track interviews your team will conduct. Build in an accountability structure, such as a scoreboard (not visible to students) tracking the number of interviews conducted, cited barriers, and resulting action steps.

Graduation Stories

Getting the most out of graduation stories depends on two critical elements: (1) leadership and (2) execution. Without these, the results will be tepid and not worth the effort. But if you execute the processes with intentionality and fidelity (as we described in chapter 2, page 35), you'll find graduation stories among the most valuable feedback you receive.

Adding graduation stories to the principal's list of things to do amid the year-end whirlwind is a tall order. For a high school principal, the end of the school year can be described as "the best of times and the worst of times"—both practically and emotionally. Practically, it's jam-packed with senior banquets, honors nights, testing, and other year-end activities, resulting in eighteen-hour days of nonstop activity. Emotionally, principals share the joys and sorrows of their seniors—from students who are celebrating full-ride scholarships to their dream schools to students who are grieving over deceased parents absent from their graduation to students who have not achieved the goal of graduation.

Yet in the middle of the bustle lies a once-in-a-student's-lifetime opportunity to gather the voices of your graduating seniors. Unlike conversation circles, graduation stories work best when their execution is left in the hands of one person—ideally the principal—or a select few people, who make a personal appeal to your senior class. This makes the activity especially vulnerable to leadership changes (more about that in a bit).

The best insurance to give graduation stories a lasting foothold in your school's culture is to execute them well. Remember that efficiency can be the enemy—robbing you of the opportunity to authentically engage with your graduates as they leave your school. Seniors get caught up in the year-end hoopla before graduation and will likely pay little heed to one more announcement, email, or link to check off an optional box. Instead, execute graduation stories with commitment, curiosity, and authenticity, and then share selected (and anonymous) stories with your faculty and community.

voices
FROM THE FIELD

We were working with a newly appointed high school principal who committed to soliciting graduation stories from his first class of seniors. Despite all the competing priorities, principal Jamie Green carved out time to talk to the class about the activity and its importance to him personally and then delegated the execution to a trusted staff member. I knew they had captured lightning in a bottle when I got this simple text from him: "Reading through my seniors' stories today. My eyes are 'sweating.' Awesome experience."

I have confidence graduation stories will be a priority for him as long as he's a school leader.

—Leigh Colburn

Student Voice Needs Survey

Your annual schoolwide Student Voice Needs Survey needs to stay fresh and relevant. Work with a small but representative committee of students to review the survey content and make any needed changes. Be sure to include any new partners or services on the survey. For example, if your school opens a health clinic, you might want to broaden the available responses to include its specific services, such as assistance with medical, dental, or vision care. You could further augment these data with a series of questions inquiring about medical causes of absenteeism.

As your schoolwide survey evolves, so will the survey you conduct with individual students. You will continually refine it to match the services you have available within your center. As a reminder, you should design the Individual Student Voice Needs Survey (see page 205) for the explicit purpose of facilitating conversation about a single student's needs so that you can better match him or her (and his or her family) to your services. Both types of surveys will continue to inform the work of your wraparound center and provide valuable data for programming and reporting.

Focus Groups and Individual Focused Conversations

As your center evolves, focus groups become the main driver for programming development, improvement, and evaluation. Consider focus groups a deeper dive into barriers and their real-time effect on students. Continually look for opportunities and service gaps revealed through your other voice processes. Then, gather a focus group of students to help flesh out the needs and brainstorm full-spectrum programming.

In addition, use focus groups to improve and evaluate the effectiveness of existing programming. Here are some examples of subgroups to invite to elicit feedback on what's working and what needs improving.

- Students participating in mentoring programs
- Students participating in tutoring

- Students who participated in an activity (or those who expressed interest but didn't participate)
- Families participating in food distribution

Finally, it's important to use the results of your work to enhance the visibility of your wraparound center and the benefits students and families gain from accessing it. Ask the student newspaper to write informative articles regarding the services available, programming, and any special activities that take place in the wraparound center. Highlight student voices on your school's walls with displays of data, voice charts from conversation circles and focus groups, student narratives, and photographs and student reviews of activities within the wraparound center. Regularly rotate the displays so they don't become stale. Whenever possible, create the displays such that they foster engagement; for example, make emoji stickers or sticky notes available for students to document their thoughts, encouragements, and responses. Creating and monitoring the displays should be the shared duty of students and someone on staff.

Assess Progress

In chapter 8 (page 187), we introduced the concept of the wildly important goal as related to connecting students and families with wraparound services and establishing measurements to support the goal. While setting up measurement systems is important when launching your services, continuing to measure is vital for sustainability. Your results not only identify areas for improvement and provide information for partner and grant sustainability but also can help continually validate your wraparound efforts' value to your community. Without feedback, you'll be flying blind in hope that your work is having an impact and will continue to receive support.

Although measurements are critical, they won't be enough to attract others to join your movement or captivate your community's attention. Even in the world of evidence-based decision making, stories matter. Nick Morgan (2014), president and founder of communications consulting firm Public Words, puts it this way: "Good stories—with a few key facts woven in—are what attach emotions to your argument, prompt people into unconscious decision making, and ultimately move them to action." Let's look at some practices that will help your team build the story of your wraparound center: telling your story, adding some facts, tying it all together, and reacting to and preventing failure.

Telling Your Story

Your wraparound center's story is ultimately the story of your students, so you can't tell it without their voice. Your students' narratives contain a treasure trove of stories running the gamut from tragedy to triumph. Approach these stories with the respect and sensitivity they deserve, and *never* expose or exploit a student's or family's situation.

Of the student voice processes we've introduced, graduation stories present the purest form of stories from students with little to gain—or lose—from sharing their unvarnished thoughts. Read graduation stories to learn from students what works and what needs improvement, setting aside relevant stories to share with your stakeholders. Likewise, develop the habit of reading *all* student narratives with an eye on both documenting efficacy and improving processes.

In addition to implementing the processes of steps 1 and 2, collect reflective feedback from your student body about interactions with your wraparound center, asking a combination of qualitative and quantitative questions, like those found in the sample student feedback form in chapter 8 (figure 8.2, page 194). Invite similar feedback from your partners.

voices FROM THE FIELD

This [wraparound] program should be implemented in more schools. Kudos to the school district for taking the risk to create something so meaningful. You have demonstrated leadership, compassion, and courage to do what is right for students. I have watched the love for students and student success incarnate in just a few months into a center that is improving the lives of your students and families. The passion and energy displayed through the constant laboring and collaborating with other entities is contagious and hopeful. The referral process has been made super easy, and services are offered immediately. Thank you for creating this partnership.

—Eunice Coley, Juvenile Probation Services

Whenever possible, seek opportunities to showcase the Center as a place that grows the seeds of resilience Barr and Gibson (2020) write about—belonging, optimism, self-worth, self-regulation, and purpose. Parents, students, staff, and partners will respond to authentic voices, open-mindedness, grace, and the opportunity to have respectful and important conversations. As we we prepared to publish this book, we were in the midst of 2020, a year that featured unprecedented uncertainty and turmoil for the United States and the world. Perhaps now more than ever, schools need wraparound centers. By leaning into this important work, you can work with your community to seek the truth, speak the truth, stretch yourself, and serve others. Through wraparound centers, schools can gather and share the stories of their community. Furthermore, schools have the opportunity to become *the place* where communities can come together to not only examine barriers but also find solutions. Most important and relevant to your work is this: the story of wraparound is a story of compassion, reconciliation, healing, and hope.

Adding Some Facts

As we discussed in chapter 8 (page 187), pointing to hard measurements (facts) of wraparound services' effectiveness is challenging because some desired outcomes are difficult to quantify, such as a sense of belonging and self-worth. Adding to that challenge are the countless variables that contribute to academic achievement, such as "students' personal factors, their interactions with others such as parents, teachers, and administrators, and lastly the larger systems that surround the student e.g. school districts, neighborhoods, local economy, political policy, and multicultural relations" (Bertolini, Stremmel, & Thorngren, 2012, p. 2). Nevertheless, people want to know the answer to the question, "Does wraparound work?"

In 2010, Joplin, Missouri, school superintendent C. J. Huff spearheaded an effort to engage his community in transforming its education system (Bright Futures, n.d.). This ultimately led to the formation of the national organization Bright Futures USA (www.bright futuresusa.org). Working in many communities, Bright Futures encourages school and community leaders to broaden their metrics of efficacy beyond academic measures to include indicators of well-being (Broader, Bolder Approach to Education, n.d.).

In chapter 8 (page 187), we also suggested tracking measures for services your center provides, such as the use of care closets, days of offset suspension, attendance, caseloads, and so on. After launching services, start to assess the impact those activities have on metrics important to the school or district, such as increasing graduation rates, increasing the number of students enrolled in honors courses, increasing attendance, decreasing cohort dropout rates, and decreasing discipline referrals (including recidivism). Teasing out wraparound services' impact on academic performance is an imperfect science at best, but it is still worth the effort, and these sorts of measurements will help you accomplish that. Choose criteria based on your school's priorities, and create cohorts of identified students for the purpose of gathering data and tracking achievement. To elaborate on the previous examples, you can specifically calculate the graduation rate of students who participated in a mentoring program, the course pass rates of students who visited your wraparound center for tutoring at least five times during a semester, or the attendance rates of students both before and after they participated in therapeutic services.

Tying It All Together

Marrying stories with relevant data will keep your stakeholders informed while also keeping them focused on your why. This marriage effectively ties together the work of your wraparound center into a compelling story. Let's revisit (in more detail) an example from Leigh's experience that we first wrote about in chapter 4 (page 103).

In 2013, when Leigh was principal at Marietta High School, teachers told her of students enrolled in honors classes who didn't have access to personal computers or Wi-Fi—putting them at a significant disadvantage. Marietta's superintendent, Emily Lembeck, approached the local Kiwanis club (of which she was a member) to gain its help in creating equity by addressing the digital divide. In partnership, the school system and the Kiwanis club developed a program called One Byte at a Time to provide laptops to low-income students taking honors classes. Across seven years, they have provided approximately 140 laptops to Marietta students, who used them during their junior and senior years. The school and club then gifted the devices to students once they graduated. Both the school district and the Kiwanis club publicized this program through various media—newsletters, websites, press releases, and the like. While the initiative is impressive in its own right, the impact of the program came to life in a student's graduation story reflecting on it:

My Graduation Story

May 12, 2017

My biggest challenge in reaching high school graduation occurred during my freshman year when I was taking Pre-Diploma IB classes and needed to have internet and computer access at home. At the time, my parents were having monetary problems. It got to the point where my family had to live with my uncle in the same house in order to pay the rent. Fortunately, living with my uncle's family allowed my parents to stabilize the money situation and provide Wi-Fi for my education. During the end of my sophomore year, I continued the IB program classes, and at the moment, I had no computer access. That was my biggest barrier to keep up with all of the IB classes. Then a survey went out, and it had to do with whether or not we had computer and internet access at home. Then, a few weeks later, I was awarded a Kiwanis Laptop Scholarship. This scholarship made a huge impact on my graduation path. With the help of the computer, I was able to always stay on top of everything that dealt with schoolwork, unlike in the past where I was getting off track for graduation. I am so thankful that programs and organizations like the Kiwanis club take into consideration the student's [sic] problems and make an effort to find a solution and afford help.

Since I had moved a lot before eighth grade, I had no idea what to expect from Marietta High School. But thankfully, Marietta High School is more than a regular high school. Its' [sic] community always goes above and beyond for their students and teachers. With all the programs, I had the opportunity to grow and learn. I became part of the Early Childhood Education Career Pathway and Healthcare Pathway as a freshman, and the teachers were amazing and always motivated me to learn and take responsibility for my future. Those teachers gave me hope for my future. Since the pathways are usually three years long, I always received help and motivation from my career pathway teachers. Thanks to them and all of their hard work, I am ready for college and ready for the workforce in my chosen career pathways.

This simple example shows how intentionally celebrating your work affirms your students, your school, your partners, and the community. It ties the stories and data of your wraparound efforts together. As longtime Kiwanian Bobby Tharpe states:

I always want the kids to realize that they aren't "lucky" to get a laptop. First of all, they are excelling with good grades even without personal connectivity. Secondly, their teachers and school leaders recognize their hard work and good character. Lastly, they live in a community [that] wants to help all its kids succeed. As a Kiwanian, I'm gratified every year at Senior Honors Night when our proud graduates are recognized for their accomplishments and then to reflect on how our club and community had a hand in their success. (personal communication, December 12, 2019)

To sustain your own efforts and marry your center's stories and data, we suggest two places to start: (1) produce an annual report, and (2) invite your community into your wraparound center.

Produce an Annual Report

Plan for and produce an annual report to share with all your stakeholders. Use this space to celebrate the successes of your students, families, school staff, and partners. This is not a time to cut corners on quality. Use graphics, photographs, and color to visually tell the story of the impact your partnerships are having. Keep enough copies of the report on hand to give to potential donors, volunteers, and partners.

Include the following in your annual report.

- Highlights and accomplishments
- The origins of your center
- A list of partners and donors
- A list of staff and services
- Your mission and values statements
- Usage data of your services (see figure 8.1, page 191)
- Calls to action (requests to donate, volunteer, and so on)
- Impact results (graduation rates; attendance or discipline data; participation data; usage or achievement data related to academic, college, and career services or programming; and so on)
- *Lots* of photos and impact statements from students, families, staff, partners, and the community

For an example of an annual report, visit the Resources page on the Centergy Project website (www.thecentergyproject.com/resources).

Invite Your Community Into Your Wraparound Center

Ideally, your wraparound center will buzz with students dropping in to participate in activities, to receive services, or to simply connect with caring adults. Your on-site partners will not be strangers to what's happening every day at your wraparound center. Your community, however, is another story. If you don't open your doors, the greater community won't have the firsthand contact necessary to get a feel for what your work is all about.

Keep your wraparound center in the news by hosting communitywide events such as the following.

- Service projects
- Parent symposiums
- Community, job, and health fairs
- Annual open houses
- Recognition events celebrating the wraparound center's anniversary
- Community forums in collaboration with partners focused on mental health and addiction or awareness events related to community-specific concerns
- Launch events for new services or partnerships

In addition, plan to host periodic tours of your center open to the community as well as educators from other districts.

About Failure

Wraparound directors must be mindful to build safeguards to protect the mission and reputation of the Center, including preventing and responding to failure. The daily work of the wraparound director is twofold: meeting needs of students and their families plus managing wraparound staff.

Misdeeds and scandal occurring within the wraparound center can prove devastating—particularly in your center's first years of operation, when you have no track record of success. To prevent scandal related to personnel, ensure background checks for all staff, all partners, and all volunteers who come in contact with students. Establish careful monitoring and protocols related to any one-on-one involvement or communication with students. Of paramount importance, all wraparound staff must handle and respond to critical situations in a timely, professional, effective, and ethical manner while also conscientiously attending to mandatory reporting of potential self-harm or harm to others.

Always be honest and as transparent as possible about data and funding, and maintain high ethical standards when it comes to reporting and spending. *Always* respect the stories and confidentiality of your students, families, and donors. Due to the collaborative nature of the wraparound center's work, communication about students, families, and donors among staff and partners is necessary, but talking outside the wraparound center, participating in gossip, and speaking of student and family concerns with nonessential staff or community members will quickly erode any and all relational trust you've achieved. Consider sensitive and identifying information about students and families to be walled in as it relates to verbal and written communication.

External issues can also put your wraparound center in the spotlight of controversial issues, especially when they involve your students wanting to take a stand. For example, on March 14, 2018, students across America staged a walkout in response to the school shooting that left seventeen dead at Marjory Stoneman Douglas High School in Parkland, Florida. The national walkout was necessarily handled by local authorities "who seemed divided and even flummoxed about how to handle their emptying classrooms" (Yee & Blinder, 2018). In cases like these, a respectful, thoughtful response can prevent the failure of broken relationships, poor press coverage, and a damaged brand.

When you create a culture that listens to your students (we hope you do!), don't be surprised if they want to take the reins on the issues of the day. We completed this book in the late summer of 2020, with many schools closed due to the COVID-19 pandemic and communities across the United States experiencing high levels of civil unrest. While you should be thoughtful in your guidance and response concerning such issues of national and global importance, this does not mean you should be timid in your advocacy for students. Be aware of how the words of you and your staff are reflected in your wraparound center's social media presence, event planning, and press coverage. Don't let it become a lightning rod for individuals and groups who don't have your holistic mission in mind; seek counsel with seasoned leaders before you speak out to align your center with or against hotbed issues in your community. When in doubt, ground yourself with the following questions.

- What is true?
- What is right?
- What is in the best interest of our students and families?

Despite everyone's best efforts, situations will occur that breach trust. Individuals who work in wraparound centers will make mistakes, like break a confidence or inadvertently jeopardize significant relationships or services. In *The Speed of Trust*, Covey (2018) explains:

> The nature of life is such that all of us will undoubtedly have to deal with broken trust at some time—maybe a number of times—during our lives. Sometimes we do something stupid. We make a mistake in a personal or professional relationship, and we're brought up short by a severely or even overdrawn Trust Account. (p. 301)

So how should you respond when trust is broken? Again, Covey (2018) asserts it is often possible to restore trust by confronting reality with trust-building responses respecting all parties involved. Such responses include the following.

- **Accept responsibility for the situation:** Don't cover up mistakes or blame others.
- **Right wrongs:** Produce an action plan to correct the situation as much as possible as well as update practices to prevent the situation from reoccurring.
- **Keep commitments:** Follow through on your promises, being careful to only promise what you can deliver.

By prioritizing trust—actively working to establish, grow, restore, and wisely extend trust—you will be positioned to turn these failures into important learning for you, your staff, and your community.

On the other hand, sometimes failure is not because of a mistake or misstep by anyone. As you engage in authentic, deep conversations with students, you will sometimes feel like you have opened a Pandora's box of need and dysfunction mixed in with the hope and promise of a better future. Sometimes, despite everyone's best efforts, a student's time with you will end in frustration or even tragedy, not triumph. At these times, be honest with yourself in your assessment of the progress your wraparound center has made while also reflecting on any mistakes or failures that occur. In *Trust First*, community leader Bruce Deel talks about his work in a troubled Atlanta neighborhood: "To commit fully to helping others, I would have to accept that many people would never be saved, not by me, not by themselves, or by anyone else" (Deel & Grace, 2019, p. 87).

The reality is that this *is* a different kind of school work. While educators are not isolated from the heartache of student struggles, signing up for this work means opening yourself up to heartbreak in a more intimate way when students drop out, overdose, go to prison, or die by suicide or some other tragedy.

In the big picture of the wraparound centers, any wrongs you or your staff commit will most likely be instances of commission rather than omission—where individuals attempted to do something and that something went awry. Failing to intervene because we know we can't succeed every time limits the positive impact we *can* have. In turning away from this work, we relegate ourselves to the sidelines where we shake our heads, wring our hands, and desperately hope for the best. Barr and Gibson (2020) quote Fred Rogers, who puts it another way:

> We live in a world in which we need to share responsibility. It's easy to say "It's not my child, not my community, not my world, not my problem." Then there are those who see the need and respond. I consider those people my heroes. (p. 59)

Navigate Leadership Changes

Every initiative depends on effective leadership, and a wraparound initiative only differs insofar as it depends on leadership of *four* areas: (1) the wraparound center, (2) the school, (3) the district, and (4) the partner agencies. When leadership changes in any of these areas, vulnerabilities open up, potentially threatening your mission, funding, and partnerships—in short, the entire effort.

Much of this book centers on establishing, developing, and deepening the relationships between a school and students that are essential to launching relevant services for students and their families. However, to keep those services up and running, you must also prioritize cultivating and nurturing the relational trust and web of relationships among students, families, faculty, administrators, partners, and the community. The best inoculant for sustainability is broad community engagement. "Indeed, the assumption that superintendents and other local leaders will come and go, a reality that poses challenges to school improvement efforts in districts across the country, makes cultivating leadership among a broader set of stakeholders critical to longevity" (Broader, Bolder Approach to Education, n.d.).

Michael D. Watkins (2013), leading expert on accelerating transitions and author of *The First 90 Days*, describes "common traps" during transition, which include "falling prey to the 'action imperative'" (p. 5), when leaders try too hard and too early to put their personal stamp on the organization. He goes on to observe that when leaders act too soon, they fail to learn—leading to bad decisions and resistance.

Further, Watkins (2013) gives good advice for new leaders, whether they be superintendents, principals, or wraparound directors:

> To succeed in your new role, you will need the support of people over whom you have no direct authority. You may have little or no relationship capital at the outset, especially if you're onboarding into a new organization. So you will need to invest energy in building new networks. Start early. Discipline yourself to invest in building up "relationship bank accounts" with people you anticipate needing to work with later. Think hard about whether there are people you haven't met who are likely to be critical to your success. (p. 201)

Let's look at tactics to approach building relationship capital at each level of new leadership—the new wraparound director, new higher leadership (principal or superintendent), and new partner leadership.

New Wraparound Director

Watkins's (2013) admonition of leaders who act too soon and fail to gain support applies especially to wraparound directors who, at most, retain dotted-line supervisory authority over partner staff. The wraparound director functions as a wraparound center's focal point by overseeing all aspects of operations, including nurturing and maintaining partnerships. Despite the title, successful directors see themselves more as colleagues than as bosses, and this understanding is essential when it comes to on-site partnered staff.

Newly hired wraparound directors should put internal and external relationships at the top of their list for the first few months on the job and spend most of their time meeting with students, faculty, administration, donors, and partners. Initially, they should reserve any changes to process for mission-critical items such as student safety and confidentiality.

If you are a new wraparound director, you can build internal relationships by becoming part of the culture—via informal and formal platforms. Create opportunities to interact casually with students and staff, such as hosting a meet-and-greet. Use a theme like "Donuts With the Director" to help drive turnout. Hold conversation circles with students, inviting feedback on an aspect of the wraparound center and assuring them you are not looking for criticism of your predecessor. Become part of the staff by asking to attend faculty and administrative leadership meetings. Seek one-on-one time with school and district leaders to find your shared mission and learn about their vision for the wraparound center.

With external relationships, carve out time to review all MOUs or established processes before scheduling one-on-one meetings with agency heads. This will help you gather greater insights from partnerships concerning what's working, what needs improving, and what will best strengthen the alliances between your school and their agencies. Then, meet with your major donors to learn their priorities for giving, such as homeless youth, military-bound students, or first-generation college attendees. Send out electronic and paper correspondence to all your donors and supporters, introducing yourself and inviting them to events at the wraparound center.

New Higher Leadership (Principal or Superintendent)

A change of leadership at the top, whether at the school or district level, perhaps presents the most serious threat to a wraparound center's sustainability. Without the enthusiastic support of higher leadership, a wraparound center has very little chance of surviving.

Adding to the action imperative, Michael D. Watkins (2013) warns new leaders of thinking they have arrived with "'the' answer," which entails the following:

> You come in with your mind made up, or you reach conclusions too quickly about "the" problems and "the" solutions. You alienate people who could help you understand what's going on, and you squander opportunities to develop support for good solutions. (p. 6)

Said another way, new principals and superintendents may violate the principle of Chesterton's fence, which essentially states, "Don't tear down a fence unless you know why it was put there" (Whelan, 2015). Without a clear understanding of a wraparound center's role, even seemingly minor changes (like alterations to the bus schedules for tutoring or tweaks to reporting relationships) can threaten the mission, organizational structures, and funding undergirding the effort.

If you are a new principal or superintendent, approach wraparound services with curiosity, and seek to understand the gestalt of the effort before imposing changes. Seek out your school and district's wraparound staff to learn about their work and its impact. Likewise, listen to stakeholders—students, faculty, administration, partners, and community members—to learn how the wraparound center affects each of them.

If you are a wraparound director with a new principal or superintendent, consider what information you would prepare for a new-donor presentation and communicate to him or her the same information about your effort's mission and impact, highlighting the many people involved in the effort. Above all else, share your student voice data story, which will be invaluable to the new leader as he or she takes the helm.

New Partner Leadership

When partner agencies change hands, roll out the welcome mat to include the new leaders in your team of community partners. Invite the new leaders to tour your center, review student voice relevant to their mission, and discuss the structure, value, and sustainability of the partnership—especially how the provided co-located services relate to their organization's mission. Involve any of their on-site service providers, if appropriate, in walking through the MOU with the new leaders to detail the full scope and potential of the partnership.

Arrange the new leaders' introductions to your school and district leadership teams. Include the new leaders on distribution lists so they receive updates. In short, go out of your way to let them know what valued members of your community they are and how much their organization's support has meant to the wraparound center's efforts. If, despite your efforts, the partnership withers, use chapter 4 (page 103) and chapter 5 (page 119) to support your review of potential new resources and find new potential partners to meet your students' needs.

Keep the Work Relevant to the Whole School

As you dig into student voice, you are likely to uncover heart-wrenching stories of students struggling with challenges such as family crises, homelessness, or grief. While those students will no doubt be at the top of your list to support, don't let the story of your wraparound center suggest it exclusively deals with trauma, drama, and emergencies, or you'll risk the wraparound center losing its appeal to all students. Media attention to your school may also reinforce the message that your wraparound center is designed for "those kids with problems"—creating a stigma around accessing services, which might dry up your walk-in traffic. All students have areas of need (albeit some have more basic or more critical needs than others), and all students and families need information and support.

To counteract the natural pull of emotionally evocative narratives, turn to your student board of directors (mentioned in chapter 7, page 163) to develop relevant programming with mass appeal. This programming might include efforts such as the following.

- After-school classes on five meals to learn to cook before graduation
- SAT or ACT boot camps
- Career talks
- Adulting 101 (lunch-and-learn sessions on topics or skills students choose)
- Mock interview training
- Résumé writing 101
- Programs on laws every student should know

Likewise, turn to your students to help create attractive spaces for meetings, such as student council meetings, homecoming committee meetings, and prom-planning meetings. Think of ways to personalize your wraparound center, like hanging poster-size pictures of current students and teachers; keep those pictures up to date so students will see familiar faces in the hallways.

The bottom line is this: the more normal you make it for students to visit your wraparound center, the more likely you'll diminish the stigma for accessing services.

Manage Funding

Much of this chapter has focused on building and maintaining social capital with your key stakeholders, from students to the broader community. But, your wraparound center needs a steady stream of funds to flourish. Fortunately, having that social capital will help maintain your funding too. The stronger your community connectedness, the easier it will be to ask for support because you'll be making requests on students' behalf from a position of trust, as opposed to at an arm's length. In fact, when you start hearing community members say "our school," you'll know you're on the right track!

However, there is much more you must do. Having a transparent annual report (page 217) that promotes accountability is directly related to the management and sustainability of funding. To further support your wraparound center's efforts, continue to increase your knowledge about local, state, and federal funding streams; review existing processes and implement new processes for making charitable giving easy; seek additional start-up capital as well as multiyear grants; and explore the potential of aligning with or starting a 501(c)(3) (see Fundraising and Other External Funding Streams, page 151).

Regarding federal and state funding, you must also be prepared for change. As was evident from chapter 6 (page 139), federal funding regulations can be complex and often depend on your state's or province's implementation strategy, not to mention your district's policies and practices. Nevertheless, staying on top of changes in funding regulations will help you adapt your budget and expectations to the ever-changing political landscape of federal and state or provincial funding. For instance, the Coronavirus Aid, Relief, and Economic Security (CARES) Act of 2020 provided U.S. school districts with financial support for services, resources, and innovation related to the COVID-19 pandemic. Always work closely with your district's leadership and funding specialist when developing your budget to determine how best to allocate funds to your priorities.

Finally, diversification of funding is critical to sustainability. Having all your eggs in one basket of funding—like one major donor, grant, or fundraiser—can expose you to excessive risk if that source dries up. In *Nonprofit Quarterly*, Mark Hager and ChiaKo Hung (2019) explain an additional problem with *resource dependence*, "which means that money (or the ways to procure it) influences how organizations behave." They stress that strings and reporting protocols can limit your autonomy and dictate your actions, becoming the tail that wags the dog. When you have limited, vulnerable, or restrictive funding streams, you stop calling the shots, which puts you in danger of no longer representing your mission and stakeholders (Hager & Hung, 2019).

To avoid this outcome, we outlined in chapter 6 (page 139) various external sources (outside of educational dollars) to ask of your community—cash donations and in-kind donations of goods and services. Continually look for opportunities to increase and diversify your community contacts, and keep potential donors informed about how they can help. Be specific with your asks, and always be prepared with a variety of them—from little asks, like buying snacks for an after-school résumé-writing seminar, to big asks, like endowing a room or program within your center. When you share your student voice data story, you'll find people genuinely happy to contribute, and you'll simultaneously stabilize the funding your wraparound center depends on.

Conclusion

In many ways, your wraparound center functions as a nonprofit where sustainability "includes the concepts of financial sustainability, as well as leadership succession planning, adaptability, and strategic planning" (National Council of Nonprofits, n.d.). Attending to these imperatives increases the likelihood that wraparound services will prove a key strategy to student success rather than another educational fad left by the wayside.

Think of wraparound work as a marathon, not a sprint. The months leading to the opening of your wraparound center will be filled with the excitement of breaking new ground. However, if silence follows the big splash of the opening, you'll have little hope of maintaining the support that will keep the lights on. Your ability to perpetuate your mission largely depends on the day-in, day-out connections with key stakeholders. Use student voice as the fuel to keep your services and partnerships relevant and robust. Maintain and continually develop authentic partnerships based on a shared mission and mutual support. Frequently let your community know the impact your team has on the lives of your students and their families.

We began this book by asking, "And how are the children?" By following the Centergy Cycle, you can create a welcoming place where students have equitable access to both services and opportunities. This hopeful work can galvanize your community and set the stage for students to achieve their full potential so that, one day, your community can declare, "The children are well. Yes, all the children are well."

EPILOGUE

With this book, we have endeavored to offer educators a practical guide for providing equity through wraparound services built on a foundation of listening to students. The impact of wraparound services doesn't have to stop there. Wraparound schools have the capacity to change communities by becoming the places where hope and social capital grow and flourish. In *Leading for Learning*, Phillip C. Schlechty (2009) talks about the interdependence of schools and communities:

> It is . . . my view that the link between the quality of schools and the quality of community life is so deep and profound that it makes no sense to work to improve the schools outside the context of improving communities as well. It is not possible to have strong schools in unhealthy communities. School improvement and community building go hand in hand. It is therefore a grave mistake to turn schools into government agencies and to remove control of the schools from local communities, especially at a time when one of the greatest crises facing the [United States] is the breakdown of communities and the loss of sources of community identity and feelings of belonging on which communities depend. (p. xi)

When we began this writing project, it was our desire you would close this book with a renewed sense of hope. The seeds you plant in your school have the potential to bear fruit in your community—and beyond—for years to come. So we close with the following poem from Margaret Wheatley (2011) writing for Resilience Circles (https://localcircles.org):

> There is no power greater than a community discovering what it cares about.
> Ask: "What's possible?" not "What's wrong?" Keep asking.
> Notice what you care about.
> Assume that many others share your dreams.
> Be brave enough to start a conversation that matters.
> Talk to people you know.
> Talk to people you don't know.
> Talk to people you never talk to.

Be intrigued by the differences you hear.

Expect to be surprised.

Treasure curiosity more than certainty.

Invite in everybody who cares to work on what's possible.

Acknowledge that everyone is an expert about something.

Know that creative solutions come from new connections.

Remember, you don't fear people whose story you know.

Real listening always brings people closer together.

Trust that meaningful conversations can change your world.

Rely on human goodness. Stay together.

PULL IT ALL TOGETHER

> *When someone listens, I feel cared for,*
> *trusted, valued, respected, and hopeful.*
>
> —High school student

Now that you have read through each step of the Centergy Cycle, we want to offer a resource that lets you examine how a school might put all this work together and apply this knowledge to a known barrier facing communities across North America—substance use. Our goal is not only to give you a holistic perspective of the Centergy Cycle but also to provide you with affirmation and information about this multifaceted barrier. We want to confirm your schools are not alone in their effort to find evidence-based, effective, and informed approaches to prevention, education, intervention, and support, as well as recovery and sustainability related to substance use disorder. The sampling of substance use data we present in this appendix is the result of a variety of published reports, conversations, and surveys with students across multiple schools.

In this appendix, we offer background information on substance abuse in the United States and provide evidence-based strategies for addressing student substance use while destigmatizing and supporting recovery. We also present ideas informed by student voice and experts in the field, plus some good news—help is on the way. We frame and apply all this content through the seven steps of the Centergy Cycle, which we are confident will give you a deeper understanding of the tangle of complicating factors that make substance use disorder so challenging to tackle.

Background: Substance Abuse and the Centergy Cycle

The CDC (n.d.a) reports the following data on substance abuse in the United States.

- Approximately 130 Americans die every day from opioid overdose.
- In 2018, 67,367 deaths were due to drug overdose, with opioid involvement in 69.5 percent of those deaths.

- In 2018, the states with the highest death rates due to drug overdose were West Virginia (51.5 per 100,000), Delaware (43.8 per 100,000), Maryland (37.2 per 100,000), Pennsylvania (36.1 per 100,000), Ohio (35.9 per 100,000), and New Hampshire (35.8 per 100,000).

- States with statistically significant increases in drug overdose death rates from 2017 to 2018 included California, Delaware, Missouri, New Jersey, and South Carolina.

As you reflect on these grim statistics, particularly the number of overdose deaths, consider that there were 58,220 U.S. military casualties in the Vietnam War (National Archives, 2019). In sum, the United States is losing more citizens to drug overdose *every* year than it lost in the totality of the Vietnam War. Consider also that, since the COVID-19 pandemic began, drug overdoses are on the rise. *Washington Post* reporters William Wan and Heather Long (2020) report a 2019 to 2020 increase in suspected U.S. overdoes of 18 percent in March, 29 percent in April, and 42 percent in May.

Consider how these numbers might reflect the impact of substance abuse on students at your school. In the report *Youth Substance Misuse and Academic Performance: The Case for Intervention*, Community Catalyst (2019) links substance use to academic struggles:

> Substance misuse during adolescence is linked to lower academic performance, student absenteeism and higher rates of high school dropout. Many young people ages 12–17 actively use substances, and that use increases during high school. . . . Youth who start using substances during adolescence are more likely to develop substance use disorders later in life. In fact, 90 percent of adults with addiction started using before the age of 18.
>
> Youth who misuse substances are more likely to receive failing grades in school. However, young people who reduce their use or stop using have demonstrated improved academic outcomes that can mirror those of students who never used substances. This means that school-based substance use prevention and early intervention services can make a difference in improving student grades and academic achievement. (p. 1)

Even more important than achievement, prevention and intervention can save lives. Our work with students and schools, individuals in recovery, and agencies supporting recovery has yielded the following information we submit as truths related to substance use.

- The United States is facing a drug epidemic in which nearly half of Americans have a family member or close friend who is addicted to drugs (Gramlich, 2017).

- Effective prevention programming is a powerful strategy for combating addiction, and early intervention is a critical component to prevention.

- Most people believe attitudes, policies, and approaches regarding substance use must change.

- Schools can play a critical role in each community's effort to address our current drug crisis and support long-term recovery.

- Shame is a powerful emotion, but hope is more powerful.

- Connection is the opposite of addiction, and recovery is real.

With this knowledge in mind, let's consider how we might use the Centergy Cycle to address this widespread crisis. A school's approach to substance use begins with gathering student voice through conversation circles, off-track interviews, a Student Voice Needs Survey, focus groups and individual focused conversations, and graduation stories. This information helps drive the effort to identify needs and establish priorities. Through these processes, school staff can generate community- and school-specific qualitative and quantitative data related to the barrier of substance use.

Given what you know about the Centergy Cycle, consider the challenge of substance abuse at your own school and how you would establish support services to address this problem. Before you begin talking to your students about substance use, you must prepare a safe environment to gain their trust to open up. When educators bring up the issue of substance use with high schoolers, the students commonly show obvious doubt and suspicion. In response to the question, "Is substance use an issue at our school?" a long pause usually occurs. Students will raise their eyebrows and exchange meaningful glances with one another before someone speaks up. Inevitably, someone asks, "You mean we're not going to get in trouble for talking about this?"

No wonder they hesitate. For starters, virtually all substance use by teens is *illegal*—the exception being tobacco use after age eighteen. For teenage students to open up, they have to feel they are safe from prosecution. One high school student summed up this sentiment this way: "It would be great if we could talk about it or get information at school but there's a constant fear of arrest and judgment at school" (personal communication, October 2, 2019).

For years, schools have used suspension, assignment to alternative settings, and expulsion as the primary discipline responses to infractions of all kinds, such as efforts addressing truancy, theft, fighting, and substance use. From a certain perspective, removing students who are in possession of or distributing drugs makes sense. Zero-tolerance methods demonstrate schools are striving to be drug-free zones, and they provide simplicity and clarity of enforcement. Administrators need to go no further than the discipline handbook to mete out consequences, sometimes despite their better judgment. However, as the following examples demonstrate, not all substance use belongs in the same category. "A beer gets you a year (in an alternative school)" is the reality of some schools with which we've worked. We've interviewed students who have been placed in alternative schools for being "in possession" of birth control pills or Tylenol because having such substances on their person rather than in the school clinic violated their school's policy.

Virtually no one argues one-size-fits-all disciplinary methods do anything to address the complicated tangle of cognitive and social-emotional issues behind substance use. Thinking deeper about this issue means acknowledging that removing students from school may actually intensify their drug use. In our experience, it exacerbates isolation, shame, and stigma—especially when accompanied by removal from positive groups like athletics or performing arts—while also compromising or denying academic progress.

voices
FROM THE FIELD

Suspending does nothing when it comes to drugs. Schools should do something that gives the students help rather than just suspend them or send them to alternative school.

—High school student

Schools should have drug kits available to parents to help them keep their kids accountable. Being able to say my parents will test me gives me an out to say no when others around me are using. It's one of the good things about being on probation.

—High school student

The school could work together with juvenile court or probation officers to coordinate required supervision visits and community services requirements and also about support groups and therapy. It would be great if some of that at school could count for probation requirements.

—High school student

We've talked to hundreds of students about substance use. Overwhelmingly, they reveal underlying issues, such as family dynamics, stress, anxiety, grief, anger, and depression, as the reasons they turn to drugs as a coping mechanism. There is one inescapable message we consistently hear from students, and they want their schools to know:

I feel like I don't prioritize school now the way I prioritize drugs. I hate that. I wish schools understood how to relate to us and our situation and maybe they could help the most right there . . . where it starts. It would take getting to know us and what is going on in our lives and why we sometimes do the things we do. (High school student, personal communication, March 9, 2019)

After speaking with students, we view substance use as a continuum from exposure to experimentation to use to dependency. We make the case that interventions begin with prevention and work through education and support to recovery. With this in mind, the rest of this chapter examines how a school would use the seven steps of the Centergy Cycle to establish wraparound services related to substance abuse.

Step 1: Identify Needs

To fully uncover your students' needs related to substance use, gather their perspective through step 1's open-ended and organic student voice processes.

- Conversation circles
- Off-track interviews
- Graduation stories

Figure A.1 shows an excerpt artifact from a conversation circle gathering students' general perspectives on academic services, behavioral and life skills, community services, and family

Source: © 2020 The Centergy Project.

Figure A.1: Artifact from a conversation circle regarding needed partnerships and clinical services.

needs. Several student groups had the opportunity to brainstorm content for this chart; other groups received colored stickers to mark the topics they believed to be the greatest needs of the students in their school. The students showed a high level of interest and need around the topic of substance use (as the large number of stickers demonstrates). We find this typical in *every* high school in which we've worked—affirming the U.S. Department of Health and Human Services' (2019) declaration of a national opioid epidemic.

Off-track interviews and graduation stories may provide qualitative data stories that will further clarify the impact student substance use is having on your students' achievement and graduation. As individual student stories emerge, collect this content as well as related attendance, discipline, and alternative school data, and organize them in an anonymous format. In the future, the school can share the information as part of the data story it needs to better inform school staff, partners, and other stakeholders about the seriousness of the issue.

Step 2: Establish Priorities

The next step is to establish priorities by collecting additional student voice data. Begin with conducting an anonymous Student Voice Needs Survey (ensure it includes questions related to substance abuse), then review the data and have your wraparound staff use the findings to conduct focus groups and individual focused conversations with students. For these conversations, facilitators choose students who have self-reported struggles, students who have referrals from family or school staff, or students who have received disciplinary consequences related to substance use.

Table A.1 (page 232) provides a broad perspective on the pervasiveness of substance use in just one geographic area. We derived this table's data from six high schools in the southeastern United States through Student Voice Needs Surveys administered in 2018 and 2019. The numbers indicate the percentage of students who expressed interest in substance abuse services on the surveys. These data informed the schools involved about the number of students and families potentially in need of support related to substance use. The voice information gathered during subsequent focus groups informed each school's plans with regard to the programming.

Table A.1: Percentage of Students Interested in Substance Abuse Services

Category	High School 1 (Large Rural)	High School 2 (Midsize Rural)	High School 3 (Small Urban Suburban)	High School 4 (Large Urban)	High School 5 (Small Urban Suburban)	High School 6 (Small Rural)
Percentage of students interested in substance abuse services for themselves	35 percent	30 percent	25 percent	37 percent	28 percent	30 percent
Percentage of students interested in substance abuse services for family members	32 percent	46 percent	26 percent	34 percent	31 percent	29 percent

Source: © 2019 The Centergy Project.

Focused conversations at these six high schools also provided a rich narrative and artifacts detailing how substance use affected the students' lives, friends, family, and schooling. These focus group artifacts and summaries documented comments from students all along the continuum of use (exposure, experimentation, use and dependency, and recovery), stories of family members with pervasive substance abuse who lived chaotic and traumatic lives, and accounts of families draining their reserves to help their children. As you'll see, these deeper discussions with students reveal substance use as a complex, impactful issue.

A Word About Mental Health, Trauma, and ACEs

In her article "Addiction Doc Says: It's Not the Drugs. It's the ACEs . . . Adverse Childhood Experiences," Jane Ellen Stevens (2017) speaks with Daniel Sumrok, director of the Center for Addiction Sciences at the University of Tennessee Health Science Center's College of Medicine. Regarding Sumrok's medical practice, Stevens (2017) notes that he has seen approximately 1,200 addicted patients in total, 1,100 of whom have an ACE score of 3 or more (out of 10). Stevens (2017) explains that students with these kinds of scores are four times more likely to use alcohol or other drugs from a young age. People with ACE scores of 5 or higher are seven to ten times more susceptible. Stevens (2017) also notes:

> Subsequent research on the link between childhood adversity and addiction corroborates the findings from the ACE Study, including studies that have found that people who've experienced childhood trauma have more chronic pain and use more prescription drugs; people who experienced five or more traumatic events are three times more likely to misuse prescription pain medications.

In figure A.2 (page 234), students candidly discuss the impact substance use has had on them, their friends, their family, and their schooling. Their comments document the prevalence of shame, stereotypes, labels, and blame in their lives. These comments also clearly record deteriorating trust among friends and family. Leaders can use such a chart with teachers and administration for professional learning, with students in health classes, and with community members and partners to provide deeper context to attendance, discipline, and survey data.

Figure A.3 (page 235) is an artifact from a focus group designed to gather student perspective about substance use. Sharing these types of data stories can help you develop empathy and understanding with the stakeholders in your school and community, which can inform your school's response to substance use.

As further evidence that substance use often occurs in tandem with other issues, students in focus groups at the six high schools these data derive from also cited experience and struggles with the following.

- Stress
- Anxiety
- Anger
- Sadness
- Grief

- Depression
- Substance use by family members
- Pain
- Loneliness

- Self-harm
- Mental illness
- Sexual identity and acceptance

voices FROM THE FIELD

Education and curriculum need to change and begin earlier—some of it in elementary school, especially if the school knows the student is growing up in a house with drugs. It should begin with a lot of intensity in sixth grade and continue through ninth grade. I bet all of us in this group used [drugs] for the first time between [ages] 9 and 12.

—High school student

I've been around drugs since I was born, basically, and you don't know anything about what I'm going through or why I use. Mainly, you labeling me as a bad kid doesn't really help me not use.

—High school student (personal communication, September 13, 2018)

I wish my school cared as much about *why* I use as they care about the fact that I am using.

—High school student (personal communication, October 16, 2018)

Figure A.4 (page 236) shows a sampling of students' ideas about how their schools can better approach substance use by students. As you read through their words, reflect on the programming and activities your school has related to prevention, education, support, and intervention, as well as recovery. Think through potential partnerships and ways to connect students and families with services.

When reviewing your own charts on this topic, make note of particularly compelling commentary, as these comments can prove beneficial for grant writers and your partners

Me

Feeling helpless and worthless

Feeling embarrassed, ashamed, guilty

Became addicted

Less energetic, lazy

Some drugs help my focus

I'm less interested in stuff I used to like.

Makes me feel nervous, sad, anxious — especially about getting caught

Changes in my personality

Changes in my group of friends — New friends / Lost friends

Makes me feel the way I want to feel

At the time I'm using, I feel smart and that I can do anything

Changes in sleep, appetite — weight gain / weight loss

Less focus, less motivated

Lonely, isolated

My Friends

I'm dishonest with my friends.

Loss of friends

Their personality has changed

It has made me not trust people or only want to be around certain people.

Some of my friendships are based on drugs.

I've realized some of my friends aren't my friends because they take advantage of me when I'm high.

I have lost some friends and had some friends die.

We've gotten in trouble.

Some of my friends want me to use so they don't use alone.

My best friend has become unmotivated and very selfish and does not care about anything else except her boyfriend who supplies her.

We trust only each other, not others.

I (we've) been arrested. Meaning curfew, legal charges, court costs, arrest, probation, community service, criminal records, fines, loss of trust, loss of employment, being out of school

What impact has substance use had on . . .

My Family

I have distanced myself from my family.

My use has caused my family to have financial debt.

My parents had lost faith in me which I am slowly earning back. My dad never really noticed a change in me, it was always my mom who knew. She's stressed about me every day and it hurt her a lot.

I've seen my mom overdose three times.

My Dad almost killed my Mom when he came home high.

My brother got shot over drugs.

Drugs made my life hard when I was young.

I've seen my parents lose their jobs over and over because of drugs.

My sister died of an overdose from black tar heroin.

My mom has been addicted all my life to meth.

My aunt died.

I'm afraid for my family and afraid of being taken from my family if I ask for help.

Getting taken from my home and put with my grandparents.

All the police officers and judges know my family.

I've been around drugs since I was born basically.

My Schooling

I'm in alternative school.

I lost motivation. I felt like nothing was fun unless I was high— like I didn't want to go to a football game, a dance, not even the stuff I liked unless I was high.

I'm in trouble and the staff has lower expectations of me.

I got arrested and got expelled for a year.

My grades have gone down and I have lost credits. I may not graduate on time. I may not graduate at all— I have a court date coming up and they might send me to jail.

School suspension

Drugs have changed what people think of me. The SROs and administrators do not trust me. They search me when other students aren't or wouldn't be searched.

It's impacted my memory. I sometimes can't remember what my teachers have taught.

I might not graduate.

Loss of ability to participate in programs/activities I care about.

My attendance is terrible.   Consequences, Judgement

Less focus/more focus – it just depends on which drugs. I buy the "study drug" and it works.

Source: © 2020 The Centergy Project.

Figure A.2: Focus group chart on the impact of substance use.

What would you want teachers or school staff to understand about a teen's struggle with substance use?

People do these things (drugs) for a reason and our struggle is real. You should learn about us and our lives before you judge us.

Drugs are really easy to get which makes using them easy and getting off of them a lot harder.

Taking drugs doesn't make me a bad person.

Sometimes students do drugs FOR the side effects.

We are all different and dealing with different things but punishments are always treating us like we are the same or that the same consequences will work best for all of us.

You can't just consequence me out of drugs.

I smoke weed and I sometimes do think it's a gateway to do other drugs. It's so easy to like how weed makes you feel. I like how I feel when I smoke pot. For me, sometimes I feel like I function and focus better after I smoke.

I don't think adults know much about what is going on today with drugs. It's mostly pot and pills for teens.

I tried to commit suicide many times when I was younger. Now I use drugs to cope instead of hurting myself. I don't have much hope about things getting better but the drugs make me feel better for a little while.

I am scared to be open with my family about drugs and how I think the drugs help me. They are judgemental and I know they will overreact. I am 16 years old and I have high grades and very high life expectations. I am always expected to do my best and I am a good girl. I do drugs to help me cope with all the pressure, stress, and anxiety.

Source: © 2020 The Centergy Project.

Figure A.3: Focus group chart on sharing student perspective about substance abuse.

What types of information, activities, events, staffing, support, and programming related to substance use do you think would benefit students?

"Schools should check on students they believe are using daily. They should make sure students are not being pressured, help them with other things (like mental illness) if they need it, and teach students the signs of addiction —especially if they are interested in getting help or quitting. Having staff or people around who can talk to us is important (someone who has experienced substance use like it is today.")

"Having free drug test kits available for parents helps teens say no when pressured. Also, random, voluntary drug testing should be an option for students who want the chance to prove they are staying clean and want to stay at school."

"Sometimes I want to cut back on my use, but I do not have successful strategies for doing so or for dealing with the stuff that is the reason I use in the first place."

"More searches are needed to keep the school stay as drug-free as possible."

"I do think having support groups for all kinds of issues could be SO beneficial. It could make people feel less alone, and being alone in your struggle is a big reason why teens use."

"Students could be matched with assistance instead of schools suspending us or sending us to alternative school. A lot of students need help with why they are using."

"Don't treat every drug referral the same. Each case should be dealt with individually. Zero tolerance should be done away with, I do think that possession and selling should be handled differently."

"After-school support from therapists and people in recovery who could mentor us (people we can relate to) would be great—having a chance to talk to people who have been through it and are trained to listen, not lecture."

Source: © 2020 The Centergy Project.

Figure A.4: Focus group suggestions for effective programming and approaches regarding substance use.

as you work to design programming. For instance, one high school student (personal communication, October 17, 2019) from a rural county told us:

> Schools just keep responding to the news and parents and community people and the events that have just happened, so they concentrate on certain drugs more than others. Last year, our school was all upset about dip and then it focused on drinking at prom time. This year, it is all about juuling. It doesn't seem to me that schools get the big picture about drug use. They just react to the one that is getting all the social and media attention at the time.

The student making this comment is correct. In most cases, schools *do* react rather than respond when it comes to substance use.

---

voices
FROM THE FIELD

Substance use curriculum really needs to be updated to be current and real. Just stop trying to scare us with scary videos and wrecked cars. We would listen more to in-person real people who are honest and straightforward. I would rather spend time listening to people who get it and are now over their drug use. We need the kind of experiences that "hit you in the feels" because you can tell the people know and care and that they are being truthful with you.

—High school student (personal communication, October 10, 2018)

I think we need an elective about life choices (risky decision making, mental health, substance use and getting clean, and sexuality). Maybe it could be for students over the age of sixteen and students could sign up with parent permission. It could be taught by nurses or therapists.

—High school student (personal communication, November 8, 2018)

Help me with coming back to school. Encourage me in my withdrawal and staying clean. Don't just try to catch me screwing up again. Being judged and having a constant fear of punishment makes it rough, and dealing with your old friends is tough too. Having something new to be involved in with new people might have helped me. If I could have a mentor or coach who has been through something similar, someone who I could meet with at school, that would have helped too.

—High school student (personal communication, February 26, 2019)

At each school when we have interviewed students about effective programming regarding substance use, they have been full of ideas on what schools should stop doing, start doing, and improve on. To be candid, it doesn't seem schools are doing much right. In fact, it seems a wholly different, updated, student- and research-informed approach is in order. In our research, one valuable resource we used is a recovery community organization called Davis Direction Foundation (www.davisdirection.org), which is directed by Missy Owen, a school counselor with more than thirty years of experience who lost one of her five children to substance use disorder (Davis Direction Foundation, n.d.). The Davis Direction

Foundation website provides a wealth of information and resources, including plans to offer for a K–12 curriculum.

Step 3: Identify Resources

Once you understand the most pressing needs and contemplate the ideas of your students and their families, you'll want to begin to map out the organizations, experts, and potential funding sources in your community. For example, when you are looking for organizations that deal with substance abuse, you might think of them in categories as represented in the Centergy Project's wraparound services model (figure I.3, page 9).

The four asset map categories in this model that most directly connect to matters of substance abuse and recovery are featured in table A.2. This table also lists the kinds of organizations most capable of supporting substance use services in these categories.

Table A.2: Organizations Providing Substance Use Services

Service	Organization
Health and Wellness	Public health agencies
	Local hospitals
	State drug prevention and substance use agencies
	Clinical providers of support and treatment
	Wellness professionals and advocates
	Community services boards
Community Services	Local recovery nonprofits
	Advocacy agencies
Safety and Justice	Law enforcement
	Drug courts
	Judges
	Juvenile court or Departments of Juvenile Justice
College and Career Transition	College and university recovery and sober-living organizations

If available, connect with organizations in these categories to learn more about your community's current situation and available programs. As we discussed in chapter 5 (page 119), one method for learning more about the mission, needs, resources, and services of such groups is to have individual meetings with group leaders. Another is to host a community gathering for representatives of these groups and present the data and information you have gained from your students.

Once you've got a lay of the land, you can educate your community and publicly identify resources available to your students, families, and staff by doing the following student-requested activities.

- Host a community gathering at your school that brings together experts to increase parents', teachers', and community members' awareness of drug uses prevalence and the intervention efforts underway.

- Invite experts into your school to conduct professional learning with staff regarding the science of addiction.

- Provide student assemblies, lunch-and-learns, and after-school activities that celebrate recovery, and give your students the ability to speak directly with individuals in long-term recovery.

- Have community and PTSA meetings to provide people in town, school staff, students, and parents with information on what to look for and how to get help.

Step 4: Establish Partnerships

Because you want to present yourself as someone who is informed but also inquisitive, a thorough review of relevant data is useful in preparing for partnership meetings. In addition to gathering student voice and identifying resources, continue to educate yourself about school and local community data, needs, and trends related to substance abuse. Valuable information on substance use can be pulled from the following sources.

- **State agency data:** Current usage statistics, trends, and state responses

- **Judicial data:** Drug-related prosecution rates and current drug-related practices, such as drug courts

- **Discipline records:** Suspension numbers based on substance use and student voice data that identifies drugs students commonly use

- **Data from local recovery community organizations and recovery advocacy groups:** Qualitative and quantitative insights regarding effective local options for substance use, support, treatment, and recovery

- **Community public safety data:** Trends regarding community arrest rates on drug-related charges and local numbers regarding first-responder administration of medications such as naloxone

- **Community public health data:** Drug overdose statistics and local health initiative data

- **School, state, and national student health surveys:** Data regarding student usage

By combining student narratives with data from your school, community, and state, you'll begin to understand the scope and complexity of substance use and its bearing on your students and their families. Carefully review your students' comments and ideas to create and establish programming addressing the full continuum of use: exposure, experimentation, use and dependency, and recovery. External partners focused on substance use will help you prioritize your efforts and can provide the expertise and staffing to deliver the types of services students request.

Building on student suggestions, a school may respond with partnerships and activities such as the following.

- Partner with local law enforcement to provide free drug test kits or coordinate a prescription drug take-back night. Many police departments have asset forfeiture money they can use for activities related to school programming, prevention, and education.

- Speak with your local hospital about providing funding, educational materials, resource packets, overdose treatment kits and training, speakers for health classes, and help in marketing and facilitating a drug take-back night.

- Collaborate with local and collegial recovery groups, state agencies, and public health agencies to learn more about SBIRT. Health class teachers or other qualified staff can use SBIRT, which is an evidence-based public health universal screening tool and a powerful resource for prevention and communication (Substance Abuse and Mental Health Services Administration [SAMHSA], 2017) to educate their students regarding the problematic use of, abuse of, and dependence on alcohol and illicit drugs. State and local agencies, as well as hospitals, can be effective resources for locating the funding for SBIRT, recovery mentoring, support groups, and activities to celebrate recovery.

- Partner with a local agency that supports young adults in recovery to brainstorm evidence-based, effective, and informed responses your school can use for early intervention and in lieu of suspension. Seek information regarding individuals in long-term recovery who are willing to share their real talk—personal narratives of their journeys to recovery.

- Collaborate with your local juvenile justice organization on how schools can partner with them regarding legal intervention, probation requirements, community service, and support activities you could hold at school.

voices FROM THE FIELD

Work with the police department or the hospitals to host drug take-back events for families to dispose of unused drugs parents have around their house. My child started using by having access to the prescription pills at my house and my parents' house.

—High school parent and recovery group leader

I think we should partner with a college or recovery group and have college students and young adults who dealt with addiction in high school and college come in to talk to us about sober living on a college campus. They could give us the facts about what alcohol and drug use is really like as you become an adult.

—High school student

Implied in the Voices From the Field box in this section is the student articulation of understanding that schools can't and shouldn't attempt these efforts on their own. By working to establish partnerships with reputable local organizations and state agencies, school districts can become informed, proactive, strategic, and positively effectual.

Step 5: Secure Funding

When considering how to fund your wraparound services related to substance use, keep in mind that the idea is *not* for your school system to spend educational dollars hiring new employees to provide mentoring, therapy, educational programming, or clinical services. Likewise, we aren't suggesting you allocate school funds to purchase drug test kits, provide educational information, or host community meetings. We do encourage you to reach out to your community and collaborate with public health, law enforcement, community service boards, local colleges and universities, and local and state recovery organizations. We recommend you consider co-locating within your building the existing expertise, programming, and resources already available in your community. Harness the resources of law-enforcement and health-care professionals and employ the wisdom of community members in recovery to better serve your students. In this way, you will address head-on the negative impact drug use and drug addiction can have on learning and graduation as well as on families.

The following two sections examine obtaining funding related to substance use from federal and state levels as well as from agencies, organizations, nonprofits, and foundations. As in chapter 6 (page 139), we focus on obtaining such funding in the United States. Be sure to conduct research into sources of potential funding specific to your community, province, or nation.

Federal and State Funding

As we established in chapter 6, federal funding is available for local innovation and collaboration through Title I, Title II, Title IV, and others. Work with your district's federal funding staff to investigate your state's flexibility and spending guidelines. The U.S. government included nearly $9 billion for programs targeting addiction between 2016 and 2019 (U.S. Department of Health and Human Services, n.d.). In addition, between these same fiscal years, the U.S. Department of Health and Human Services opened up $2.12 billion in funding specifically for opioid treatment and recovery (Bipartisan Policy Center, 2019). These funds are largely intended for both state and local community collaborative initiatives to stem the tide of abuse. Sadly, many of these funds remain untapped because communities are not working together to write compelling funding requests that are innovative and demonstrate a collaborative, grassroots effort that is responsive to local data and student voice. In districts with school-based health centers, inquire about Medicaid funding availability for universal screenings and recovery support services related to substance use disorder.

In addition to federal options, chances are high that your community and state are working to develop strategies to deal with substance use, especially in the area of opioid and prescription drug abuse. Explore the feasibility of aligning yourself with these efforts and funding opportunities. For instance, Leigh was able to fully implement SBIRT as a universal screener with all ninth-grade students at no cost to her district. She was able to facilitate screening in health classes because she learned the Hilton Foundation was seeking five high schools to participate in the training and pilot the tool using young adults in recovery to administer the screenings. In summary, simply ask, listen, and learn. Opportunities to collaborate and join existing prevention and recovery efforts are available in many communities.

Funding From Agencies, Organizations, Nonprofits, and Foundations

Work with your partners that specialize in health and recovery services—as they may have their own grant writers—to identify funding streams from agencies, organizations, nonprofits, and foundations. In our experience, school districts' partners are often eager to help address adolescent substance abuse. Together, you may be able to apply for collaborative grants for programming and staff funding from sources such as the following.

- Public health organizations such as SAMHSA, which is a part of the U.S. Department of Health and Human Services

- Hospital foundations

- Public, private, and nonprofit organizations such as Community Catalyst, the Center for Social Innovation, the National Alliance on Mental Illness, and the Hilton Foundation

- State agencies such as the Department of Behavioral Health and Developmental Disabilities, the Department of Corrections (restorative justice funding), and the Department of Community Health

In addition to these sources, explore grants available to your community, such as the following.

- Police department asset forfeiture funding and public safety grants
- Community-improvement grants
- Community health and wellness grants

It is important for U.S.-based school leaders to acknowledge that the United States is in the midst of a substance use epidemic impacting families as well as communities, and full-spectrum services require community collaboration and response. Unfortunately during the COVID-19 pandemic of 2020, overdose and fatality rates are soaring (Wan & Long, 2020). Finding partners and funding sources to address the downstream impact of escalating substance use will become an imperative for school districts. Although battling substance use and empowering recovery typically falls outside the expertise of a school district, communities quickly grasp the positive and impactful role schools can play in prevention, education, and early intervention.

Step 6: Create Your Structure

At this point, you've got rich data from your student voice processes, and you've identified partnerships and potential funding. Now, it's time to pull those together to create a structure—the programming, staffing, activities, and services you'll be offering to address substance abuse in your school community.

Develop your programming around your student voice data. As you have seen throughout this appendix, students struggling with substance use tell us they are not interested *at all* in the advice of adults who have no familiarity or expertise with drug use or the students' experiences. Instead, they want access to someone who has experienced substance use "like it is today," and they want to hear real people's stories. They desire wisdom, empathy, and informed support, not judgment or well-intended sympathy. In addition, they prefer non–school system employees when it comes to discussing drug use to avoid the stigma and fear of legal consequences.

Figure A.5 (page 244) lists examples of programming opportunities agencies and service providers in the field of substance use disorder have brought to us. To offer streamlined access to services, you'll often decide to co-locate your partners' staff in your building on a part-time or full-time basis. For example, you may provide a designated space for parole officers working with your students and a private space for support groups and other group activities run by a facilitator or clinician in long-term recovery. In figure A.5, you will see some overlap with the insight provided through student voice. In some cases, you might also classify strategies in more than one category, but we elected to record these strategies only once. Start with a few, and grow from there. Don't try to bite off too much at once.

Step 7: Connect Students and Families With Services

Now that you have your structure in place, you're ready to connect your students and their families with robust services based on their needs. Make it easy for students to access services through self-referrals; disciplinary interventions and administrative referrals; or referrals from family, staff, or friends.

Your procedures for connecting students and families with services should include the following.

- Marketing all services and activities related to substance use
- Obtaining parental permission (when necessary)
- Setting up communication protocols between school staff and partners
- Establishing safeguards for mandatory reporting
- Collecting data on services' utilization

In addition to performing these procedures, offer alternatives to out-of-school consequences for drug possession or substance use as this is an effective strategy to help students experimenting or struggling with substance abuse stay on track academically. *Connection is the opposite of addiction, and recovery is real* is a common mantra in the recovery community. Unfortunately, many schools respond to students' substance use by removing the students from all activities that provide a sense of optimism, belonging, self-worth, self-regulation, and purpose. By allowing suspended students to displace their suspension time in your wraparound center, you can give them tutoring that catches them up on schoolwork, gain an understanding of co-occurring concerns they are facing, and connect them with a support network that they and their families need.

Substance Use Full-Spectrum Services and Programming
Prevention
Hosting prescription drug take-back events
Offering updated, relevant curriculum inclusive of research- and evidence-based prevention strategies
Broadly distributing information on the impact substances (including nicotine) have on brain chemistry and mood regulation
Using SBIRT as a universal screening, education, and prevention tool
Having a schoolwide assembly where you simulate a drug overdose at a party utilizing local first responders, local medical staff, and a local coroner
Education
Cohosting and organizing community gatherings on the collective impact of local substance use
Empowering data sharing with the police department, public health agencies, the court system, the coroner's office, the primary health-care agency or hospital, or the fire department
Offering parent training tools like the Cobb Overdose Prevention Effort (COPE) House used in Cobb County, Georgia (Cobb County Government, 2018). For more information, see http://www.cobbcounty.org/board/news/cobb-overdose-prevention-effort.
Providing PTA programming regarding the science of addiction that includes a panel of practitioners presenting information on evidence-based intervention and support strategies (National Institute on Drug Abuse, 2018)
Providing school staff training on the science of addiction
Providing information to students and parents regarding Good Samaritan overdose-immunity laws (which forty U.S. states and the District of Columbia have)
Support and Intervention
Making drug test kits available at schools and community gatherings
Offering overdose treatment devices, such as Narcan, in schools and training key school personnel (such as the school nurse, the school resources officer, and a certified athletic trainer) in the use of these devices
Providing information on where students can receive support (including 24–7 access to support) if they or their friends are struggling with substance use or mental health challenges
Conducting student conversation circles and focused conversations with real talk regarding substance use to gather student voice
Conducting school assemblies, lunch-and-learns, and after-school programming that feature people in recovery and community members who interface with the downstream impact of substance use, addiction, and overdose (emergency medical technicians, coroners, public health workers, health-care practitioners, police officers, judges, and so on)
Hosting intervention and support groups with facilitators trained in long-term recovery, such as certified addiction counselors (levels I and II), certified addiction recovery empowerment specialists, or coaches who have received Recovery Coach Academy training from the Connecticut Community for Addiction Recovery
Sponsoring mentorships between students and young people in recovery
Networking with the juvenile court or the local Department of Juvenile Justice with regard to students on probation for possession or use
Establishing restorative discipline practices (services not focused on consequences)
Sustainability and Recovery
Hosting recovery groups with facilitators trained in long-term recovery, such as certified addiction counselors (levels I and II), certified addiction recovery empowerment specialists, or coaches who have received Recovery Coach Academy training from the Connecticut Community for Addiction Recovery
Hosting activities and events that celebrate sobriety and recovery
Partnering with local college recovery groups on programming regarding the transition to college, college life, and sober living on a college campus
Scheduling a transition meeting with every student returning from a treatment facility to plan support and connect the student with services and a designated point of contact for assistance

Figure A.5: Potential substance use full-spectrum programming.

voices
FROM THE FIELD

The Georgia Council on Substance Abuse (GCSA) is a proud community partner working alongside the [Graduate Marietta Student Success Center]. So often, school districts want to "put out" and "put away" students who are struggling with substance use. From the beginning, we have appreciated the fact that the Center is led by student voice, and its staff listens to [students] about what gets in the way of academic achievement and graduation. These honest conversations with students take courage and compassion on the part of the administration and the students. Getting to speak with and engage students about their choices around risky and harmful substance use has been both enlightening and encouraging. GCSA commends the thoughtfulness and respect the Graduate Marietta Student Success Center has for its student body, parents, faculty, and surrounding community.

—Neil Campbell, executive director, Georgia Counsel on Substance Abuse

Be sure to look for ways to involve student advocates in community campaigns and public events. For substance use, you may invite students to help with community gatherings, assemblies, and recovery or sobriety celebration events.

As you reflect on the many details in these seven steps, Leigh would like to share one memorable experience addressing substance use in her work.

Wraparound Services: A Life Saved

By Leigh Colburn

One afternoon during early January 2016, a student, Sarah (not her real name), came to the Graduate Marietta Student Success Center to serve several days of a deferred suspension she incurred for a substance use infraction. Prior to the winter break, a teacher had taken her to the school nurse because she appeared to be zoned out and potentially under the influence of something. Barely coherent, she admitted to taking Xanax to calm what she described as *test anxiety*. The school called her parents to come get her, informing them we would follow up when she was able to tell us more.

When Sarah arrived at the Center, our wraparound staff met with her and then subsequently set up a meeting to meet her parents as well. A junior honors student in the school's most rigorous coursework, Sarah had no discipline record, and she was horrified at her situation. In a conversation with a young co-located female staff member in recovery, Sarah admitted she'd been purchasing Xanax for some time. She felt she needed something to help her deal with a variety of physical and emotional symptoms she believed were due to school-related stress and anxiety. She also told us that, over Thanksgiving break, she had experienced jitters, shaky hands, and increased emotionality and irritability, among other symptoms—all of which got much worse before exams. Sarah and her friends concluded the pressure of exams was too much for her to handle, so she purchased more Xanax to help her deal with her test anxiety. She took two just before an exam . . . and that's how she landed in the nurse's office.

Sending Sarah to an alternative school, which our district's discipline policy would have sanctioned, seemed to be the wrong thing to do in this situation. Fortunately for her, the school administration agreed. I was concerned (incorrectly as it turned out) the symptoms she described experiencing over the break were related to withdrawal, and I assumed Sarah was probably not telling us the full extent of her substance use. Still, I talked with Sarah and her parents about seeing a therapist to help her with her anxiety and to further investigate the extent of Sarah's unprescribed use of Xanax. Given the circumstances, they didn't argue.

Also fortunately for Sarah, not only did her parents take my advice, but they went a step further. In addition to making an appointment with a therapist, they took her to a doctor for a complete physical, where they discovered she had diabetes. The symptoms she experienced were *not* due to text anxiety. They were due to a blood-sugar imbalance that had likely been triggered not by her pending finals but by her diet changes over the break, during the holidays, and during high-stress times. Sarah didn't need discipline; she needed insulin and support.

Imagine what a miscarriage of justice it would have been if we had operated by the book and sent Sarah to an alternative setting, derailing her academic path for the "crime" of foolish and flawed self-diagnosis and self-medication. Thank goodness we had resources and staff in place to dig into the situation with a mind toward investigating root causes, listening without judgment, and using restorative practices. Thank goodness her parents also responded in an appropriate and thoughtful manner.

Scenarios such as this play out in one form or another in schools across North America, and it takes the empathy and diligent work of wraparound staff, school faculty, parents, and community members to achieve the kind of successful outcome I relate here. Addressing substance use prevention, education, intervention and support, and recovery is not just critical work for your school to emulate; it is a human and moral imperative that can save students' lives.

REFERENCES AND RESOURCES

Adelman, H. S., & Taylor, L. (2005). *The school leader's guide to student learning supports: New directions for addressing barriers to learning.* Thousand Oaks, CA: Corwin Press.

Adelman, H. S., & Taylor, L. (2016, February). *ESSA, equity of opportunity, and addressing barriers to learning* [Policy brief]. Los Angeles, CA: UCLA Center for Mental Health in Schools. Accessed at http://smhp .psych.ucla.edu/pdfdocs/essaanal.pdf on May 7, 2020.

Allison, M., & Kaye, J. (2005). *Strategic planning for nonprofit organizations: A practical guide and workbook* (2nd ed.). Hoboken, NJ: Wiley.

Anderson, M., & Perrin, A. (2018, October 26). *Nearly one-in-five teens can't always finish their homework because of the digital divide.* Accessed at www.pewresearch.org/fact-tank/2018/10/26/nearly-one-in-five -teens-cant-always-finish-their-homework-because-of-the-digital-divide on March 5, 2020.

Anderson-Butcher, D., Lawson, H. A., Bean, J., Flaspohler, P., Boone, B., & Kwiatkowski, A. (2008). Community collaboration to improve schools: Introducing a new model from Ohio. *Children and Schools, 30*(3), 161–172. Accessed at http://cayci.osu.edu/wp-content/uploads/2015/03/Community -collaboration-to-improve-schools-Introducing-a-new-model-from-Ohio.pdf on March 5, 2020.

Association for Supervision and Curriculum Development. (n.d.). *Whole School, Whole Community, Whole Child.* Accessed at www.ascd.org/programs/learning-and-health/wscc-model.aspx on April 15, 2020.

Association for Supervision and Curriculum Development. (2015). *Elementary and Secondary Education Act: Comparison of the No Child Left Behind Act to the Every Student Succeeds Act.* Accessed at www.ascd.org/ASCD /pdf/siteASCD/policy/ESEA_NCLB_ComparisonChart_2015.pdf on March 5, 2020.

Association for Supervision and Curriculum Development & Centers for Disease Control and Prevention. (2014). *Whole School, Whole Community, Whole Child: A collaborative approach to learning and health.* Alexandria, VA: Authors. Accessed at www.ascd.org/ASCD/pdf/siteASCD/publications/wholechild/wscc -a-collaborative-approach.pdf on March 9, 2020.

Balfanz, R. (2019). An integrated approach fosters student success. *Education Next, 19*(3). Accessed at www.educationnext.org/integrated-approach-fosters-student-success-forum-should-schools-embrace -social-emotional-learning on March 5, 2020.

Barr, R. D., & Gibson, E. L. (2013). *Building a culture of hope: Enriching schools with optimism and opportunity.* Bloomington, IN: Solution Tree Press.

Barr, R. D., & Gibson, E. L. (2020). *Building the resilient school: Overcoming the effects of poverty with a culture of hope.* Bloomington, IN: Solution Tree Press.

Bertolini, K., Stremmel, A., & Thorngren, J. (2012). *Student achievement factors.* Brookings: South Dakota State University College of Education and Human Sciences. Accessed at https://files.eric.ed.gov /fulltext/ED568687.pdf on March 5, 2020.

Bipartisan Policy Center. (2019, March). *Tracking federal funding to combat the opioid crisis.* Washington, DC: Authors. Accessed at https://bipartisanpolicy.org/report/tracking-federal-funding-to-combat-the -opioid-crisis on March 10, 2020.

Brault, R. (2014). *Round up the usual subjects: Thoughts on just about everything.* Scotts Valley, CA: CreateSpace.

Brendtro, L. K., Brokenleg, M., & Van Bockern, S. (2019). *Reclaiming youth at risk: Futures of promise* (3rd ed.). Bloomington, IN: Solution Tree Press.

Bright Futures. (n.d.). *Our history: A bright idea.* Accessed at www.brightfuturesusa.org/domain/57 on April 14, 2020.

Broader, Bolder Approach to Education. (n.d.). *Bright futures in Joplin, Missouri.* Accessed at www.bold approach.org/case-study/bright-futures-joplin-mo on March 10, 2020.

Brown, M. H., Lenares-Solomon, D., & Deaner, R. G. (2019). Every Student Succeeds Act: A call to action for school counselors. *Journal of Counselor Leadership and Advocacy, 6*(1), 86–96.

Bryk, A. S., Sebring, P. B., Allensworth, E., Luppescu, S., & Easton, J. Q. (2010). *Organizing schools for improvement: Lessons from Chicago.* Chicago: University of Chicago Press.

Cameron, W. B. (1963). *Informal sociology: A casual introduction to sociological thinking.* New York: Random House.

Carney, T. P. (2019). *Alienated America: Why some places thrive while others collapse.* New York: HarperCollins.

Carver-Thomas, D., & Darling-Hammond, L. (2017, August). *Teacher turnover: Why it matters and what we can do about it.* Washington, DC: Learning Policy Institute. Accessed at https://learningpolicyinstitute.org /sites/default/files/product-files/Teacher_Turnover_REPORT.pdf on March 5, 2020.

Center, T. (2018, December 4). *CityViews: To reduce teacher turnover, city must increase support.* Accessed at https://citylimits.org/2018/12/04/cityviews-to-reduce-teacher-absences-govt-must-show-up-with-support on March 5, 2020.

Center for Popular Democracy, Coalition for Community Schools, & Southern Education Foundation. (2016, February). *Community schools: Transforming struggling schools into thriving schools.* Washington, DC: Authors. Accessed at https://eric.ed.gov/?id=ED585872 on March 10, 2020.

Center for Promise. (2017, March 28). *Youth in poverty six times more likely to experience detrimental levels of adversity than higher-income peers* [Press release]. Accessed at www.americaspromise.org/press-release /youth-poverty-six-timesmore-likely-experience-detrimental-levels-adversity-higher on October 8, 2019.

Centers for Disease Control and Prevention. (n.d.a). *Drug overdose deaths.* Accessed at www.cdc.gov/drug overdose/data/statedeaths.html on March 5, 2020.

Centers for Disease Control and Prevention. (n.d.b). *The Whole School, Whole Community, Whole Child model.* Accessed at www.cdc.gov/healthyyouth/wscc/pdf/wscc_fact_sheet_508c.pdf?s_cid=tw-zaza-1081 on March 5, 2020.

Chetty, R., Hendren, N., Kline, P., & Saez, E. (2014). Where is the land of opportunity? The geography of intergenerational mobility in the United States. *Quarterly Journal of Economics, 129(4),* 1553–1623.

Child Mind Institute. (2016). *2016 children's mental health report.* Accessed at https://childmind.org/report /2016-childrens-mental-health-report on March 5, 2020.

Child Trends. (2019, March 7). *Adverse childhood experiences.* Accessed at www.childtrends.org/?indicators= adverse-experiences on February 21, 2020.

Children's Museum of Atlanta. (2018). *Our purpose.* Accessed at https://childrensmuseumatlanta.org/our -purpose on July 22, 2020.

Civil Rights Act of 1964, Pub. L. No. 88–352, 78 Stat. 241 (1964).

Coalition for Community Schools, Communities in Schools, and StriveTogether. (n.d.). *Letter of intent framework: Students at the center challenge.* Accessed at http://files.constantcontact.com/b14ce16e301 /a490c663-d4f4-494d-bc7a-6bbb9f50dddd.pdf on August 14, 2020.

Cobb County Government. (2018, November 5). *Cobb overdose prevention effort.* Accessed at www.cobb county.org/board/news/cobb-overdose-prevention-effort on March 5, 2020.

Community Catalyst. (2019, June). *Youth substance misuse and academic performance: The case for intervention.* Accessed at www.communitycatalyst.org/resources/tools/sbirt-resources/pdf/Link-Between-SUD-Academic -Achievement_CC_2019.pdf on March 10, 2020.

Conzemius, A. E., & O'Neill, J. (2014). *The handbook for SMART school teams: Revitalizing best practices for collaboration* (2nd ed.). Bloomington, IN: Solution Tree Press.

Coronavirus Aid, Relief, and Economic Security Act of 2020, Pub. L. No. 116–136 (2020).

Covey, S. M. R. (2004). *The 7 habits of highly effective people: Restoring the character ethic* (Rev. ed.). New York: Free Press.

Covey, S. M. R. (2018). *The speed of trust: The one thing that changes everything.* New York: Free Press.

Curtin, S. C., Warner, M., & Hedegaard, H. (2016, April). *Increase in suicide in the United States, 1999– 2014* (Data Brief No. 241). Hyattsville, MD: National Center for Health Statistics. Accessed at www.cdc .gov/nchs/products/databriefs/db241.htm on March 5, 2020.

Darling-Hammond, L., & Cook-Harvey, C. M. (2018, September). *Educating the whole child: Improving school climate to support student success.* Palo Alto, CA: Learning Policy Institute. Accessed at https:// learningpolicyinstitute.org/sites/default/files/product-files/Educating_Whole_Child_REPORT.pdf on March 5, 2020.

Davis Direction Foundation. (n.d.). *About.* Accessed at https://www.davisdirection.com/about on August 11, 2020.

DeBray, E., & Blankenship, A. E. (2016). Foreword: The aftermath of ESSA's devolution of power to states: A federal role in incentivizing equity and building state and local capacity. *Education Law and Policy Review, 3,* ix–xxvii.

Deel, B., & Grace, S. (2019). *Trust first: A true story about the power of giving people second chances.* New York: Optimism Press.

Derefinko, K. J., García, F. I. S., Talley, K. M., Bursac, Z., Johnson, K. C., Murphy, J. G., et al. (2019). Adverse childhood experiences predict opioid relapse during treatment among rural adults. *Addictive Behaviors, 96,* 171–174.

Development Services Group & Child Welfare Information Gateway. (2015). *Promoting protective factors for children and youth in foster care: A guide for practitioners.* Washington, DC: U.S. Department of Health and Human Services, Administration on Children, Youth and Families, Children's Bureau.

DiMaria, L., & Gans, S. (2020, March 22). *How to recognize internalizing symptoms in depressed children.* Verywell Mind. Accessed at www.verywellmind.com/internalizing-behaviors-and-depression -1066876 on July 21, 2020.

Dingerson, L. (2015, December). *Investing in what works: Community-driven strategies for strong public schools in Georgia.* Atlanta, GA: Southern Education Foundation and Annenberg Institute for School Reform.

Doerr, J. (2018). *Measure what matters: How Google, Bono, and the Gates Foundation rock the world with OKRs.* New York: Portfolio.

Doll, B., & Lyon, M. A. (1998). Risk and resilience: Implications for the delivery of educational and mental health services in schools. *School Psychology Review, 27*(3), 348–363.

DuFour, R., Dufour, R., Eaker, R., Many, T. W., & Mattos, M. (2016). *Learning by doing: A handbook for Professional Learning Communities at Work* (3rd ed.). Bloomington, IN: Solution Tree Press.

Early, T. J., & Vonk, M. E. (2001). Effectiveness of school social work from a risk and resilience perspective. *Children and Schools, 23*(1), 9–31.

Economic Opportunity Act of 1964, Pub. L. Nol. 88–452, 78 Stat. 508 (1964).

Education Amendments of 1972, 20 U.S.C. §§ 1681–1688 (2018).

Elementary and Secondary Education Act of 1965, Pub. L. No. 89–10, 20 U.S.C. § 6301 (1965).

Engelhardt-Cronk, K. (n.d.). *Understanding in-kind contributions: What US nonprofits need to know.* Accessed at www.missionbox.com/article/56/understanding-in-kind-contributions-what-us-nonprofits-need-to-know on March 5, 2020.

Every Student Succeeds Act of 2015, Pub. L. No. 114–95, 20 U.S.C. § 1177 (2015).

Family Educational Rights and Privacy Act of 1974, 20 U.S.C. § 1232g, 34 (1974).

Family Youth and Services Bureau. (n.d.). *State Personal Responsibility Education Program fact sheet.* Accessed at www.acf.hhs.gov/fysb/resource/prep-fact-sheet on August 10, 2020.

Federation for Community Schools. (2017). *Strategies for braiding funds under the "Every Student Succeeds Act" to support community school development* [PDF file downloaded August 2017].

Felitti, V. J., Anda, R. F., Nordenberg, D., Williamson, D. F., Spitz, A. M., Edwards, V., et al. (1998). Relationship of childhood abuse and household dysfunction to many of the leading causes of death in adults: The adverse childhood experiences (ACE) study. *American Journal of Preventive Medicine, 14*(4), 245–258. Accessed at https://doi.org/10.1016/S0749-3797(98)00017-8 on February 21, 2020.

Fisher, C., Hunt, P., Kann, L., Kolbe, L. J., Patterson, B., & Wechsler, H. (2010). *Building a healthier future through school health programs.* Accessed at www.cdc.gov/healthyyouth/publications/pdf/PP-Ch9.pdf on March 25, 2020.

Foundation Group. (n.d.). *What is a 501(c)(3)?* Accessed at www.501c3.org/what-is-a-501c3 on August 7, 2020.

Fullan, M., Gardner, M., & Drummy, M. (2019). Going deeper. *Educational Leadership, 76*(8), 64–69.

Gamson, D. A., McDermott, K. A., & Reed, D. S. (2015). The Elementary and Secondary Education Act at fifty: Aspirations, effects, and limitations. *RSF: The Russell Sage Foundation Journal of the Social Sciences, 1*(3), 1–29.

Georgia Department of Education. (2019a, January). *Title II, part A LEA handbook.* Atlanta: Author. Accessed at www.gadoe.org/School-Improvement/Teacher-and-Leader-Effectiveness/Documents/Title%20II,%20Part%20A%20Documents/FY19%20Resources/Handbook/Title%20II,%20Part%20A%20Handbook%2001.11.19.pdf on March 5, 2020.

Georgia Department of Education. (2019b, November 20). *Title IV: Part A student support and academic enrichment.* Atlanta: Author. Accessed at www.gadoe.org/School-Improvement/Federal-Programs/Documents/Title%20IV%20Part%20A/FY20%20Title%20IV%20Part%20A%20Handbook%2011.24.19%20[1].pdf on March 6, 2020.

Georgia Network to End Sexual Assault. (n.d.). *Step Up. Step In.* Accessed at www.gnesa.org/page/step-step-0 on April 22, 2020.

Gramlich, J. (2017, October 26). *Nearly half of Americans have a family member or close friend who's been addicted to drugs.* Accessed at www.pewresearch.org/fact-tank/2017/10/26/nearly-half-of-americans-have-a-family-member-or-close-friend-whos-been-addicted-to-drugs on March 6, 2020.

The great opioid epidemic. (2016, December 11). *Washington Post.* Accessed at www.washingtonpost.com/opinions/the-great-opioid-epidemic/2016/12/11/77bd8998-be4d-11e6-91ee-1adddfe36cbe_story.html on March 5, 2020.

Green, L. (2018, May 15). *Nine ways Title IX protects high school students.* Accessed at www.nfhs.org/articles/nine-ways-title-ix-protects-high-school-students on March 9, 2020.

Greenwald, R. (2005). *Child trauma handbook: A guide for helping trauma-exposed children and adolescents.* New York: Haworth.

Hager, M., & Hung, C. (2019, April 10). Is diversification of revenue good for nonprofit financial health? *Nonprofit Quarterly.* Accessed at https://nonprofitquarterly.org/is-diversification-of-revenue-good-for-nonprofit-financial-health on March 6, 2020.

Hammond, Z. (2015). *Culturally responsive teaching and the brain: Promoting authentic engagement and rigor among culturally and linguistically diverse students.* Thousand Oaks, CA: Corwin Press.

Hardie, E. (2019). Giving teens a place at the table. *Educational Leadership, 76*(8), 18–23.

Hendershott, J. (2009). *Reaching the wounded student.* Larchmont, NY: Eye On Education.

Hendershott, J. (2016). *7 ways to transform the lives of wounded students.* New York: Routledge.

Hess, F. M. (2009, October). Cages of their own design. *Educational Leadership, 67*(2), 28–33. Accessed at www.ascd.org/publications/educational-leadership/oct09/vol67/num02/Cages-of-Their-Own-Design.aspx on July 17, 2020.

Hughes, M., & Tucker, W. (2018). Poverty as an adverse childhood experience. *North Carolina Medical Journal, 79*(2), 124–126.

Improving America's Schools Act of 1994, Pub. L. No. 103–382, H.R. 6–103 (1994).

Institute for Educational Leadership & Coalition for Community Schools. (2017). *Community schools: A whole-child framework for school improvement.* Washington, DC: Authors. Accessed at www.community schools.org/assets/1/AssetManager/Community-Schools-A-Whole-Child-Approach-to-School -Improvement.pdf on March 6, 2020.

Interdisciplinary Group on Preventing School and Community Violence. (2013). December 2012 Connecticut school shooting position statement. *Journal of School Violence, 12*(2), 119–133.

Jennings, P. A. (2018). *The trauma-sensitive classroom: Building resilience with compassionate teaching.* New York: Norton.

Jensen, E. (2019). *Poor students, rich teaching: Seven high-impact mindsets for students from poverty* (Rev. ed.). Bloomington, IN: Solution Tree Press.

Johnson, S. (2019, November 13). *Linking accountability and partner support to improve outcomes for Georgia students.* A presentation to the CCSSO Annual Policy Forum.

Kolbe, L. J. (2002). Education reform and the goals of modern school health programs. *The State Education Standard, 3*(4), 4–11. Accessed at http://wvde.state.wv.us/healthyschools/documents/Education_Reform.pdf on March 9, 2020.

Lacoe, J. (2013). *Too scared to learn? The academic consequences of feeling unsafe at school.* Working Paper #02–13. Institute for Education and Social Policy.

Lawson, H. A., & Anderson-Butcher, D. (2001). In the best interests of the child: Youth development as a child welfare support and resource. In A. L. Sallee, H. A. Lawson, & K. Briar-Lawson (Eds.), *Innovative practices with vulnerable children and families* (pp. 245–265). Des Moines, IA: Eddie Bowers.

Lyke, B., & Byrd, S. (2018, August 23). Restorative justice creates a culture of safety [Blog post]. *Education Week.* Accessed at https://blogs.edweek.org/edweek/learning_social_emotional/2018/08/restorative_justice _creates_a_culture_of_safety.html on November 8, 2019.

McChesney, C., Covey, S., & Huling, J. (2012). *The 4 disciplines of execution: Achieving your wildly important goals.* New York: Free Press.

Miller, D. (2017). *Building a StoryBrand: Clarify your message so customers will listen.* New York: HarperCollins.

Miller, W. R., & Rollnick, S. (2013). *Motivational interviewing: Helping people change* (3rd ed.). New York: Guilford Press.

Minahan, J. (2019). Trauma-informed teaching strategies. *Educational Leadership, 77*(2), 30–35.

Monterey Bay Aquarium. (n.d.). *About us.* Accessed at www.montereybayaquarium.org/about-us on July 22, 2020.

Moore, K. A., Caal, S., Carney, R., Lippman, L., Li, W., Muenks, K., et al. (2014, February). *Making the grade: Assessing the evidence for integrated student supports* (Publication No. 2014-07). Bethesda, MD: Child Trends. Accessed at https://childtrends-ciw49tixgw5lbab.stackpathdns.com/wp-content/uploads /2014/02/2014-07ISSPaper2.pdf on May 7, 2020.

Morgan, N. (2014, May 14). Decisions don't start with data. *Harvard Business Review*. Accessed at https://hbr.org/2014/05/decisions-dont-start-with-data on March 9, 2020.

Naar-King, S., & Suarez, M. (2011). *Motivational interviewing with adolescents and young adults*. New York: Guilford Press.

National Academies of Sciences, Engineering, and Medicine. (2017). *Pain management and the opioid epidemic: Balancing societal and individual benefits and risks of prescription opioid use*. Washington, DC: The National Academies Press. Accessed at www.ncbi.nlm.nih.gov/books/NBK458661 on March 9, 2020.

National Archives. (2019). *Vietnam War U.S. military fatal casualty statistics*. Accessed at www.archives.gov /research/military/vietnam-war/casualty-statistics on March 10, 2020.

National Association of Secondary School Principals. (n.d.a). *ESSA fact sheets*. Accessed at www.nassp.org /policy-advocacy-center/resources/essa-toolkit/essa-fact-sheets on March 9, 2020.

National Association of Secondary School Principals. (n.d.b). *Every Student Succeeds Act (ESSA) overview*. Accessed at https://principalsmonth.org/igx_temp/essa/ESSA_FactSheets.pdf on March 9, 2020.

National Association of Secondary School Principals. (n.d.c). *Why Title III matters*. Accessed at www.nassp .org/policy-advocacy-center/resources/essa-toolkit/essa-fact-sheets/title-iii-language-instruction-for-english -learners-and-immigrant-students on August 7, 2020.

National Council of Juvenile and Family Court Judges. (2006, October 24). *Finding your ACE score*. Accessed at www.ncjfcj.org/publications/finding-your-ace-score on February 21, 2020.

National Council of Nonprofits. (n.d.). *Nonprofit sustainability*. Accessed at www.councilofnonprofits.org /tools-resources/nonprofit-sustainability on December 18, 2019.

National Institute on Drug Abuse. (2018). *Drugs, brains, and behavior: The science of addiction*. Accessed at www.drugabuse.gov/publications/drugs-brains-behavior-science-addiction/preface on March 9, 2020.

National Museum of Natural History. (n.d.). *About the museum*. Accessed at https://naturalhistory.si.edu /about on July 22, 2020.

The Nature Conservancy. (n.d.). *Our mission, vision, and values*. Accessed at www.nature.org/en-us/about -us/who-we-are/our-mission-vision-and-values on July 22, 2020.

No Child Left Behind Act of 2001, Pub. L. No. 107–110, § 115, Stat. 1425 (2002).

Nonprofit Risk Management Center. (n.d.). *Drafting a memorandum of understanding*. Accessed at https://nonprofitrisk.org/resources/e-news/drafting-a-memorandum-of-understanding on March 9, 2020.

NonProfit Times. (2015, June 9). *4 ways to strengthen collaborative grant proposals*. Accessed at www.the nonprofittimes.com/npt_management_tips/4-ways-to-strengthen-collaborative-grant-proposals on March 9, 2020.

North, R. A. (2017). *Motivational interviewing for school counselors*. Author.

Parker, D. (2019). *Building bridges: Engaging students at risk through the power of relationships*. Bloomington, IN: Solution Tree Press.

Partnership for the Future of Learning. (n.d.). *Community schools playbook*. Washington, DC: Author. Accessed at https://communityschools.futureforlearning.org/assets/downloads/community-schools -playbook.pdf on March 9, 2020.

Peoria Public Schools. (2016, August 16). *Wraparound center* [Video]. Accessed at www.youtube.com/watch ?v=8O8XFZr8qUQ on July 12, 2020.

Pew Research Center. (2019, September 19). *Why Americans don't fully trust many who hold positions of power and responsibility.* Accessed at www.pewresearch.org/politics/2019/09/19/why-americans-dont-fully -trust-many-who-hold-positions-of-power-and-responsibility on August 7, 2020.

Pink, D. H. (2018). *When: The scientific secrets of perfect timing.* New York: Riverhead Books.

Platt, R. (2019). What's love got to do with it? *Educational Leadership, 77*(2), 42–46.

Putnam, R. D. (2015). *Our kids: The American Dream in crisis.* New York: Simon & Schuster.

Quaglia, R. J., & Corso, M. J. (2014). *Student voice: The instrument of change.* Thousand Oaks, CA: Corwin Press.

Quaglia Institute for School Voice and Aspirations. (2016). *School voice report 2016.* Accessed at http://quagliainstitute.org/dmsView/School_Voice_Report_2016 on July 16, 2020.

Rea, D. W., & Zinskie, C. D. (2017). Educating students in poverty: Building equity and capacity with a holistic framework and community school model. *National Youth-at-Risk Journal, 2*(2), 1–24.

Rice, F. P., & Dolgin, K. G. (2008). *The adolescent: Development, relationships, and culture* (12th ed.). Boston: Allyn & Bacon.

Rogers, J. (2019). For school leaders, a time of vigilance and caring. *Educational Leadership, 77*(2). Accessed at www.ascd.org/publications/educational-leadership/oct19/vol77/num02/For-School-Leaders,-a-Time -of-Vigilance-and-Caring.aspx on April 22, 2020.

Sappa, A. (2019, July 2). Opinion: "What teachers and schools need is for the whole community to see education as its job." *The Hechinger Report.* Accessed at https://hechingerreport.org/opinion-proven -community-school-models on March 9, 2020.

Sasse, B. (2018). *Them: Why we hate each other—and how to heal.* New York: St. Martin's Press.

Schlechty, P. C. (2009). *Leading for learning: How to transform schools into learning organizations.* San Francisco: Jossey-Bass.

Schrobsdorff, S. (2016, October 27). Teen depression and anxiety: Why the kids are not alright. *Time.* Accessed at https://time.com/4547322/american-teens-anxious-depressed-overwhelmed on March 9, 2020.

Sinek, S. (2011, July 5). *How great leaders inspire action* [Video file]. Accessed at https://simonsinek.com /discover/how-great-leaders-inspire-action on September 10, 2019.

Skerritt, M. (Director). (2017). *Angst.* Elephant in the Room Productions.

Smithsonian National Museum of Natural History. (n.d.). Accessed at https://naturalhistory.si.edu/about on October, 7, 2020.

Society for Public Health Education. (2019). *Working with students: Using youth voice to promote healthy schools.* Accessed at www.sophe.org/wp-content/uploads/2019/10/Using-Youth-Voice-to-Promote -Healthy-Schools.pdf on March 9, 2020.

Southwest Educational Development Laboratory. (2013). *Partners in education: A dual capacity-building framework for family–school partnerships.* Austin, TX: Authors. Accessed at www2.ed.gov/documents /family-community/partners-education.pdf on April 15, 2020.

Stevens, J. E. (2017, May 2). *Addiction doc says: It's not the drugs. It's the ACEs . . . adverse childhood experiences.* Accessed at https://acestoohigh.com/2017/05/02/addiction-doc-says-stop-chasing-the-drug-focus-on-aces -people-can-recover on March 9, 2020.

Stevens, J. E. (2019, May 21). *Bad news–good news: Each additional ACE increases opioid relapse rate by 17%; each ACE-informed treatment visit reduces it by 2%* [Blog post]. Accessed at www.acesconnection.com/blog /bad-news-good-news-each-additional-ace-increases-opioid-relapse-rate-by-17-each-ace-informed-treatment -visit-reduces-it-by-2 on March 9, 2020.

Substance Abuse and Mental Health Services Administration. (2017). *Screening, brief intervention, and referral to treatment (SBIRT).* Accessed at https://www.samhsa.gov/sbirt on August 11, 2020.

Success Center for Sexual & Reproductive Health. (n.d.). *Reducing the risk*. Accessed at www.etr.org/ebi /programs/reducing-the-risk on August 10, 2020.

Terrasi, S., & de Galarce, P. C. (2017). Trauma and learning in America's classrooms. *Phi Delta Kappan, 98*(6), 35–41.

Tippett, K., & Boyle, G. (2012, July 11). *Turning inspiration into action* [Video file]. Accessed at www.youtube.com/watch?v=S9MkHqIMBfc on April 2, 2020.

Tisch, J. M., & Weber, K. (2004). *The power of we: Succeeding through partnerships*. Hoboken, NJ: Wiley.

TopNonprofits. (n.d.). *50 example mission statements*. Accessed at https://topnonprofits.com/examples /nonprofit-mission-statements on July 22, 2020.

Trujillo, T., & Renée, M. (2013). Democratic school turnarounds: Pursuing equity and learning from evidence. *Voices in Urban Education, 36*, 18–26.

Ueland, B. (1993). *Strength to your sword arm: Selected writings*. Duluth, MN: Holy Cow! Press.

U.S. Department of Education. (n.d.). *Programs: Title II—Preparing, training, and recruiting high-quality teachers, principals, or other school leaders*. Accessed at www2.ed.gov/policy/elsec/leg/essa/legislation/title-ii .html on April 22, 2020.

U.S. Department of Education. (2018, March 1). *Family Educational Rights and Privacy Act (FERPA)*. Accessed at www2.ed.gov/policy/gen/guid/fpco/ferpa/index.html on March 10, 2020.

U.S. Department of Health and Human Services. (n.d.). *HHS by the numbers*. Accessed at www.hhs.gov /opioids/about-the-epidemic/hhs-by-numbers/index.html on July 26, 2020.

U.S. Department of Health and Human Services. (2013, July 26). *Summary of the HIPAA security rule*. Accessed at www.hhs.gov/hipaa/for-professionals/security/laws-regulations/index.html on March 10, 2020.

U.S. Department of Health and Human Services. (2019). *What is the U.S. opioid epidemic?* Accessed at www.hhs.gov/opioids/about-the-epidemic/index.html on July 26, 2020.

Vogels, E. A., Perrin, A., Rainie, L., & Anderson, M. (2020). *53% of Americans say the internet has been essential during the COVID-19 outbreak*. Accessed at www.pewresearch.org/internet/2020/04/30/53-of -americans-say-the-internet-has-been-essential-during-the-covid-19-outbreak on August 6, 2020.

Voting Rights Act of 1965, Pub. L. No. 89–110, 79 Stat. 437 (1965).

Walker, T. (2019, October 18). *"I didn't know it had a name": Secondary traumatic stress and educators*. Accessed at https://neatoday.org/2019/10/18/secondary-traumatic-stress on March 10, 2020.

Wan, W., & Long, H. (2020, July 1). "Cries for help": Drug overdoses are soaring during the coronavirus pandemic. *Washington Post*. Accessed at www.washingtonpost.com/health/2020/07/01/coronavirus-drug -overdose on July 27, 2020.

Wardle, T. (2007). *Strong winds and crashing waves: Meeting Jesus in the memories of traumatic events*. Abilene, TX: Leafwood.

Watkins, M. D. (2013). *The first 90 days: Proven strategies for getting up to speed faster and smarter* (Updated and expanded ed.). Boston: Harvard Business Review Press.

Wells, L. (2018, April 10). *Capturing kids' hearts*. A presentation for Flippen Group Training, Tinley Park, IL.

Wheatley, M. (2011, May 31). *Turning to one another* [Blog post]. Accessed at https://localcircles.org/2011 /05/31/turning-to-one-another-by-meg-wheatley on March 10, 2020.

Whelan, E. (2015, February 10). Chesterton's fence. *National Review*. Accessed at www.nationalreview.com /bench-memos/chestertons-fence-ed-whelan on March 10, 2020.

Yee, V., & Blinder, A. (2018, March 14). National school walkout: Thousands protest against gun violence across the U.S. *New York Times*. Accessed at www.nytimes.com/2018/03/14/us/school-walkout.html on July 27, 2020.

Youth Mental Health Canada. (2019, April 15). *Youth mental health stats in Canada*. Accessed at https://ymhc.ngo/resources/ymh-stats on July 15, 2020.

Youth.gov. (n.d.). *Risk and protective factors*. Accessed at https://youth.gov/youth-topics/juvenile-justice/risk -and-protective-factors on March 10, 2020.

INDEX

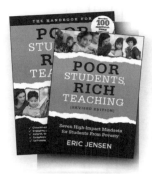

Poor Students, Rich Teaching, Revised Edition
The Handbook for Poor Students, Rich Teaching
Eric Jensen

You have the power to change the lives of students from poverty. Rely on the new edition of Dr. Eric Jensen's best-selling book *Poor Students, Rich Teaching* and its companion handbook to help you fully embrace the mindsets that lead to richer teaching.
BKF887 BKF888

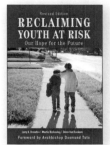

Reclaiming Youth at Risk
Larry K. Brendtro, Martin Brokenleg, and Steve Van Bockern

Empower your alienated students to cultivate a deep sense of belonging, mastery, independence, and generosity. This fully updated edition of *Reclaiming Youth at Risk* merges Native American knowledge and Western science to create a unique alternative for inspiring troubled youth to thrive and overcome.
BKF914

Community Connections and Your PLC at Work®
Nathaniel Provencio

In a PLC, every student, teacher, staff member, parent, and family member is vital to the operation of the school. Emphasizing transparency, mutual trust, and clarity of purpose, this resource helps create highly engaged communities collectively committed to learning for all.
BKF962

Messaging Matters
William D. Parker

Harness the power of messaging to create a culture of acknowledgment, respect, and celebration. Written specially for leaders, this title is divided into three parts, helping readers maximize their role as chief communicators with students, teachers, and parents and community.
BKF785

Yes We Can!
Heather Friziellie, Julie A. Schmidt, and Jeanne Spiller

Utilizing PLC practices, general and special educators must develop collaborative partnerships in order to close the achievement gap and maximize learning for all. The authors encourage all educators to take collective responsibility in improving outcomes for students with special needs.
BKF653

Solution Tree | Press

a division of Solution Tree

Visit SolutionTree.com or call 800.733.6786 to order.